SIMPSON'S STUDIO, Conway, Iowa,

Jones School photo, Conway, Iowa, ca. 1892. Wiate Phillips is second from the left on the top row; Waite is fourth. Fred is in the second row at the far right and Nell is in front of Fred in the first row. Below, the twins in their Western Union uniforms, ca. 1900. At right, Genevieve Elliott at sixteen, a photograph of her childhood home in Knoxville, Iowa, and Waite and Genevieve's certificate of marriage.

Detach this and give to one of the P...

Certificate of

THIS CERTIFIES, That on the ___30___

at ___Knoxville___ in

according to law and by authority and license under

___Walt Phillips___ JOINED I...

Given under my han...

f. B. Elliott residence - Knoxville Iowa

A gusher come[...]
for the Lewcin[...]
Oil Company, [...]
1900. Inset, S[...]
Number One, [...]
Waite Phillips [...]
Company. Ab[...]
right, the Phil[...]
brothers in [...]
Bartlesville in [...]
Fred, Waite, [...]
L.E., and Fran[...]
Below right: [...]
Genevieve wit[...]
Helen Jane, th[...]
Phillipses' first [...]
in 1911.

WAITE PHILLIPS BLDG., TULSA, OKLA.—66

PHILLIPS TEST IS
MAKING 120 BARRELS

Second Hole on Jane Reed
Farm Drilled 24 Feet in Sand
for Good Showing

Waite Phillips second test on
Jane Reed farm, in the north
corner of the northwest quart
the southeast quarter of sectio
13-11, was drilled in the sa
feet and the well is making 12
rels an hour. The No. 1
n is making 2,400 barrels
Waite Phillips and
test in se

Postcard of the Philtower in Tulsa. The entrance to Villa Philbrook, the Phillips family home in Tulsa, 1930. Elliott and Helen Jane Phillips in the Philbrook garden, 1931. The brothers at Woolaroc for a "cow theives and outlaws reunion" in 1930, after the merger of Independent Oil & Gas Company and Phillips Petroleum: from left, Fred, Waite, Ed, L.E., and Frank. Phillips family and friends at Fish Camp, 1927. Waite, at the far right, rides his paint horse, Dalhart. Next to him are Elliott on Headlight and Helen Jane on Calvin.

BOOKS BY MICHAEL WALLIS

OIL MAN:
THE STORY OF FRANK PHILLIPS
AND THE BIRTH OF PHILLIPS PETROLEUM

ROUTE 66: THE MOTHER ROAD

PRETTY BOY:
THE LIFE AND TIMES OF CHARLES ARTHUR FLOYD

WAY DOWN YONDER IN THE INDIAN NATION:
WRITINGS FROM AMERICA'S HEARTLAND

MANKILLER: A CHIEF AND HER PEOPLE

EN DIVINA LUZ:
THE PENITENTE MORADAS OF NEW MEXICO

SONGDOG DIARY:
66 SOUVENIRS OF THE AMERICAN WEST

Beyond the Hills:

The Journey of Waite Phillips

BY MICHAEL WALLIS

KENNY A. FRANKS
SERIES EDITOR

GINI MOORE CAMPBELL
ASSOCIATE EDITOR

OKLAHOMA HERITAGE ASSOCIATION
TRACKMAKER SERIES

Manufactured in the United States of America

OKLAHOMA HERITAGE ASSOCIATION
201 NORTHWEST FOURTEENTH STREET
OKLAHOMA CITY, OKLAHOMA 73103

ISBN 1-885596-02-2 hardback;
1-885596-03-0 paperback
Library of Congress Catalog No. 95-70411

DESIGNED BY CAROL HARALSON

Second Printing 2002

OKLAHOMA TRACKMAKER SERIES

*Frontispiece photographs: A formal portrait
of the Phillips family in Conway, Iowa, ca.
1885. Top row, standing: Frank and
Jennie. Second row, seated, left to right:
L.E., Lewis, the twins, Lucinda. Front,
center: Ed.
Waite and Genevieve in a postcard photo
soon after their wedding, ca. 1909.*

For Allen "Storm" Strider,
the consummate son of Oklahoma

For Suzanne Fitzgerald Wallis,
my life partner and best friend

...ly group taken in Concord about 18...

CONTENTS

PART V

BRIGHT LANDS WEST ~ 1942-1964

ACKNOWLEDGMENTS

There is absolutely no question that this biography could not have been written without the assistance and input provided by Elliott and Virginia Phillips, the son and daughter-in-law of Waite and Genevieve Phillips. From Day One their desire to see to it that we produced a balanced and accurate account of the life of Waite Phillips helped guide me through the development of this biography.

Thanks to Elliott and Virginia, I had at my disposal literally scores of files filled with personal correspondence, family records, photographs, and documents.

Elliott, or Chope, as family and friends call him, is every inch the tenacious and fair-minded cattleman who looks you dead square in the eye and never pulls a punch. That sort of candor is always welcomed whenever a writer attempts to tell someone's life story. Chope's lovely wife, Virginia, is not only gracious but, like her husband, a wealth of information regarding the family. I appreciate their hospitality while I spent long days at their ranch near Watrous, New Mexico, poring through file cabinets, storage boxes, and photograph albums.

I remain ever grateful to both of them for their generous support and invaluable counsel.

Other members of the Phillips family were also important sources of information to me. They include Anne Phillips, the granddaughter of Fred Phillips, Waite's younger brother, and Flint Breckinridge, the great-grandson of Waite and Genevieve Phillips.

The Oklahoma Heritage Association, founded in 1927 by prominent state leaders and headquartered in the historic Oklahoma Heritage Center in Oklahoma City, is publishing this book as part of its Oklahoma Trackmaker Series.

Much of the credit belongs to Robert J. LaFortune. The seeds for the biography were planted by this Tulsa business and civic leader who not only has strong ties to both Philbrook and Philmont but also maintains his office in Waite Phillips' former business suite in the historic Philtower Building in downtown Tulsa. It was Bob LaFortune who first approached Oklahoma Heritage Association with the suggestion for the book and helped act as a liaison in assembling the team required to produce such a work.

When Dr. Paul F. Lambert, the dedicated executive director of Oklahoma Heritage Association, approached me to see if I would be interested in writing this book, I did not hesitate. I had already written another biography about the Phillips family — *Oil Man: The Story of Frank Phillips and the Birth of Phillips Petroleum* — and I knew full well the importance of telling the story of yet another family member — Waite Phillips.

My sincere thanks and appreciation go to Dr. Paul Lambert and also to Dr. Kenny A. Franks, who serves as director of heritage education as well as the series editor, and to Gini Moore Campbell, associate editor.

Hazel Rowena Mills, a fine editor and dogged researcher who has assisted me with several of my literary efforts, once again answered the call. My deepest thanks go to you, Rowena.

Many bravos need to be directed to Carol Haralson, a sensitive and talented artist who lent her enormous skills to the design of this book. Carol and I have worked together in the past, and, thankfully, the good folks at Oklahoma Heritage Association agreed with me that to give this biography a special look, we could call on none more talented than Carol.

Allen Strider, a native Oklahoman who lives and breathes the state's history and heritage, was especially helpful to me during the research and writing. Allen accompanied me on several research trips and gave me the benefit of his wisdom on more than one occasion. My sincere thanks to you, good friend.

The leadership and staff at both the Philmont Boy Scout Ranch near Cimarron, New Mexico, and the Philbrook Museum of Art in Tulsa, Oklahoma, bent over backwards to see to it that I was given complete access to their files and facilities. Both Philmont and Philbrook remain everlasting tributes to the legacy left by Waite Phillips.

At the Philmont Boy Scout Ranch, I need to single out Stephen Zimmer, director of the Philmont Museum and Seton Memorial Library. Stephen himself has authored some very fine books and articles about Waite Phillips, the Phillips family, and Philmont — the wilderness haven that has benefited so many young people for so many years. Special praise also goes to C. M. Buenger, former general manager at Philmont, and to Bill Spice, the capable executive who took over the post during the book's development.

And at the Philbrook Museum of Art, I will remain eternally grateful to many staff members whom I consider my friends and neighbors. Tom Young, a real asset to the museum as assistant registrar and librarian in charge of the Chapman Library, was especially helpful to me. Tributes need also go to Marcia Y. Manhart, executive director; Dr. Lydia Wyckoff, curator of Native American art; Lynne S. Butterworth, director of communications; and Denise Montgomery, museum shop manager. Thank you, one and all.

Several others also merit special recognition for their help and support with this project. They include: the late Fred L. Dunn, Jr.; Dottie Bayazeed; Karolyn K. Garland, Amoco Production Company; Jeanne Parks Chelsea; A. Blaine Imel; H. John Trinder III; Patricia McClintock Hilton; Patricia Kennedy McClintock Schmidlapp; Grant McClintock; Margery Mayo Feagin Bird; Elizabeth Greis McBirney Mason; Mike McGraw; Steve Smith; William B. Michaels; the staff and management of the Saint James Hotel, Cimarron, New Mexico; the Tulsa City-County Public Library; the *Tulsa World;* and the World Publishing Company library.

Also, my gratitude goes to the Frank Phillips Foundation, Inc., and to the staff and management at the Woolaroc Museum and Wildlife Preserve near Bartlesville, Oklahoma. At Woolaroc, I want to especially acknowledge Dick Miller, general manager; Robert R. Lansdown, museum director; Kenneth D. Meek, curator of collections; and Linda Stone-Laws, curator of art.

Last, but certainly never least, all thanks possible to my wife and partner, Suzanne Fitzgerald Wallis, a woman who not only encourages our feline muses, Beatrice and Molly, to stay on the job as I work, but also lends her own magical inspiration, encouragement, and unbounded love to anything worthwhile that I manage to get done.

MICHAEL WALLIS

Tulsa, Oklahoma, 1995

A SPECIAL NOTE TO READERS

This book was greatly enhanced because Elliott and Virginia Phillips, the son and daughter-in-law of Waite Phillips, provided the author with their own personal remembrances and several previously unseen files of written documentation — mostly business correspondence and internal memorandums. Even more important, they also shared with the author a detailed private journal, or diary, written by Waite Phillips himself, listing virtually all of his daily activities during his entire life.

This detailed diary and financial records journal, known among family members as the "Black Book," has been excerpted throughout the text of this book so others may read the actual words of Waite Phillips.

The citations from the daily diary, personal and business correspondence, and other written material are adequately dated and noted within the text itself, therefore eliminating the need for the use of formal footnotes.

THESE TWIN BOYS WERE NOT OUTSTANDING ONES EXCEPT
AS TO THEIR UNUSUAL ENERGY AND THEIR INTENSE
INTEREST IN NATURE AND EXPLORING WHAT LAY BEYOND
THE HILLS OF THEIR FARM HOME, ESPECIALLY THE
COUNTRY THEY VISUALIZED IN THE WEST WITH ITS
MOUNTAINS, STREAMS, AND DESERT LANDS.

~ WAITE PHILLIPS DIARY, 1886-1899

THE ONLY THINGS WE KEEP PERMANENTLY
ARE THOSE WE GIVE AWAY.

~ WAITE PHILLIPS EPIGRAMS, 1964

YOU CAN SEE WHAT A RESTLESS PERSON MY FATHER WAS.
HE WAS ALWAYS WANTING TO SEE WHAT WAS ON THE
OTHER SIDE OF THE MOUNTAIN. UNLIKE HIS BROTHER
FRANK, HE NEVER GOT MARRIED TO ANY OF HIS
BUSINESSES, COMPANIES, OIL, RANCHES, OR HOMES. HE
REALLY COULDN'T UNDERSTAND PEOPLE WHO PUT DOWN
ROOTS.

~ ELLIOTT PHILLIPS, 1993

1883-1902

I
WAITE &
WIATE

Body and spirit are twins: God only know which is which.

ALGERON CHARLES SWINBURNE, 1880

SIMPSON'S STUDIO. Conway, Iowa.

Overleaf: A gathering of Iowa young people photographed August 4, 1899, just before Waite and Wiate left home. Waite kneels in the front row, fifth from left. Left: The twins, Conway, Iowa, ca. 1897. Below: Lucinda Josephine Faucett Phillips and Lewis Phillips, Waite Phillips' parents, ca. 1915. Bottom: The Phillips family in Conway, Iowa, in 1896 at Waite's maternal grandparents' golden wedding anniversary celebration.

A Phillips gathering at the farm near Conway, Iowa, summer of 1899.
Top row: Waite's father, Lewis, his sister, Lura, and his mother,
Lucinda. Seated, second row: Waite, Wiate, Ed , L.E., Frank and
Frank's wife, Jane (holding their son, John), Waite's sister, Nellie.
Seated, bottom row: Waite's brother, Fred, and his sister, Jennie. The
family dog, Spot, is perched behind the twins. In oval frame, a formal
portrait of Waite made ca. 1906.

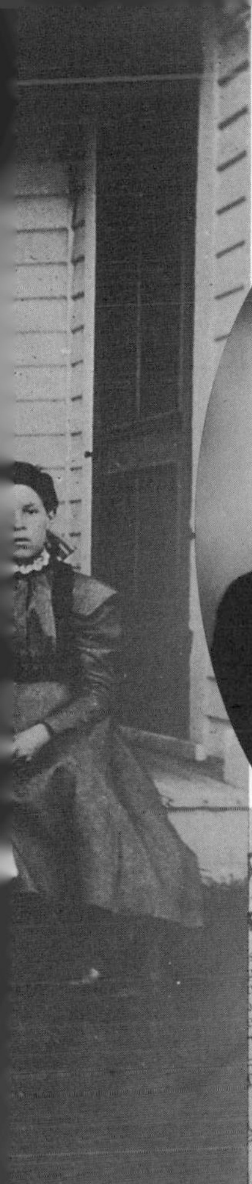

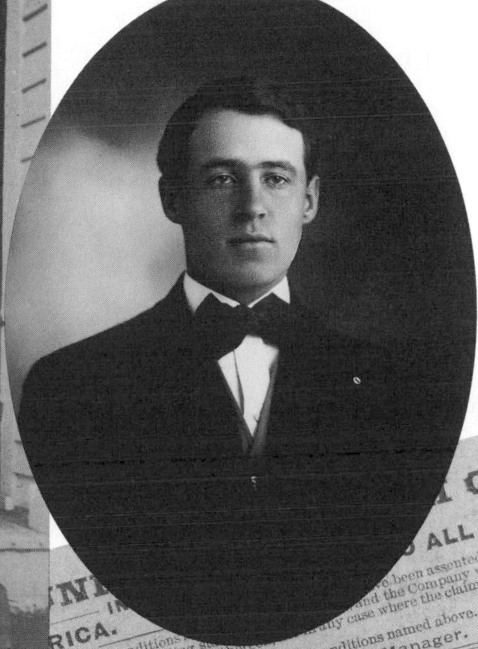

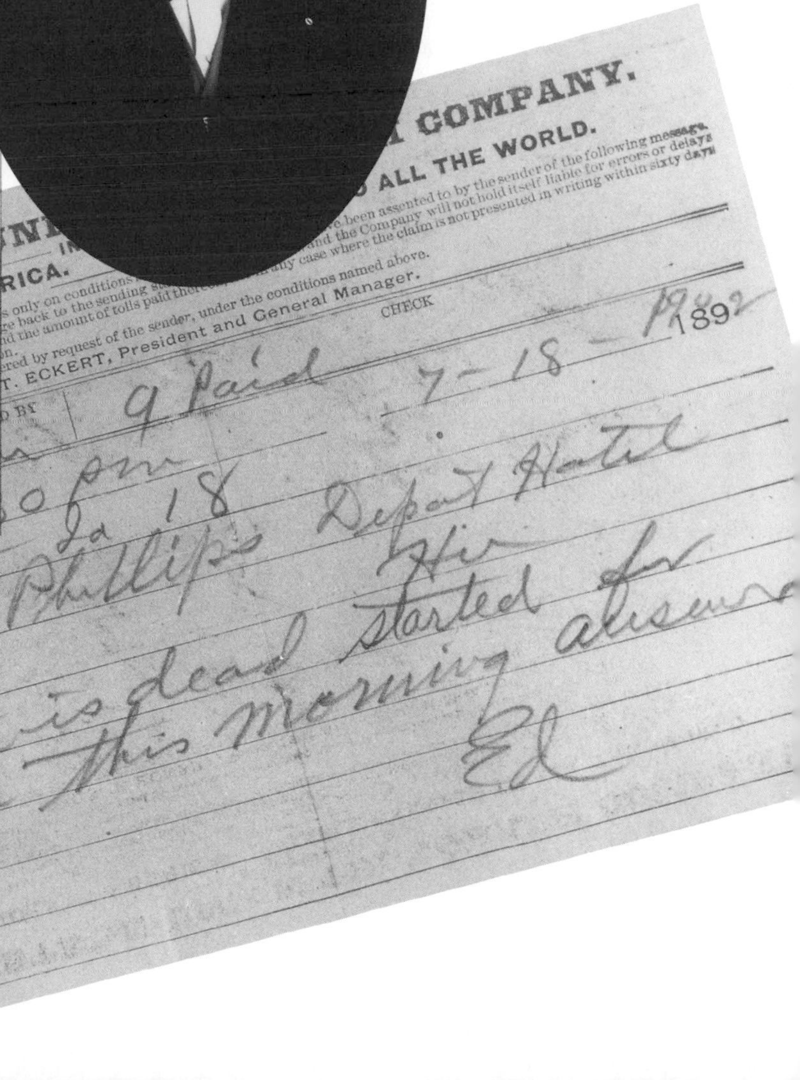

COMPANY.
ALL THE WORLD.
...been assented to by the sender of the following message.
...and the Company will not hold itself liable for errors or delays
...any case where the claim is not presented in writing within sixty days
RICA.
...s only on conditions ...
...e back to the sending ...
...d the amount of tolls paid thereo...
...ered by request of the sender, under the conditions named above.
T. ECKERT, President and General Manager.
CHECK
...D BY | 9 Paid 7-18 190 1892
...30 pm
ED at Grant, Ia 18
Ed a Phillips Depot Hotel
Hi
Wiate is dead started for
Home this morning answer
Ed

CHAPTER ONE

THE TWINS

First there were two.

They were twins. Twin boys. Their time to be born came on the nineteenth day of January in the year 1883.

From the outset it was evident these brothers were loyal sons of Capricorn. True to the symbol of their zodiacal sign — the goat — both of them would grow to become as determined and fiercely driven as a pair of rams scaling the mountains in quest of greener meadows.

They were identical twins, the result of one fertilized egg dividing into two equal parts early in its development. Each of the halves became one of the twins. As a result, their features were exactly the same. So were their hair, eye, and skin color, as well as their blood groups. Even their body scent was alike. If anyone had tried to gauge the twins' cardiovascular measurements, he or she would have found a near perfect match. The twins' hearts beat as one. In a sense, they were the same person.

On that frigid January day, news of the birth of the twin boys got around pretty quickly and naturally aroused plenty of curiosity. That was surely to be expected, especially in predictable Iowa, home to Protestant Yankee pioneers who did their level best to achieve an unalterable state of normalcy. Twins — be they white-faced calves or human babies — were something not quite normal.

But then, when it came right down to it, Iowans were not unlike the rest of the world in their attitude toward twins. Ever since there has been a human race, all sorts of explanations have been sought for the phenomenon of twins. Myths, legends, religious beliefs, and superstitions developed around twins in almost every civilization. Stories of twins occurred during biblical times and throughout Greek and Roman mythology. In ancient Rome, the best known twins were the city's builders — Romulus and Remus. Castor and Pollux, the most famous twins in the Greek myths, were revered as the tutelar gods of navigation, and their names were given to the two main stars in the constellation Gemini.

In some cultures, twins were associated with magic and miracles. Certain Native American tribes believed twins were the reincarnation of revered ancestors. It was said that they could read mortals' minds. Often, divine honors were paid to newborn twins because it was thought that they possessed supernatural powers. Still other cultures believed that twins brought good fortune or had second sight. Sometimes, one twin symbolized evil and the other good. One twin embodied darkness and the other light. One represented the sun, while the second infant was the incarnate moon.

The birth of twins during a bountiful harvest might have been thought of as a good omen, perhaps even a visit from the gods. If, however, the babies' arrival coincided with flood, famine, drought, or some other disaster, the twins also could be taken as a harbinger of evil.

There may have been some genuine wonder at the Iowa farmhouse where these twin boys were born in 1883, but certainly there was no talk of magic or omens. They were the sons of a hardworking couple grounded in the Methodist church, a strict work ethic, and the soil of the midlands. Their growing family already included a daughter and three other sons. Another daughter — the eldest child and a big sister the twins never knew —

forever rested in a country graveyard after having succumbed to diphtheria when she was almost seven.

The supernatural was not discussed on this frigid day in January, less than one month after the winter solstice. The family members only considered themselves doubly blessed as first one healthy boy and then, just a few minutes later, another was delivered in the soft featherbed.

The babies' father, Lewis Franklin Phillips, a Civil War veteran who had marked his thirty-ninth birthday just two weeks before the twins' birth, was quietly proud and pleased that he now had two more sons to help someday with the chores. The twins' mother, Lucinda Josephine Faucett Phillips, was thirty-four years old and not nearly at the end of her childbearing duties. All told, Lucinda gave birth to ten children. In the next decade after the twins' birth, she had two more daughters and yet another son.

The Phillipses' forty-acre farm was a mile east of the Taylor County town of Conway in southwestern Iowa. Dr. H. B. Liggett had been summoned from his home in Conway to the Phillips place early that day. He grabbed his bag, pulled on a heavy coat, and rode out lickety-split in his horse-drawn buggy. The good doctor knew the Phillips family very well. He had looked down the throats and into the ears of all of the children. Liggett also was well acquainted with the route to the farm. He had made the short journey down the narrow dirt lane on several occasions.

The twins' birth was rather unremarkable. There were no complications. Both of the boys were delivered with relative ease. Both of them appeared to be sound and without any noticeable blemish. The first twin was welcomed with a firm swat on his behind. He was still squawking when, moments later, the second boy made his appearance.

Lucinda and Lewis Phillips had long before decided what they would call the twins if they were both boys. They named the first-born twin Wiate, perhaps a variation of Wyatt or Wyatte from the British *gwy,* meaning "water." The younger of the twins ended up with something very close to his slightly older brother's name. Only two letters were reversed. They called him Waite, from the Old English *waad,* meaning "a road."

On January 19, 1883, identical twin boys, named Wiate and Waite, were born on a 40-acre farm one mile west of Conway, Iowa. Mother attended by Dr. H. B. Liggett. — WAITE PHILLIPS DIARY, 1883-1886

Before he bundled up and returned to Conway, Dr. Liggett looked over each of the infants one more time just to be sure, and again proclaimed them both fit. They were laid together in Lucinda's arms to nurse beneath the goose-down quilts and flannel spread. Later, the older siblings tiptoed into the shadowy room to squeeze their mother's hand and to take their first peeks at their new brothers' wrinkled faces, the color of cherry pulp.

Stoves and fires sputtered and sparked inside the snug house. Just outside the windows stretched endless fields of corn stubble and the skeletons of orchards slumbering under icy skies. Beyond and above the purple horizon, the twin boy stars in the constellation Gemini — Castor and the somewhat brighter Pollux — blinked awake. And higher in the dark winter heavens, the ghost of an old man moon lit the way for a weary country doctor going home.

CHAPTER TWO

PILGRIM ROOTS

Twin brothers Waite and Wiate were born into what many people living in the 1880s in the midlands of America might have called the quintessential family.

At first glance, the Phillips clan of Iowa closely resembled the classic mixed-breed mutt dog — durable and steadfast, with distinct strains of purebred European stock and just a hint of aristocracy. On both sides, they boasted an enviable procession of forebears ranging from early colonists to rugged pioneers. A prominent Pilgrim leader and even a European monarch were extolled as distant ancestors.

An explanation of the family lineage, both paternal and maternal, was a definite component in all of the Phillips children's upbringing. And soon after they were weaned off their mother's milk, the youngsters flourished on country cooking spiced with ample doses of family history and heritage. True stories and tall tales were passed around the crowded supper table, right along with platters heaped with fried chicken and bowls of steaming lima beans or succotash.

Soon, the twins would learn from their big brothers and sister that on their father's side they were ninth-generation descendants of Miles Standish. Any child growing up in Iowa — the quintessence of America — surely would have been thrilled beyond belief to boast of kinship to the English colonist remembered chiefly for his role in the saga of John Alden and the "Puritan maiden" Priscilla Mullens.

Undoubtedly, Waite and Wiate were not told during the family chats that Captain Standish bore little or no resemblance to the dashing figure portrayed in the standard history books of those times. Nor was he as depicted in "The Courtship of Miles Standish," a famous poem with no historical basis, penned only twenty-five years before the twins' birth by the prolific and popular bard Henry Wadsworth Longfellow.

> *The twins' paternal grandparents were Daniel Phillips, whose ancestors came from Wales, England, and Marilla Phillips (née Standish), who was a descendant of Captain Miles Standish of the Mayflower.* ~ WAITE PHILLIPS DIARY, 1883-1886

In truth, Standish was a paid soldier of fortune. In 1620, at the age of thirty-six, he sailed from Southampton, England, with the Pilgrims on the *Mayflower*. After the ship landed at Plymouth, Massachusetts, he was chosen military captain of the colony. According to some historians, the Native Americans who encountered Standish and his company of armed men greatly feared him.

Standish was recognized not only as an accomplished and zealous Indian fighter but also for his business prowess. As assistant to the governor, and for six years the treasurer of the colony, the enterprising Standish — astute as any in financial negotiations and transactions — helped to save his fellow colonists thousands of dollars.

An aptitude for commerce and a reputation for making instant decisions — but not his competence as a formidable mercenary — would be passed to future generations. The Standish business acumen and talent for being on time materialized in at least some of the Phillips sons born in the late nineteenth century.

Thanks to family records scribbled in Bibles and genealogical charts, the bloodline separating the Phillipses of Iowa from their famous early American ancestor was fairly easy to follow, even for farm youngsters. Waite and Wiate, like the other Phillips children, eventually would be able to reel off fluently the family names and dates as if reciting memorized Scripture or nursery rhymes.

The children knew, for example, that Rose Standish, the captain's first wife, died during the initial trying winter in America without bearing any children. By 1624, Standish had remarried. He and his second wife, Barbara, had six children. Their second son, Josiah, born in 1634, served as an officer in King Philip's War. In 1656, the year Miles Standish died, Josiah married Sarah Allen.

That couple's first of five offspring, Samuel Standish, was born just to the north of Plymouth on the Atlantic coast at Duxbury, Massachusetts. Samuel wed Deborah Gates of Stow, Massachusetts. Their son, also named Samuel, born in Preston in far eastern Connecticut in 1713, married Abigail Brown Backus, a native of Canterbury, Connecticut. Later, he served as a soldier in the militia at Bennington, Vermont.

Samuel and Abigail eventually moved to Massachusetts, where a son, Asa Backus Standish, was born in about 1760. He married Abigail Aimee Albee at Granville, New York, in 1784. From that union came Matthew Kettle Standish, born at Auburn, New York, on January 8, 1794. He wed Esther Curtis of Sheffield, Massachusetts. Their daughter, Marilla Standish, married into the Phillips family. She was Waite and Wiate's grandmother, and she lived until 1900.

Marilla, born on May 14, 1819, at Richmond in Ontario County, New York, was barely twenty years old when on June 2, 1839, she pledged herself in marriage to Daniel Phillips.

The second oldest of five sons, Daniel was born July 10, 1811, in Tioga County in northern Pennsylvania. His parents were Spencer and Susanna Stiles Phillips, hardworking settlers of solid Welsh stock. Besides Daniel's ancestors who had migrated to

America from Wales, family records also revealed that one of the more prominent family members was Thomas Phillips. It was this Phillips who supposedly had been hired by William Bradford of the Plymouth colony to build a church and meetinghouse in Duxbury. Job Stiles, an ancestor on Daniel's mother's side, was known as the first male child born in the colony of Connecticut, in 1634.

After their marriage at Oswayo in neighboring Potter County, Pennsylvania, Daniel and Marilla migrated to southern Ohio. They made their home near Pomeroy in Meigs County, not far from the Ohio River. Regarded by his family and friends as a tireless and vigorous worker, Daniel Phillips earned his living as a lumberman. Often, his work took him far from home, aboard the stout rafts that transported cut timber to destinations dotting the banks of the Mississippi and Ohio rivers.

As the family grew, Daniel decided to spend more time with his loved ones. He left his work on the great rivers to become a farmer. On the family's land near Pomeroy, Lewis Franklin Phillips was born on January 4, 1844. With two older sisters, Lewis was the Phillipses' firstborn son. Five more children would follow. An examination of the dutifully recorded family accounts shows that young Lewis was considered to be not only a "promising child" but also "a great favorite with his grandfather Standish."

In 1847, the family left Ohio and moved to Jackson County, Iowa, just west of the Mississippi River bordering Illinois. Settlers by the wagonload, anxious to take land which had belonged to Native American tribes, poured into Iowa. It joined the Union as the twenty-ninth state in 1846, two years after Lewis Phillips' birth.

Daniel tilled the fertile soil while Marilla created a classroom in their home. She faithfully taught school to her own brood as well as to many other children from nearby farms. But before long, word of even better farmland spread across the countryside. Daniel listened to the whispered rumors and became restless.

When Lewis was about eleven years old, the Phillips family packed up and moved yet again. They went farther west and settled on a farm in Story County on the fringes of the black-earth country just north of Des Moines.

Within two years, the state constitution was revised and the capital was moved from Iowa City to Des Moines. In that same year, 1857, a band of Sioux warriors killed white settlers near the town of Spirit Lake, in the northwestern part of the state. Although it was the final Indian uprising in Iowa, the white politicians feared that the incident would discourage future settlement. They were wrong. Attracted by the richness of the earth, significant numbers of homesteaders flocked to Iowa like a plague of locusts.

The deep topsoil provided Daniel Phillips with a decent living, and his eight children were not afraid of hard work. They pitched in and did their share. Before trudging off to school, Lewis and his brothers and sisters slopped the hogs, fed the poultry, and worked their way down a long list of other daily chores.

As with many other aspects of life in rural America at that time, the school year was regulated by crops. Terms were scheduled so youngsters could help with the planting and later with the harvest.

The rolling Iowa pastures and fields stretched on forever. For Lewis Phillips and his friends, landlocked in the corn belt of America, the future seemed as golden as a tub of fresh butter. But the idyllic life of even an Iowa farm boy would not last long. Storm clouds brewed heavy and dark on the horizon.

CHAPTER THREE

LEW AND JOSIE

By the time Lewis Phillips reached his sixteenth birthday, it was becoming clear that life was about to change dramatically for him and for the entire nation. Throughout the autumn and winter of 1860 and into early 1861, young Lewis heard very little but talk of the approaching war between the northern and southern states. Most folks figured it was about to erupt at any time.

Lew, as most folks called him, and two older boys who were his best chums attended the district school seventeen miles northeast of Des Moines. Like everyone else, they spent more and more of their time in heated discussions about the threat of war. Just as the school term was concluded for spring planting in March, Abraham Lincoln was inaugurated as the sixteenth president of the United States. Although armed conflict appeared to be all but certain, the three boys decided they could not sit around chewing the fat and listening to gossip. They needed to hunt gainful employment. Lew hired out to a local carpenter, and his two friends went to work as farmhands.

They barely had started with their new professions when the clouds of war burst. On April 12, 1861, Confederate artillery opened fire at the Union garrison at Fort Sumter in Charleston harbor. Volunteers hurried to join armies forming in the North and the South. The much feared Civil War was on. Although he was most anxious to join up and don the Union blue, Lew listened to his parents, who implored him to wait and see how long the war would last.

Then on July 21 at the First Battle of Bull Run, named for a small stream near Manassas in northeast Virginia, the Federal troops were given an old-fashioned country licking. They fled in retreat. Lew Phillips could wait no more. On the following Sabbath, he and his two chums got together to plot their future. As Lew Phillips explained in a memoir he compiled and published in 1911, "Some Things Our Boy Saw in the War," the three youths thought they had but one option. "Now we will go," he wrote.

The very next morning, Lew and his friends trekked to Des Moines and enlisted in the Union army. They enrolled their names, took a solemn oath to obey their officers at all times, and marched off as buck privates to camp at Council Bluffs. Originally accepted in Company I in the Fourth Iowa Infantry, Lew soon ended up in the artillery. Because of a surplus of men, Company I was taken out of the regiment to become the Second Iowa Battery.

Orders were issued, and Lew's outfit boarded riverboats bound for Saint Louis, where the farmboy turned carpenter would train to be a cannoneer, practicing artillery drills with guns left over from the Mexican War.

Before the soldiers left Iowa, a delegation of women from Council Bluffs appeared to present the gallant boys with beautiful silk battle flags and state banners. In his memoir, Lew Phillips noted that the Iowa ladies "knew the boys would defend them and return them to the state in due time. The battery did return its flag to the state in due time, all battered and torn, with its staff shot in two and spliced together with iron bands."

It did not take very long for Lew and his comrades to find themselves in the thick of the fray. Many years later as an old man back home in Iowa, he recalled his first battle when he wrote:

"Minié balls and cannon shot were now cutting limbs off the trees above us and strewing the ground, and soon the wounded began coming to the rear, some being carried on stretchers, some crawling and others using their rifles as crutches. Here our boy had his first sight of good red blood that was being so freely shed for his country in those days. Do you think he was sick? Yes, he was. Never having been able to endure the sight of human blood, he tried to look in some direction where there was none in sight; but it was everywhere."

The war lasted much longer than most people had thought. Lew Phillips served with the Second Iowa Battery for the duration. For thirteen dollars a month and for the defense of Old Glory, he and his outfit fought bravely at the sieges of Nashville and Vicksburg and at Corinth and Tupelo and other places throughout the South. Like so many others from both sides of the conflict, Lew quickly lost all traces of his youth and developed into a hardened soldier. As he put it in his written account of those war years, "As long as there was an enemy in sight our boy was as full of fight as a young bulldog."

Lew survived fever and illness and the horrors of close combat. He put up with meals of hardtack and raw bacon washed down with vile camp coffee. His hearing was impaired forever by the incessant roar of artillery, and he was wounded by enemy gunfire. He watched many men die.

At long last, the bloody conflict was concluded. Back in Davenport, Iowa, in August 1865 — four long and arduous years after he had enlisted — Corporal Lewis Phillips was discharged from the Union army.

Upon his discharge he was a Corporal and as a result of his duty as a cannoneer he received ear injuries which later on in his life caused partial deafness and complete deafness during his last 15 years. ~ WAITE PHILLIPS DIARY, 1883-1886

Lew returned home and once again began to work as a carpenter and farmer. He also met the young woman who was to become his wife and the mother of his ten children.

Lucinda Josephine Faucett was her name. It was said that when he first caught sight of Miss Faucett, five years his junior, Lew declared her to be "the most beautiful girl in his section" of the state.

Josie, as her closest friends and loved ones called her, came from a family with a heritage just as varied and interesting as that of Lew Phillips.

The Faucetts traced their ancestral line to France. From there in the mid-1700s William Faucett, a Huguenot emigrant, fled to Ireland, where he lived for many years before moving to America. By 1783, he had settled in North Carolina. After marriage to a local girl, Faucett oversaw a successful farm and raised a family. One of his sons, James Faucett, born April 19, 1789, married Elizabeth Jeffers, and they became the parents of twelve children. Their eighth child, born August 31, 1826, was Thomas Linch Faucett, who twenty-three years later became the father of the beguiling Miss Josie.

By the time Thomas reached his sixth birthday, the Faucetts — bitterly opposed to slavery — had left the South and their extensive cotton and tobacco operations. They moved to a two-hundred-acre farm near the town of French Lick in southern Indiana. Besides farming, the family also owned a tavern and rented rooms to stage passengers traveling the busy road between Vincennes and Louisville.

On October 24, 1846, twenty-year-old Thomas wed Mary Jane Tate, less than a month after she had turned sweet sixteen. Mary Jane's family was of Scottish and Dutch descent. Although they had no written proof or any convincing evidence, the Tate family always claimed to be descendants of Mary, Queen of Scots, who had been beheaded in 1587 for supposedly having plotted the death of her cousin Queen Elizabeth I of England.

Hearty North Carolina pioneers, the Tates eventually moved to Indiana, where Mary Jane was born in 1830. Mary Jane and Thomas Faucett brought a dozen children into the world. Their second, arriving at their Orange County, Indiana, home on August 13, 1849, was Lucinda Josephine, or Josie.

Josie's father not only farmed but also worked as a blacksmith and sold grindstones. He moved his family from Indiana to an eighty-acre farm in Illinois, and then in 1864, while the Civil War still raged, they settled in Iowa. There Faucett was awarded a steel-welding contract for the first railroad to enter Des Moines. He also worked a 160-acre farm, and found time to devote to his deep religious convictions by acting as a Methodist preacher and evangelist. According to family records, Faucett frequently commented during his sermons, "I hammer iron all week and hammer the Gospel into people's hearts on Sunday."

After a whirlwind courtship, Lew Phillips asked for the hand of Miss Josie, whom he later wrote was "a rarely beautiful girl, bright and good as she was fair." Her parents were pleased to give their consent. The handsome young man who wished to be their son-in-law had a reputation as a hard worker.

On July 3, 1867, Lew Phillips, the twenty-three-year-old war veteran, and Josie Faucett, almost eighteen and the daughter of a blacksmith-Methodist minister, were united in marriage at Des Moines. The young couple set up housekeeping at Mitchellville, just to the east of Des Moines and south of the Skunk River. Their first child, a daughter they named Etta, was born at their home there in 1868. She was followed in 1871 by a second daughter, Mary Jennie, or as most people called her, Jennie.

The Phillips family seemed to be secure in the Iowa home. But, much like their ancestors on both sides, Lew and Josie became restless. They wanted to break the routine. They were anxious to see what life was like elsewhere. They looked to the West.

CHAPTER FOUR

AMERICAN GOTHIC

Just as the expanding American frontier had lured generations of their elders farther west, it drew Lew and Josie Phillips to follow their instincts.

Only five years into their marriage, they left Iowa behind. In 1872, they packed up their belongings and their best expectations and turned westward.

In an ox-drawn wagon filled with china dishes, tools, and their two small daughters, Etta and Jennie, the Phillipses moved far beyond the Missouri River. They crossed rough terrain and virgin prairies covered by a thick rug of alluvial soil until they reached the North Loup River valley in Nebraska, which had been a state for less than five years.

. . . they moved to Greeley County, Nebraska, to homestead a farm by preferential right of their father being a Civil War veteran. ~ WAITE PHILLIPS DIARY, 1883-1886

Josie set about to make her family as comfortable as possible in a sod house while Lew built a stout cabin with hand-hewed red cedar logs. To supplement the food he raised on the homestead, Lew hunted for prairie chickens, deer, pronghorn antelope, and other game. He also journeyed to distant canyons to cut more of the fragrant cedar logs, and hauled them more than eighty miles to market in Grand Island, just above the Platte River.

Almost as soon as the family had settled, Lew became a familiar figure around the nearby town of Scotia. In the autumn of 1872, he met with others in the town to help organize Greeley County. The following year, he was elected the first county judge. In that capacity, he was credited with having issued the first marriage license granted in the county. Like some of the other Civil War veterans who homesteaded in those parts, Lew signed on with the Greeley County Guards, and the governor named him a second lieutenant.

The same month Lew was chosen as county judge held another benchmark for the family. On November 28, 1873, a third child — the Phillipses' first son — was born at the family's log cabin. They named the boy Frank Faucett Phillips. News of his arrival quickly circulated throughout the Loup River valley.

Frank was the only one of the Phillipses' ten children to be born in Nebraska. By the end of the following year, Lew and Josie were ready to go home.

They had suffered through isolation and lonely times. They had braved threats of Sioux warriors, blizzards, prairie fires, hailstorms, and other dangers of the frontier. Then during the summer of 1874, a great scourge of grasshoppers chewed its way across the country. Everything in the way was devoured. It was considered one of the worst insect plagues in history. After the huge clouds of grasshoppers finally passed, not a blade of grass or a stalk of corn was left standing. Lew Phillips surveyed his decimated farm and wept bitter tears. He later said that he felt as though he had been transported back in time to a Civil War battlefield.

In September 1874, the Phillipses left their devastated homestead. Like the Union soldiers after the first Battle of Bull Run, the family retreated. Lew and Josie tucked their three small children into a wagon and retraced the route they had taken two years before. They went back to Iowa and started all over again.

Eventually, after staying with some of their relatives, they ended up in Taylor County, named for President Zachary Taylor. Located sixty miles east of the Missouri River near the southwestern corner of Iowa, the county was perched on the border facing Missouri. On a forty-acre farm a mile outside of Conway, a town laid out by a railroad company in 1872, the Phillipses licked their spiritual wounds and rebuilt their lives. But more suffering was to come.

Little more than a year after their return to Iowa, the Phillipses' eldest child, Etta, became gravely ill with diphtheria. On October 1, 1875, the little girl died. Consolation of family members and friends, hard labor in the fields, and evenings spent with the Good Book helped Lew and Josie suffer the tragic loss.

There were other comforts. On August 8, 1876, less than a year after Etta's death, another baby was born. Delivered by Dr. Liggett, this second Phillips son was named Lee Eldas, or L. E., as the family called him. The newest baby boy cost his parents seven dollars in physician's fees, including a half-dollar for a bottle of colic medicine.

Dr. Liggett returned to the Phillipses' farm on July 3, 1879 — Lew and Josie's twelfth wedding anniversary — to deliver Edd Raleigh. This third Phillips son soon was known simply as Ed.

Then Waite and Wiate — the family's double blessing — came along in 1883.

Josie fussed over her twin babies as much as she did over the other children. Always mindful of the young daughter she had lost, Josie made sure the rest of her brood stayed healthy and strong. She also wanted them to remain aware of their strong family roots. Often, she spoke of her kinfolk and of Lew's.

She told of past family adventures all the while she cooked at the big iron stove or, in the evening, when she sewed new school clothes and darned socks by a kerosene lamp. Family members recalled Josie reciting her litany of stories as she bathed her twin sons from head to foot in a basin of tepid water and lathered them with castile soap.

A firm believer that "cleanliness is one of the grand incentives to health," as purported by the leading child-care authorities of that time, Josie followed the basic and commonsense rules of infant hygiene. That meant her twins got plenty of water for the skin, plenty of milk for the stomach, plenty of fresh air for the lungs, and plenty of sleep for the brain. Fortunately for Waite and Wiate, life on a farm in Iowa was tailor-made for youngsters on such a regimen.

They were trained to work diligently in farm duties but allowed reasonable time for . . . recreational pleasures. ~ WAITE PHILLIPS DIARY, 1886-1899

Three years after the twins were born, Lew Phillips was presented with an opportunity to expand his operations, so he sold the farm. That money, supplemented with an additional eight hundred dollars he had borrowed, allowed Lew to double his acreage by acquiring an eighty-acre farm almost four miles to the north of his first Taylor County place.

The last three of the Phillips children were born on the new farm. Nell, or Nellie, was born on July 28, 1886, Fred on October 2, 1889, and finally in 1893 Lura, who shared her oldest brother Frank's birthdate of November 28. Lew and Josie were pleased with their six sons and three daughters, even though by the time the last child was born, the older ones were leaving the nest.

Their father managed the farm and worked on it intermittently with his building business and their mother was most proficient in household duties and others having to do with feeding, clothing and taking care of her large family. Those were the days before any modern conveniences, such as exist today, were invented or in use in Taylor County, Iowa where they lived but life without such conveniences was good and wholesome at the time.

By hard work and frugal methods they gave their children the best
of care and all necessities of life. ~ WAITE PHILLIPS DIARY, 1886-
1899

Like any sensible Iowa farmer, Lew was overjoyed to have
strong sons to assist him on the farm. The presence of so many
helping hands at home also meant that Lew could earn more
wages elsewhere. For years, he toiled long and hard as a master
carpenter, amateur architect, and building contractor. He was
credited with the construction of many fine homes and barns
throughout the region.

Waite and Wiate thrived on their parents' farm. Both of them
spent as much time as possible outdoors. When they were not
going to school or taking care of farm tasks, the twins hunted,
fished, or trapped in the nearby forests. They scouted the freshly
plowed fields and thickets for arrowheads, and listened to old-
timers recite the legends of Native Americans who had hunted
and held council meetings in those same woods.

In the summertime, the two boys followed their older
brothers to swimming holes on the branches of the One Hundred
and Two River. During the winter months, long after nightfall,
they skated on the frozen streams or farm ponds by the light of
bonfires.

All in all, Waite and Wiate did well on a combination of hard
work and play. Despite the drudgery of the farm, their boyhood
together was mostly comfortable and simple. Those early years in
rural Iowa imprinted the rest of their lives.

Boys are fortunate to grow up in a farm or ranch environment
and this was especially true with these twin boys. ~ WAITE
PHILLIPS DIARY, 1886-1899

CHAPTER FIVE

BROTHERLY LOVE

Waite and Wiate were inseparable.

That fact could have been chiseled in granite by anyone who met the boys. And as the twins grew older, that single truth became quite apparent to the rest of the Phillips family. The brothers were a matched set. The tie, or psychological thread, binding them together was so strong that even if anyone had wanted to try, it could not have been severed.

Josie noticed it first. When her twin sons were still infants, she observed that they hardly ever competed with each other, even at feeding time. They might fuss a little bit, but the commotion never lasted too long. Instead, the two boys vied together against others. It was as though Waite and Wiate were taking on the rest of the world.

Like some other twins, the two brothers were so much alike that they seemed to read each other's mind. They were a complete unit. When one spoke, the other could finish the sentence.

Hardly anyone, including many of their own family members, could tell the twins apart. As the brothers grew, folks who knew them searched for differences constantly. There were none to be found easily. Nonetheless, folks peered into the boys' blue-gray eyes vainly looking for differences. Not only did the twins look exactly alike, but they wore identical clothes. Even the cowlicks in their brown hair matched.

From a distance, the boys' parents had a tough time saying which twin was which. It got to the point that when some mischief took place and either Waite or Wiate was thought to have been involved, Lew and Josie punished both of the twins just to be sure they got the true culprit. The puzzling thing was, there were no indications that the twins minded much receiving the punishment. Whether it was Lew's leather strap out behind the barn or a school-yard fistfight, they took their licks together and with little complaint.

Waite and Wiate never minded being twins, but enjoyed being each other's best friend and confidant.

And when one of the pair was hurt or became ill, the family noted that usually the other twin complained that he too felt the hurt or would become sick just like his brother. What the Phillipses did not know at that time was that the boys were experiencing the mysterious phenomenon of sympathetic pain sometimes associated with twins who were especially close.

Practically from the start of their lives, Wiate, the eldest twin, emerged as the leader of the twosome. He and Waite became a most formidable duo and, if they put their minds to it, they were as strong-willed as a pair of plow mules. Consequently, the twins had their share of altercations.

Although they normally did not compete against each other, a sibling dispute over a penknife or some other trophy sometimes took place. On very rare occasions, they fought between themselves, and some of those bouts were fierce. When Frank and L. E. tried to separate the punching and kicking twins, it was as though Wiate and Waite were striking out at their own mirror images. It was almost as though they were attacking themselves. And perhaps they were.

But most of the time, the twins remained strong allies, just as they had been from birth. They took up for each other, and each prided himself on knowing his twin's whereabouts at all times. Over the years, they developed a heightened sense of telepathy, the transference of thought between minds — a term coined by English writer F. W. Myers just a year before the twins' birth. Each insisted that he always could sense when his twin was in danger or in trouble.

Like the other Phillips children, the twins received a brief and rather basic grammar-school education. For most of their formal academic training, the boys attended a country school about one mile north of their farm. Together, Waite and Wiate slaved over McGuffey's readers, learned the three Rs, and managed to complete the sixth grade. Their favorite teachers were Maude Jones and Guy Liggett, a good friend of the older Phillips boys.

Another of the twins' preferred teachers was their own brother L. E., who, at age seventeen, enrolled in Western Normal College at Shenandoah, Iowa. He made his way through a two-year course of study by working as a janitor and waiting on tables for his room and board. At the end of the course, L. E. received a teacher's certificate and for a few years taught in several rural districts. By 1899, he had left teaching to team up with his pal, Claude Fisher of Creston, Iowa, as an insurance solicitor.

By the time L. E. started peddling insurance policies, the eldest of the Phillips brothers, Frank, already was long settled in Creston, where he owned and operated the town's leading barbershops. A natural-born entrepreneur, Frank had left the family farm by 1890 as a teenager. He struck out on his own and headed west to try his luck as a barber in the silver boom town of Aspen, Colorado. After his stint in the Rockies, Frank packed up his shears and straight razor and migrated to several points in Utah Territory before finally returning to Iowa.

Waite and Wiate corresponded with their big brother throughout his years in mining and railroad camps and rowdy towns. They looked up to their brother and were as itchy as Frank was to escape their father's farm and seek high adventure in the great American West.

The twin boys were afflicted with motion sickness which is an inconvenient affliction when living on a farm. However, they made frequent trips to Conway to attend church and Sunday school, also to Lenox, Sharpsburg and Clearfield to accompany their mother to market to trade farm products for food it was not possible to raise on the farm. The only trips outside Taylor County were to Creston, Iowa with their mother while babies and another one when about 12 years old to visit their brother Frank in Council Bluffs where he worked as a barber. ~ WAITE PHILLIPS
DIARY, 1886-1899

As they entered their teenage years, Waite and Wiate had plenty of friends, but their best chums — other than each other — were George Nagel and Fred Cooper. Those local lads also enjoyed the outdoors and shared the twins' dreams of Wild West escapades.

Unquestionably the best looking of all the Phillips boys, the handsome twins, sun-tanned and muscular from their labor on the farm, caught the eyes of many of the girls they encountered at school and church. The two boys developed a special adolescent interest in the Alderson girls, Emma and Minnie. They also paid particular attention to a set of twins, Edna and Effie Beach, who lived near Lenox.

Waite and Wiate's romance with the Beach girls was ideal, because only another set of twins could understand fully what it was like to be bonded forever to another person. Edna and Wiate made up one of the couples, and Waite and Effie the other.

With all four of them being twins, there were no attempts by either set to play the classic trick of passing off one twin for another. Edna and Effie always knew who was Waite and who was Wiate, and the two brothers never had any trouble telling the Beach twins apart. There was no use in anyone trying any shenanigans.

Before too long, carefully crafted notes, penned in india ink on stationery or scrawled in pencil on school paper, were being sent back and forth between the Beach and Phillips households. Edna and Effie addressed their young beaux as "Kind Friend" or "Dear Friend," and signed off with a stylish "Au revoir," or the more traditional, "I remain as ever your friend."

The correspondence was innocent and sweet. In a single paragraph in a letter of June 3, 1899, Effie told Waite of her father's rheumatism acting up and of how much she missed seeing Waite. The coy Effie went on to say, "Did Wiate tell you about the pretty May basket I got? I wonder who hung it? Wiate said he knew but he wouldn't tell me. Do you know? I have an idea but I don't know how good it is."

Picnics of deviled eggs and gingersnaps shared with a pair of beguiling lasses beneath a shady elm were close to pure nirvana for Waite and Wiate. But the brothers had more on their minds. They were also smitten with the promise of adventure. Tales of Teddy Roosevelt and his elite Rough Riders, of gold miners and silver kings, and of the so-called Wild Bunch led by Butch Cassidy and his sidekick, the Sundance Kid, proved every bit as tempting to Waite and Wiate as the winsome Beach sisters.

These twin boys were not outstanding ones except as to their unusual energy and their intense interest in nature and exploring what lay beyond the hills of their farm home, especially the country they visualized in the West with its mountains, streams, and desert lands. ~ WAITE PHILLIPS DIARY, 1886-1899

Late at night, after the rest of the family was fast asleep, the twins peered into the dark sky. They made out faces on the moon and watched as lightning bugs blinked awake in the damp honeysuckle. The boys thought about the world outside Taylor County and beyond Iowa. In their own remarkable twin language, they whispered their most secret dreams to each other.

CHAPTER SIX

ODYSSEY

The twins began their great western journey together on a crisp autumn day just weeks before the nineteenth century ran out of steam. Their wanderings lasted for two years nine months.

In October 1899 the twin boys followed the pattern of their two oldest brothers, Frank and L. E., by leaving their farm home to secure work in the western country. ~ WAITE PHILLIPS DIARY, 1899

Waite and Wiate were sixteen years old when they went to the Conway railroad station and boarded the train for Saint Joseph, Missouri. Their older brother Ed and their younger brother Fred remained at home with their sisters to carry on the chores. The night before the twins left, Josie prepared a special supper in their honor. She was saddened to see her boys depart, and Lew was not much in favor of the twins leaving either. Yet the Phillipses did not try to stop their sons. They knew better. The twins' minds were made up.

Waite and Wiate took only a few clothes and personal items. "Traveling light" was how Frank had told his kid brothers to go. They vowed to write home as often as possible, and they extracted promises of letters from their family and from the Beach sisters.

Just before the train left, the boys stuck their heads out a car window and waved good-bye. None of the strangers standing on the platform could tell the twins apart, but the boys' mother and the others in the family knew which was which. Josie's eyes went back and forth between Waite and Wiate as the train pulled away. It was as though she were memorizing every detail and feature of the twins. She stood there watching her sons until the train was out of sight, chugging south towards Missouri.

The boys did not linger very long in Saint Joseph. They crossed the Missouri River and went to work as hired hands on a farm outside Leavenworth, Kansas. But their employment was cut short when, as Waite pointed out in his diary, "they became homesick by doing such familiar work." They headed off to nearby Kansas City and secured railroad passes to work for the Union Pacific at Rock Springs, in southwestern Wyoming.

At long last, they found themselves deep in the American West. What the twins also discovered in Wyoming was a barren and lonesome land of scrub and sage, forbidding buttes, and snowy peaks. It was a land inhabited by the Wild Bunch, free-running antelope, and reckless cowboys. The twins were ecstatic. It was everything they had dreamed of — and then some.

Their experience with the railway in Wyoming made the brothers eager to see and do more. They also intended to retrace some of the route taken by their older brother Frank during his trek through the West as a barber and railroad worker years before.

From there [Rock Springs, Wyoming] they journeyed westward to Ogden, Utah and from there to Salt Lake City where during the months of November and December they worked for the Western Union Telegraph Company as messenger boys. Had pictures taken in Western Union uniforms which later on became prized possessions on account of unusual similarity. ~ WAITE PHILLIPS DIARY, 1899

While en route from Ogden to Salt Lake City, the twins encountered a man whom they later identified in letters and in Waite's diary only as Johnson. He was about fifty years old when he met the twins but, despite the vast age difference, Johnson became a good companion. Waite and Wiate ended up sharing an apartment with Johnson in Salt Lake City. Waite's letter to Josie on December 31, 1899 — the very last day of the century — mentioned a "gentleman . . . who has treated us better than any brother could."

Their new friend not only looked out for the twins, but also gave them their first real insight into the brutal world of big business. The brothers learned that several years before, Johnson had been a member of the American Railway Union back in Chicago. He told the boys that in June 1894, to help striking Pullman Palace Car Company workers, he and other members of his union had responded when Eugene Debs called for a general sympathy strike of all railway employees. Johnson explained that the strike was necessary because Pullman officials had reduced the company's payroll and wages, but had not cut prices at the company store or reduced rents for workers' homes.

Before the strike ended, deputy marshals and federal troops were called in, resulting in many deaths and injuries as well as the loss of millions of dollars in wages and property. Because of his participation in the strike, Johnson was banned from further railroad employment. Waite listened to all of Johnson's stories of strikes and workers' hardships and took them to heart.

He and his twin brother also thought that Salt Lake, far larger than any other city they had lived in, was a pleasant enough spot. While they were there, they did their best to answer all the correspondence that came their way from Iowa.

On January 28, 1900, just nine days after the twins' seventeenth birthday, Waite hastily scribbled a letter to his parents. He began by mentioning all the letters they had received, and then he described the large crowds that turned out every

Sabbath for services at the Mormon Tabernacle. Waite also offered reassurances for Lew and Josie.

"So you think we would be rambling home before long," he wrote. "I hope you don't take it in that light. If we intended to do that we never would have left. I found that the world is using me better than I expected it to but, of course, you have to treat it right first."

Soon after that letter was posted, the twins, accompanied by Johnson, left Utah for faraway Nome and the gold fields of Alaska. They traveled via train as far as Butte, Montana, by way of Pocatello, Idaho. Johnson pushed on to the northwest, but the twins wanted to build up a grubstake, so they stayed. They worked for a short time in a Butte smelter and then moved to Wardner, a town in far western Idaho named for a local prospector.

The brothers found lodging in Wardner with a family named Wright. They also secured jobs. At first the twins worked at the Bunker Hill, a bonanza mine that yielded loads of galena ore, a mixture of lead and silver. After a while, they changed jobs and went to the Nabob Mine. It proved to be demanding and strenuous, especially for a pair of seventeen-year-olds.

Less than a year before the twins started to work at the Nabob, the mine had been the scene of a bloody riot. Disgruntled workers who had been denied a fifty-cent increase in their pay of three dollars per day clashed with troops during a massive strike. Conditions and wages had not improved one iota since the strike had ended. Waite and Wiate each took home just three dollars a day. Each of them shelled out a full day's wages every week to cover their board. They also went to work every Sabbath, something unheard-of back in Iowa.

In a letter dated March 17, 1900, Wiate attempted to convince Josie that all was well. "There is no use in worrying about us Mother," he wrote. "Your boys know more about the world than you think. We never worry or regret anymore. There is no use in it." Wiate went on to discuss the weather, trout fishing, and the general beauty of the Coeur d'Alene country, with its vast deposits of lead, silver, and zinc. "The lady here says to me the other night, 'When you go up to bed throw down your pants and I will mend them.' It sounded quite familiar to me."

In the spring of 1900, as Buffalo Bill and his entourage performed their best tricks at New York's Madison Square Garden and across the nation, the Phillips brothers continued their own Wild West journey. By April, they had left for Seattle to meet their friend Johnson. After a quick stop in Spokane, the twins reached their destination, but they could not find hide nor hair of Johnson anywhere in the city. Finally, they decided to abandon the trip to Alaska because, as Waite put it in his journal, "it seemed everyone was headed in that direction."

Later that spring, after even more open-road traveling, the twins signed on with the Great Northern Railway. They put in a brief hitch waiting on tables in Yakima, but mostly they spent long hours belowground with picks and shovels in their calloused hands.

> *Worked, until June, in tunnel built for Great Northern R.R. under Everett, Washington. Then embarked on steamship Golden Gate at Seattle for San Francisco, California. Worked on highway near Alameda, California, and at Golden Gate Hotel in San Francisco. Waite had operation for absess [abscessed tooth] at City Hospital.* ~ WAITE PHILLIPS DIARY, 1900

Busy as they were, the twins still managed to keep up a regular correspondence with family and friends back in Iowa. "Ma, I don't look bad now, but I lost about twenty pounds while I was in California," Waite wrote from Everett on July 18, 1900. "I am alright now, only my teeth, one of them bothers me. I will get it fixed soon." He described evening strolls on the beach, taking salt baths, and gathering wild berries. He also mentioned the catches of fine trout and salmon that fetched two bits a fish at market.

That same month, the twins took a train journey to Portland, Oregon, back to Seattle, then north to Sedro Woolley. They briefly worked in a shingle mill near the village of Edgcomb, visited Vancouver, British Columbia, and then went on to Spokane. By summer's end, Wiate had decided to go to the big cowboy roundup at Pendleton, Oregon. Waite had other plans. He opted to leave his twin temporarily. He went to Missoula, Montana, and from there to the more remote settlement of Lothrop to take a job in a lumber mill.

Although they had been apart briefly in the past, this was the first time that Waite and Wiate were separated for a significant length of time. It was a difficult several months for both brothers. A melancholy epistle which Wiate sent to his parents in the fall of 1900 from Ogden, Utah, best summed up how the twins felt.

Dear Folks,

Well, I will drop you a line today to assure you I'm still among the living.

I have been waiting here a week for a letter from Waite and just received it today. I will start for Lothrop in the morning.

To tell the facts I'm getting a little too lonesome without him.

I have rheumatism until I can scarcely move. My fingers are so sore that I can hardly straighten them out. It has been snowing and raining here since last Saturday.

How do you all feel?

Well, you might write me a letter with Waites at Lothrop.

Hoping this finds you all well.

I am as ever,

Wiate

CHAPTER SEVEN

TRAIL'S END

Even though Waite and Wiate were apart from each other during the late summer and entire autumn of 1900, they were having the time of their lives. While Wiate tramped about in the wilds of Canada and moseyed through Utah, Wyoming, and back to the Pacific Northwest, Waite stuck to the heavily forested high country of western Montana.

Always ready to try a new adventure, Waite left the lumber mill that fall and joined up with men eager to spend the long winter trapping pine martens — small weasel-like mammals with soft, thick, valuable fur. Waite's new companions were Louis Vrolick, a young man from Holland; Frank Hawkins of Maryville, Missouri, just below the Iowa line and Taylor County; and last but not least, a salty local character named Bitterroot Bill, the one member of the quartet who supposedly possessed the most "woods wisdom."

This curious collection of fur trappers outfitted for a long winter's stay high in the rugged Bitterroot Range of the northern Rocky Mountains along the Montana-Idaho border. They secured packhorses and laid in plenty of provisions, utensils, and warm clothing. In November, they moved from Petty Creek to Fish Creek, a primary tributary of the Clark Fork River. From that point, the trapping party took over a prospector's old cabin near the mouth of Cash Creek.

By that time, Wiate, en route to rejoin his brother, found the best way to communicate with Waite was through their mother in Iowa. Besides letters, the twins also relied on their uncanny ability to track each other down.

At the fur trappers' cabin, surrounded by Douglas firs, lodgepole pines, and deepening drifts of snow, provisions soon were running low. By December, Waite had been chosen to fetch fresh supplies. Without complaint, he accepted the challenge and left the others behind, hiking thirty miles over the Fish Creek Trail back to Lothrop.

Once he arrived, Waite found his twin waiting for him. It was a joyous reunion. Wiate explained that he had found his way to Lothrop several weeks before, just as he had promised in the sad letter to their parents. Soon after arriving, he struck out for the mountains to find Waite and the others. Wiate followed the blazed trail until it stopped. Darkness overtook him, along with a fierce blizzard, forcing him to spend the night huddled on a mountainside. With his feet badly frostbitten, Wiate inched his way back to Lothrop, where he gradually regained his health at a friendly homesteader's cabin. That is where Waite found him.

The brothers acquired fresh packhorses and provisions, and returned together up the steep mountain trails to the cabin. But the twins found that the other trappers were gone. Bitterroot Bill, who had grown tired of the escapade and refused to pay his share of expenses, had deserted the party. Inside the cabin, a note from Vrolick explained that Hawkins, the Missouri lad, had accidentally shot himself while deer hunting. Two bones were badly broken in Hawkins' arm, so Vrolick had taken him out to find a doctor. About a week later, Vrolick returned.

On February 2, 1901, when Wiate went back to Lothrop to return the packhorses, he got off a letter to Lew and Josie. "Waite and I took some grub up to our cabin a few days ago and I just got the packhorses back yesterday," he wrote. "This is a bad time to pack into the mountains for the trail is very slick. As we were going up, one of the horses slipped on a side hill trail and rolled over and down the bank about 300 feet.

"I intended to go back today but could not. I am glad that I did not now for I received your letter. If I had gone up without receiving your letter we may not have gotten it for two months."

Wiate's letter to Iowa also was filled with plenty of news for each of his siblings still living at home. He wrote of hikes through the forest on Norwegian snowshoes, and a hungry mountain lion that had wiped out the boys' supply of freshly killed deer. He added his thoughts about the Boer War then dragging on in South Africa. He also wrote of a recent dream.

"I had a funny dream the other night. I dreamed that Waite and I were home and Pa said that he didn't want us to come home again until we were 21. He said he thought the best thing we could do would be to go to South Dakota. He said you folks would write to us often. But it was only a dream.

"Now, Ma, I don't think we will ever separate again. That is the reason I came back here from Seattle so as to be with Waite."

The twins and Vrolick stayed at the cabin through the rest of the winter. By late spring of 1901, their supplies were dwindling again. They were tired of eating mostly venison and beans. The three of them returned to Lothrop and civilization. They sold off their pelts and took Hawkins' share of the profits to him. Still recovering at a hospital in Missoula, he was in good spirits but his wounded arm had been amputated.

That April, the twins sent a joint letter to their folks in Iowa, letting them know that they had survived the rigors of life in the Bitterroots. "Just came from out of the mountains about a week ago," they wrote, "so you see we haven't had a chance to write before for this is the first time we have been out since we last wrote. But we have come out for good this time and I have hair down over my shoulders."

It was not entirely clear which twin had the long hair, but the scrawl looked to be Waite's. The letter also had news of the twins' companion, Louis Vrolick, whom they affectionately called Oom Paul. The boys teased their sister Nellie that their Dutch pal was going to visit Iowa to see her.

But neither Oom Paul nor the Phillips twins showed up in Iowa. Vrolick returned to Holland. Waite and Wiate still had gypsy feet, and continued their great adventure throughout 1901.

In May, they went to Spokane and then eastward to Roslyn, Washington, before heading north to Nelson, British Columbia, to strain and struggle in the Black Bear Mine. By late summer, they had returned to the States and found jobs in the harvest fields of North Dakota and Minnesota.

That August, the folks back in Iowa, then living close to the town of Gravity, received a letter mailed from Ada, in western Minnesota. Pausing at the Northwestern Windward Hotel, where room rates were one dollar a day, the twins wrote of the sweltering temperatures and described gathering plums, hazelnuts, and chokecherries along the banks of the Wild Rice River. Soon they were off for Minneapolis, Chicago, and Upland, Indiana, to toil in a sweltering glass factory.

Instead of cutting across the midlands so they could go home to rest for a spell and gobble down some of Josie's good cooking, Waite and Wiate continued to circle Iowa. They still had many more places to see.

Saint Louis was next on their busy agenda. Then they headed due south, passing through some of the same country their father had come to know as a young Union soldier almost forty years earlier. They spent time in the dense woods of Arkansas, sweating for a tie and timber contractor near the town of Marked Tree.

Late in the year, they signed on with a railroad grading crew not far from Hope, Arkansas. Despite the town's name, the boys almost lost all hope when they were defrauded of their winter wages by a labor boss who dreamed up fictitious commissary charges.

At the close of 1901, Waite and Wiate left Fort Smith on a

train that whisked them across Indian Territory and into Oklahoma Territory. Until March 1902, the boys again earned a living at railroad construction, this time between the Indian Territory towns of Durant and Madill.

In April to Oklahoma City, then to Newton, Kansas where twins became separated. Reunited at Denver, Colorado much by chance at a restaurant there and then to Cheyenne, Wyoming. Railway freight engineer becoming attracted to the twins insisted they accompany him in engine cab from Cheyenne to end of his run at Rawlins, Wyoming. ~ WAITE PHILLIPS DIARY, 1902

At Rawlins, the boys found some luck. As Waite put it in his journal, they "broke the gambler's bank playing blackjack," leaving them with plenty of money to continue their seemingly endless journey. Although there was no record of just how much the boys had won, Waite believed they had enough to settle down in Ogden and open a cigar store.

The morning after their big win at the card table, the twins caught a train for Utah. They stopped in Echo and took the night train to Ogden. They paid a week's rent in advance at a hotel, bought new clothes and pocket watches, and enjoyed a hot meal. Wiate put the pocket change left from their supper tab into a slot machine and hit the jackpot, which caused him to go on another gambling rampage. The boys headed for the gaming tables and played cards all night long. By dawn, all the twins' money was gone. As was the custom at that time, the dealer gave each of the brothers a silver dollar. They pocketed the money and secured free train passes. After a few days, the twins took off for Nevada to help build concrete culverts for the Central Pacific Railroad.

The twins had started their great journey in October 1899, and they had trekked through almost every one of the western United States, parts of Canada, the Midwest, and the Indian Nations. As the spring of 1902 drew to a close, it was apparent that they had no intentions of slowing their pace.

*After resting and having additional interesting experiences, the
boys with their blanket rolls journeyed over the Sierra Divide by
railroad freight train, on customary free ride basis of that period
of western development, to Roseville, California, where they
worked in a brick plant.*

*Then to Portland, Oregon — worked on river boat. North
Yakima, Washington — worked on irrigation project. Then to
Sprague, Washington where they worked in Sprague Hotel.*
~ WAITE PHILLIPS DIARY, 1902

A letter came for the boys at their hotel in early June 1902.
Postmarked at Gravity, Iowa, the letter was written by the twins'
brother, Ed. It was dated June 3 and was filled with love and concern.

"Your letter just came this morning and it makes us all feel
good to hear from you and know you are alright," wrote Ed.
"Mother and Father never cease worrying about you boys. I
believe if you knew how much they worry when they don't hear
from you so long you would not fail to write at least once a week
no difference if it were only a card. They would know where you
are and that you were alright. It seems that you don't stay in one
place. . . ."

Waite and Wiate liked their newest home base. Located thirty-six miles southwest of Spokane, the town of Sprague boasted a
colorful past, including a former sheriff who was Buffalo Bill
Cody's cousin. The twins lived and worked at the Hotel Sprague,
where proprietor J. S. Lucas charged guests one or two dollars per
night, depending on the size of the room. The brothers decided
that working at the hotel was a pleasant change from the manual-
labor jobs they had held in the past.

But despite the comfortable surroundings, by the time the
Fourth of July rolled around the twins knew they were facing yet

another difficulty. Wiate was not feeling well. He had been bothered with what was described as an "abdominal disturbance" earlier that year in Portland. Now his stomach ailment was kicking up again. And true to form, when one of the twins felt badly, so did the other.

Finally, a doctor was summoned to the hotel. After a quick examination of Wiate, the doctor declared that the young man had to be hospitalized at once. With the generous assistance of Lucas, the twins' employer, Wiate was transported on a cot in a baggage railway car to Spokane. Waite was by his side.

Wiate was rushed to Sacred Heart Hospital, a three-story brick edifice with a brand-new wing, just east of the center of the city. Spokane's first and most venerable hospital, Sacred Heart had been maintained by the Sisters of Providence since it opened in 1886.

While the good nuns tried to comfort Waite, the attending physicians diagnosed his twin's problem as acute appendicitis. They said his condition was most serious. They recommended an immediate operation. Waite quickly asked for advice from friends back in Sprague, and he wired for financial assistance from the family in Iowa.

In a response letter, the boys' employer, Lucas, wrote that he was "glad to hear the boy is doing alright. We are anxious to see him get well and as long as your brother sends you money don't fail to give him all the care that is necessary for him to have as he will require the best of care for several days. We are getting along pretty well and you [might] just as well stay with him until he is entirely out of danger . . . don't spare anything that will be a benefit to him."

Back in Iowa, Frank Phillips, the most prosperous family member, quickly wired a draft for three hundred dollars for Wiate's medical care.

On July 13, with Waite pacing the long, dark hospital corridors, the surgeons operated on the gravely ill Wiate. For three days afterward, Waite hardly left his brother's bedside. Physicians checked Wiate's vital signs, then walked away frowning and shaking their heads. The quiet sisters in black habits, with saintly faces framed in white — looking like true angels of mercy to Waite — offered constant prayers and comfort to both the twins.

Waite tried to boost his brother's spirits. He leaned over Wiate and told him everything was going to be all right. He recalled their high times in the past. He whispered of plans for further adventures.

But there would be no more new escapades for the twins. Their grand journey was completed. Their time together was done. Peritonitis had set in and the poison had spread.

On Wednesday, July 16, 1902, after nineteen spirited years of living life to its fullest, the time came for Wiate Phillips to die.

Waite watched his twin draw a final breath. After the doctor and the priest had left and the nurses had closed Wiate's eyes and pulled the crisp sheet over his face, Waite remained motionless. One of the nuns handed Waite a small packet containing his brother's few possessions. Still Waite did not move. He sat by the bed. He waited, wishing it were all only a terrible dream.

But it was not a nightmare. It was all true. Waite was alone. His partner was gone. His twin brother was dead.

11
SHADOW
CHASER

Life itself is but the shadow of death, and souls departed but the shadows of the living. All things fall under this name. The sun itself is but the dark simulacrum, and light but the shadow of God.

SIR THOMAS BROWN, 1658

Genevieve Elliott as a baby, Knoxville, Iowa, 1887. Waite Phillips and classmates at Shenandoah Commercial Institute and School of Penmanship, 1903. Waite is on the far left. Genevieve with friends, ca. 1903. Genevieve is on the far left. An oil-well site in Indian Territory, ca. 1907. Waite is on the far left.
Following pages: Genevieve, early 1900s. A letter from Genevieve's father consenting to her marriage to Waite.

REX
COAL

WAITE PHILLIPS.

REPRESENTING
THE REX COAL & MINING CO.
CRESTON, IOWA.

Knoxville National Bank

Knoxville, Iowa, 10/19 190

Mr. Waite Phillips

Bartlesville Okla

My Dear Waite

It is with regret and
pleasure I give my cons
to your marriage with
my daughter Genevieve
I regret to loose her
yet am pleased that
her choice is one
who I hone every reason
to believe will treat
her kindly and do all
in his power under
all circumstances to
make her happy

CHAPTER EIGHT

HOMECOMING

When his twin brother died in the Sacred Heart Hospital ward in Spokane, Waite Phillips felt as though half of himself had perished. It was an overpowering tragedy. He could not comprehend something that made absolutely no sense to him. Life without his best friend and confidant was unthinkable.

Unquestionably, his twin's passing caused the most profound pain of Waite's life. It was a loss he carried forever. He would never again feel completely whole. Many decades later, when Waite was an old man and his life was nearly at its end, he found himself still looking for his vanished twin. Even then, the eternally youthful Wiate haunted his brother's dreams.

There really were few people whom Waite could turn to for support and relief. In the Spokane of 1902, there were no psychotherapists or analysts, no psychologists or professional counselors to help Waite deal with his enormous grief, depression, hopelessness, and apathy.

There were only a few gentle and sympathetic nuns. They remained steadfast and did all they could to console Waite. Their tender mercies brought at least some solace. The sisters prayed for the dead twin's soul and for the living twin's life. They told Waite that the extreme anguish he felt would diminish in time. The sisters implored him to return to where his and his brother's lives had begun.

Waite listened to the nuns. He knew they spoke the truth. He would go home. There really was no other choice. He would take his dead twin and they would return to Iowa and to their own — the Phillips family and the others who always had loved them.

With money left from what Frank had wired to Spokane, Waite employed a local mortician to see to Wiate's body. He used the rest of the money for train tickets back to Iowa.

Dr. J. D. Buchanan, billed in Spokane as a leading "funeral director and embalmer" who dealt in "wholesale and retail funeral furnishings," was hired to take care of Wiate's body. Dr. Buchanan arrived at Sacred Heart Hospital in his best horse-drawn hearse. He took the corpse back to his establishment on Riverside Avenue and prepared Wiate for the long trip home. Buchanan washed and shaved the dead boy, embalmed the body, and dressed Wiate in new underwear and a burial robe. He placed him in a metal-lined casket and delivered it to the depot. Buchanan's total fees, including care of the body, coffin, and transportation, came to $230. But because Waite had cash in hand and was able to pay the invoice in full, Buchanan sliced eighty dollars off that substantial total, making the final bill $150.

On July 18, 1902 — a sunny Friday — Waite and Wiate Phillips began their last trip together. On the train, Waite had time to reflect. The long journey allowed Waite to read a letter received that summer from Edna, one of the Beach twins from Lenox, Iowa. Edna was Wiate's best sweetheart. "Dear Love of Old," her letter began.

> Well, my goodness I thought you were never going to answer but you say you "will ans. immediately" so I suppose the distance is the cause of my anxiety.
>
> Why, Wiate, what makes you so anxious lately to receive my letters? You didn't used to care so much whether you heard from me or not. But I rather think homesickness is the cause of the mystery, isn't it? Poor boy

— you have my sympathy, though it isn't as deep, probably, as it might be if it came from one having more experience with homesickness than I have.

I believe if I should ever get the chance to travel and see some of this great world, my joy would be so great that no thought of poor old Lenox would ever enter my head again. Oh, how heartless! I'll take it back, for I have many and very dear friends here in this old town and I know if I should have to part from them forever it would be almost as bitter as death.

But I really don't see how you boys can stay away from your folks so long; loved as you were and are! My! How gladly they would welcome the wanderers! I would like to be an invisible witness to such a scene.

So you have been in the hospital, dear? What was the trouble with you? Poor boy, to think of you being sick away off there with no one but strangers to wait on you! Were they kind to you? You write you could be near me only — only what Wiate? Only you don't want to? No, I don't know My Girl's A Dream but I've heard it. Perhaps that's all she is Wiate — only a dream.

Oh, dear, life seems to be not worth the pain of living. I get tired of the same old rigmarole every day. And, yet I must live and each day must smile when the world is glad; must laugh in the old time way though my heart be heavy and sad.

Home is the best place, Wiate. I think you had better decide in its favor. I think I'd stop the running around too, dear, if I were you. You've surely seen a great deal of the U.S. anyway. . . .

Riding in the baggage car with his brother's coffin, Waite looked at the postmarks on the envelope. Edna's letter had followed the twins around Washington from North Yakima to

Prosser until finally it caught up with them at Sprague. Those guileless words from the girl he had left behind were in the last letter Wiate Phillips ever received.

During the trip home, Waite probably pulled out the small packet of Wiate's belongings. There were rolling papers, a Prince Albert tobacco tin, a few trinkets, tintype photographs, and not much more. Those were Wiate's last possessions, his worldly goods. Waite carefully tucked them away in his bedroll. He kept those few cherished items close to him for the rest of his life.

The train made its way through country that the twins had traversed during their lengthy trek. Waite listened to the miles click by on the steel rails while the train moved eastward and at last passed into Iowa. At Council Bluffs, L. E. came to meet the train and accompany his brothers, both living and dead, the rest of the way home. Working as a traveling coal salesman, L. E. had learned of Wiate's death when he received a wire on July 18 sent from Gravity by his brother Ed. It simply stated, "Wiate is dead. Started for home this morning."

L. E. rode with Waite and Wiate on that last stretch downstate across the West and the East Nishnabotna and the Nodaway rivers to Taylor County and the town of Gravity. An undertaker and the entire Phillips family, all as somber as midnight, waited at the train station.

This seems a proper place in the diary to record a comparison of these twin brothers. While classified as "identical" by medical science, the older one — Wiate — was somewhat superior in intelligence and considerably more so in the qualities of leadership and the spirit of adventure (he also liked to gamble and I — Waite — was the conservative one). It is interesting to contemplate the importance of these qualities as to results, had the older twin brother lived to continue the almost certain partnership which heretofore existed between them. ~ WAITE PHILLIPS DIARY, 1902

On a sweltering July morning filled with stark sunshine, the family laid Wiate to rest in Lexington Cemetery near Bedford. He did not repose there very long. Only a short time later, his coffin was reinterred at Gravity Cemetery, because it was closer to Lew and Josie's newest home. It was the graveyard where they themselves eventually would be buried.

Despite his continuing grief, all of this activity must have made Waite smile. He, of all people, understood the irony of the situation — that even in death, his twin could not stay still, but had to make yet one more move before yielding to a final rest.

CHAPTER NINE

RECOVERY

A return to life in Iowa, encircled by loved ones and the cornfields, nurtured Waite Phillips. Like his elders, dating to even before the venturesome Captain Standish splashed ashore at Plymouth, Waite put a great deal of stock in the curative powers that resulted from a combination of hard work and play. The daily dose of labor and sport among his familiars was just the healing tonic Waite required to balm his profound grief.

He approved of the newest family home that his father had acquired during the twins' long absence. It was built on a 120-acre farm one mile west of Gravity. Breathing fresh country air saturated with the aroma of manure, freshly mowed hay, and wild blossoms did not do Waite any harm.

Perhaps his mother's cooking and her loving hands were the most therapeutic of all remedies for melancholy and loneliness. Josie Phillips and the family were rock solid and steadfast. They were always there for Waite, particularly through those first few difficult months after Wiate's death. And even though he knew that he never would mend fully from the deep wound, Waite was able to gain strength and go on with his life.

Last half of July with family on farm and renewed acquaintance-ship with old friends. Considerable emotional adjustments necessary as a result of loss of brother. ~ WAITE PHILLIPS DIARY, 1902

In early August, a letter came for Waite from Lenox. It was written by Edna Beach, Wiate's sweetheart. The letter was filled with news of her twin sister, Effie, and other mutual chums. Edna's warm words fortified Waite. Edna also broached the sensitive subject some people had tiptoed around with Waite — his deceased brother. Although still lamenting Wiate's death, she wrote of the twin they both had loved, the twin they missed so much.

"Poor boy come up, I have no doubt you are lonesome," Edna wrote. "It's too bad. Oh, I do wish I could help you! Nothing can ever bring him back, but, dear, we'll meet him in heaven above." As with much of the other correspondence from his early life, Waite cherished the letter forever.

That same month, Waite also tried to get his mind on other matters and at the same time better himself. Braced with encouragement from his older brothers, Waite landed a position as a grocery clerk in Gravity. He went to work for Roy W. Coan, the store owner and the man who had married Waite's oldest sister, Jennie. Waite took his new job quite seriously. He left his parents' farm and boarded in a spare room at his sister and brother-in-law's home in town.

Much later in his life, Waite learned the truth about that job. He found out that his brothers Frank and Lee Eldas had paid all of his earnings, and not Coan. Anxious for his little brother to garner practical experience in the world of business, Frank earnestly believed that every dollar he forked over to Coan to cover Waite's wages was worth it.

During the years, Frank began to take more interest in Waite. For his part, Waite always had looked up to L. E. and held him in high regard. Yet it was also true that Waite especially thought of the paternalistic Frank, the oldest Phillips brother, as the ideal role model.

Far beyond his instinctive talent for deal making, everyone could see that Frank possessed a genuine entrepreneurial style.

Waite told his pals that his big brother was not afraid to take chances. That gutsy behavior made the difference when it came to success, thought Waite. But besides having the steel nerves of a jewel thief, Frank also had the good luck of a high-stakes gambler — the sort who was undaunted by the occasional bad cut of the cards or roll of the dice.

Frank's luck seemed to be holding well. Almost a decade older than Waite, Frank had been very busy — and very successful — while the twins made their extended jaunt around the country. Frank quickly parlayed his Creston barbershops into popular tonsorial parlors. A skilled salesman, Frank even came up with a hair restorative which could help prevent baldness, he bragged.

Perfumed rainwater was the principal ingredient in the hair tonic. Frank dubbed it Mountain Sage, and peddled the concoction as fast as he could get it into bottles. Young Waite and the rest of the family always marveled at the popularity of Mountain Sage, because even in his early twenties, Frank was already as bald as a newborn's behind. Frank's sales ability gave genuine meaning to the cliché about being able to sell ice to Eskimos.

In 1897, a couple of years before the twins left on their odyssey, Frank had had the good fortune of marrying Jane Gibson. She was fondly called Betsie by those who loved her, including her protective father, John Gibson, the premier banker and civic leader of Creston, Iowa, and Frank's best customer.

Although he presented the newlyweds with a nest egg of twenty thousand dollars and he was impressed by Frank's prowess with the shears and straight razor, John Gibson wanted much more for his daughter than life as a barber's wife. That was especially the case by December 1898, when a baby arrived in Creston — a bouncing grandson promptly named John Gibson Phillips by the doting Frank and Jane.

A successful entrepreneur and investor with his hands in several ventures such as mining operations, real estate developments, and a mahogany-import business in the Philippine Islands, Gibson became Frank's mentor. He took his son-in-law under his wing, convincing him to give up barbering to learn the banking and bond business.

But not even Frank's continuing rise up the ladder of success could prevent heartaches. In July 1902, just a few days after Wiate had died in Spokane, word reached Frank and Jane Phillips in Creston that Jane's mother, Matilda Gibson, was also dead. Tillie, as her Iowa friends knew her, had died of cholera while accompanying her husband on a business trip to the Philippines. Faced with the sudden death of his brother, Frank also consoled his heartbroken wife while her mother was laid to rest in a Manila tomb thousands of miles from home. Just as the nuns at the hospital where Wiate died had told Waite that the passage of time would heal his wounds, Frank comforted his young wife with the same advice.

It was true. When the autumn of 1902 came round, life was settling down again for the Phillips family in Iowa.

"I had a nice long letter from Waite this morning, which was very cheerful," Frank wrote his parents that October. "He seems to be well satisfied with his place in Gravity. I understand that Roy has purchased the entire stock, and I am glad of it. I hope he will feel that the conditions there justify him in reaching out to such an extent that he can provide a better position for Waite until he becomes thoroughly familiar with the details of the mercantile business, as Waite seems to feel that he would prefer that line to any other business he could choose. I enjoyed Waite's visit to Creston very much and we had a good visit over matters in general, and among other things we agreed to keep up a regular correspondence and exchange letters every week."

Life was smoothing out for all the Phillipses. In September, Ed married Anna Beveredge in Gravity, and they moved into a cottage that Lew Phillips built for them on his farmland.

Another marriage within the family soon followed. On November 26, 1902, L. E. wed Lenora Carr, from Bedford, Iowa, whom everyone called Node, a name of endearment pronounced Nodie. L. E. and his bride took up residence in Knoxville, Iowa, where he accepted a position as secretary and manager of a new venture, Hawkeye Mining Company.

For the rest of the year, Waite continued to work as a grocery clerk and delivery boy for his brother-in-law's store in Gravity. But he was once again feeling restless. As the Christmas holidays approached, Waite knew that despite what he had told Frank about wanting to remain in the mercantile business, he was ready to try something new.

By January 1903, Waite had quit working for Coan at the grocery and had relocated to Shenandoah, in Page County, just west of Taylor County. Waite moved there to improve himself by attending the Shenandoah Commercial Institute and School of Penmanship, departments of Western Normal College. The six-month course of study he enrolled in would be the last of his formal education.

Waite worked hard at his courses in business and bookkeeping, commercial law, grammar and rhetoric, penmanship, and mathematics. He liked most of his instructors, but his favorite was Laviece Chambliss, the English teacher. Waite carried on a correspondence with Miss Chambliss and regularly sent her gifts of money until her death in September 1956.

Lew Phillips was glad that Waite, then twenty years old, wanted to return to school, and he told his son not to worry about expenses. Besides the tuition, Waite needed money for room and board, to get some teeth filled, and for covering a few incidentals.

"Am getting along very well so far so don't worry about me," Waite wrote on February 21, 1903, to his parents — with a new flair and flourish, thanks to his penmanship course. "I think I am getting my money's worth, and as soon as I see that I am not, I will quit."

That never happened. Waite did not quit. He lasted the entire session, and on July 13, 1903, he was awarded a diploma. The impressive document certified that "Waite Phillips has completed the regular business course of study and practice as prescribed by this institution. And upon a proper examination, is found worthy of graduation. We therefore by his presence declare him an intelligent and competent accountant, and as such cheerfully commend him to the favor of the business community."

Also found later in life that the older two brothers paid my tuition and living expenses there. My father later reimbursed them and I reimbursed him. ~ WAITE PHILLIPS DIARY, 1903

CHAPTER TEN

GENEVIEVE, SWEET GENEVIEVE

With his diploma and a new suit of clothes in his satchel, Waite was ready to enter the world of business and make his mark.

In August 1903, he moved to Iowa's coal-mining country. There Waite found a niche in Knoxville, Iowa, the seat of Marion County, southeast of Des Moines. He accepted the position of bookkeeper at Hawkeye Coal Company, where L. E. was a stockholder, secretary, and manager of the firm. Frank and some of his Creston associates were also major Hawkeye stockholders.

Waite's starting salary was forty dollars a month, and that time none of his big brothers paid the wages under the table. He wore a necktie and suit every day of the week, including Sunday, when he attended services at the Methodist church.

L. E. and Node allowed Waite to take a room at their home — a pleasant two-story frame residence with a front porch ideal for visits on evenings and Sunday afternoons. By October, there was a nephew for Waite to play with when he came home from work. L. E. and Node named their firstborn Philip Rex. The middle name was for George B. Rex, president of Hawkeye Coal.

Waite kept his nose to the grindstone, making frequent visits to the company mine in connection with his clerical duties. He also got around Knoxville as much as possible. There were all kinds of parties and a whirl of social activities, so he made many new friends, especially among local young people. His natural good looks and boyish charm made him particularly popular with the young ladies.

One afternoon late in that summer of 1903, one of his many acquaintances, Miss Tony Kauffman, introduced Waite to a young woman who would remain a key part of his life forever and ever. She was a pretty lass, just turned sweet sixteen. Her name was Genevieve Elliott.

We attended dances together and she taught me that social art.
~ WAITE PHILLIPS DIARY, 1903

Waite admitted later that at their very first meeting, he was struck hard by the charming Miss Elliott. Although she was still very much a young girl, four years his junior, Genevieve's grace and style absolutely enchanted Waite. He had never met anyone quite like her. She was refined and poised, but not at all stuck up like some of the other young women. She also happened to be the daughter of the wealthiest banker in town.

Born in Knoxville on June 17, 1887, Genevieve was the youngest daughter of John Brown Elliott and Nora Miller, considered to be two of the proverbial pillars of the community.

Genevieve's mother was born in Knoxville on December 2, 1856, the youngest child of Admiral Miller and his wife, Eliza Chapman. Educated in the Knoxville schools, Nora later attended college at Ames. She then went back to the family home on East Montgomery Street, the tree-lined avenue that would be her abode throughout her life.

Nora suited Knoxville, and the town seemed just right for Nora — especially after she met and began her courtship with John Elliott, descendant of an esteemed Puritan religious leader and grandson of Irish immigrants.

Elliott, born in 1852 in Poland, Ohio, was the son of Jared K.

Elliott and Mary Brown. Jared, also a native of the town of Poland, was a son of Daniel Elliott of Connecticut. Through Daniel, the lineage was traced to John Eliot, famous in early colonial history as a Puritan apostle to Indian tribes in Massachusetts and as translator of the Bible into local Indian dialects. Recognized on both sides of the Atlantic as the embodiment of efforts to Christianize Native Americans, the zealous Eliot represented the epitome of New England Puritanism.

John Elliott's mother did not come from such illustrious roots. Mary Brown was born in Ireland and immigrated to the United States with her parents when she was a little girl.

Equally proud of their colonial heritage and Irish blood and anxious to settle in new lands, the Elliotts of Ohio headed west in the early 1860s as the Civil War raged. With their three sons and two daughters, they settled on a farm near Knoxville in Pleasant Grove township, Marion County. John Elliott attended public schools and then returned to Ohio to complete a three-year course of study at Poland College.

Back in Iowa, Elliott read for the law and was admitted to the state bar in 1876. On November 27, 1878, he married Nora Miller. He served two terms as a Democrat in the legislature, and entered banking. Working his way up through the executive ranks, Elliott became cashier of Knoxville National Bank in 1884, and many years later was made president. By this time, all of his business associates knew Elliott as J. B. and regarded him as one of the major influences and powers in their community.

The two Elliott daughters — Helen and Genevieve — were always proud of their parents and of the family's high standing in the small Iowa town where they resided.

At the time of her death in 1931, Genevieve's mother was described in one newspaper account as "a woman of unusual physical beauty and charm, a born social leader, yet withal she remained unspoiled, always courteous and gentle, ever thoughtful of others."

As much as she adored her mother, Genevieve also was very close to her father, a distinguished man with a dignified bearing and friendly manner.

Among the most cherished images from Genevieve's youth was a photograph made by Snodgrass Studio in Knoxville. In the photo are Genevieve, her parents, and others posed in and around the Elliott family's brand-new motor carriage — the first car to arrive in Knoxville.

The photographer placed several people inside the automobile, parked in the shade of a gum tree in front of the Elliott home. He posed Genevieve's mother at the front of the touring car. She was resplendent in her long frock with her hat tied with a scarf around her smiling face. J.B. Elliott, in his best banker's suit, bow tie, and summer straw hat, stood at the rear of the car with his arms behind his back. Next to Elliott was Genevieve, in a duster and gloves with her long hair fashionably piled and pinned beneath a hat. Her head was turned ever so slightly and there was just the hint of a smile on her lips.

The photograph of the Elliotts and their shiny new motorcar was made at about the time Genevieve was introduced to Waite Phillips. It remained a candid and revealing portrait of Genevieve, the young woman whom everyone called Veva — her favorite name of endearment.

Holding Genevieve — the lithe Veva — in his arms as she taught him to dance beneath paper lanterns rejuvenated Waite. She caused him to live once again and not feel empty as he had felt ever since his twin died. Waite looked forward to Sunday afternoon walks through town with Genevieve, tall lemonades shared on the cool front porch, and fancy dinner parties. As he tended to his bookkeeping tasks at the coal office six days a week, the serenade of dance music played in his head.

Waite became especially interested in an old song, the lyrics written in 1869 by George Cooper, a close friend and occasional collaborator of Stephen Foster. Cooper wrote the words to the song right after the death of his young wife. The nostalgic melody remained popular with all lovers of close harmony. Waite knew every word and could sing it loud and clear. It was his favorite song.

O, Genevieve, I'd give the world
To live again the lovely past!
The rose of youth was dew impearled;
But now it withers in the blast.
I see thy face in every dream,
My waking thoughts are full of thee;
Thy glance is in the starry beam
That falls along the summer sea.

O, Genevieve, sweet Genevieve,
The days may come, the days may go,
But still the hands of mem'ry weave
The blissful dreams of long ago.

Fair Genevieve, my early love,
The years but make thee dearer far!
My heart shall never, never rove,
Thou art my only guiding star.
For me the past has no regret
Whate'er the years may bring to me;
I bless the hour when first we met,
The hour that gave me love and thee!

CHAPTER ELEVEN

QUICKSILVER DAYS

A steady job with a decent salary and a cozy room at his brother's home did not stop Waite from once again becoming gypsy footed and anxious to roam. Not even squiring around the most desirable damsel in town was enough to quell what Waite called his "wanderlust tendencies."

> *Continued with Hawkeye Coal Co. work and with the usual*
> *social activities of a young man 21 years old from January 1 until*
> *April 1. Then instinctively feeling restless and the need for change*
> *made a trip to St. Louis, Mo. and worked in the Southern Hotel*
> *there.* ~ WAITE PHILLIPS DIARY, 1904

For a young fellow such as Waite still itching for adventure or, as he put it, "instinctively feeling restless," Saint Louis was the one place on earth to be during 1904. It was a thriving city — the fourth largest in the country. More importantly, it was the site of the Louisiana Purchase Centennial — considered by many to be the grandest, perhaps even the finest world's fair ever staged.

Waite was right there in the thick of things for the grand opening, on April 30, 1904. It was a cold and crisp Saturday. The ceremony included music and prayer and plenty of speeches. Waite spied John Philip Sousa, the vigorous bandmaster and composer, immaculate in his smart uniform. Later that day, Sousa would lead his band and a chorus of four hundred voices in his

"Hymn of the West," written for the occasion.

William Howard Taft, the rotund secretary of war, showed up in Saint Louis to deliver the principal address. Four years later, Waite would vote for Taft in his successful election as president of the United States on the Republican ticket.

After Taft's speech, the president of the Louisiana Purchase Exposition Company, David R. Francis, former Saint Louis mayor and former Missouri governor, rose and walked to a telegraph machine. As his finger pressed the key, he exclaimed in a clear voice for all to hear, "Open ye gates! Swing wide ye portals! Enter herein ye sons of men! Learn the lessons here taught and gather from it inspiration for still greater accomplishments!"

The touching of the telegraph key in Saint Louis alerted President Theodore Roosevelt in Washington, D.C. Having served as the nation's president since the fall of 1901, after William McKinley's assassination, "Teddy" Roosevelt, like Waite, was an outspoken advocate of life in the Wild West. Waite heartily approved of "T. R." Later that year, when Waite voted in his first election, he cast his ballot for Roosevelt in his sweeping victory over Alton B. Parker.

Most likely, neither Waite Phillips nor Roosevelt was thinking of the distant November election on that chilly April day. Standing on the tips of his toes in the midst of the huge crowd in Saint Louis, Waite intently listened and watched. At 12:15 p.m. in the nation's capital, Roosevelt received the telegraph signal sent from afar. At once he pressed a golden button, setting lights ablaze in Saint Louis and signaling the formal opening of the world's fair.

At that moment, Waite looked up as ten thousand flags suddenly fluttered from their masts, fountains exploded in geysers of water, and Sousa lifted his baton. The yearlong celebration started with the blare of trumpets and thousands and thousands of people, including an excited young man from Iowa, all cheering themselves hoarse.

The Southern Hotel, where Waite worked as a desk clerk, stayed packed with guests, as did the 108 other hotels in the city limits by the time the fair opened. Waite tended to his clerking duties but spent as much time as possible at the world's fair. He ratholed away most of his earnings, and rode crowded city street-cars to the spacious site.

Open six days a week but closed on Sunday by order of the United States Congress, the world's fair was everything that had been promised. Waite did not miss an attraction or event. He took it all in — every ornate hall, palace, and pavilion — and went back for more. He went to the Plateau of States to see the many state and territorial buildings, such as the one representing Oklahoma. It later was transported to El Reno, Oklahoma Territory, to serve as a meeting place for the Elks Lodge. Of course, Waite also visited his home state's building, which eventually was shipped in pieces to Iowa to become an asylum for alcoholics.

But of all the many enticements, Waite was especially drawn to the Pike. This was a mile-long stretch where folks could view sights from around the world, feast on the newly invented ice-cream cone, or ride an enormous Ferris wheel. Its thirty-six cars, each of which seated sixty people, provided a bird's-eye view of the sprawling, 1,275-acre fairgrounds.

Undoubtedly, the only way his Saint Louis fair experience would have been more enjoyable for Waite was if Wiate could have been there with him. But besides still missing his twin, Waite confessed in letters to friends that he also felt a pang of longing for sweet Genevieve in Knoxville. Miss Elliott would have been just the right person for Waite to toast with a stanza of "Meet Me in St. Louis, Louie."

Apparently a month of adventure was enough to appease Waite's "wanderlust tendencies" — at least for a short while. After only a little more than thirty days, he bade farewell to his co-workers at the Southern Hotel and the sights and sounds of the glittering world's fair. At the cavernous Union Station, he caught an Iowa-bound train and headed back to Knoxville.

Waite picked up his former routine without missing a beat. He resumed living with L. E. and Nora, joined the local Masonic lodge, visited his parents at Gravity and, on a part-time basis, returned to his job at Hawkeye Coal. Besides his bookkeeping duties, Waite also handled some sales work and served as an assistant superintendent at the mine.

He also went calling on Genevieve at the J. B. Elliott home. The young couple continued right where they had left off, with dance lessons and social instructions. Still, Waite was careful not to sever his social relationships with several other young ladies of charm and circumstance who resided in the area. Although he was definitely smitten by Miss Elliott and preferred her over all others as his partner at the various jubilees and dances, the fidgety Waite still was not prepared to make any sort of romantic commitment.

From Jan. 1 to March continued same duties with Hawkeye Coal Co. The coal reserves becoming rapidly depleted, however, and with railroad car trouble it was decided by the directors and management to close the mine, sell the equipment, and quit operations. ~ WAITE PHILLIPS DIARY, 1905

Being out of work was not something altogether foreign to Waite, and he was not particularly worried about his prospects. Besides, his big brothers Frank and L. E. had other irons in the fire, and Waite hoped that he eventually would be able to hook up with them.

Waite had not been the only Phillips brother to take in the world's fair. On business for his father-in-law, Frank also had visited Saint Louis. He was there just prior to the official opening, and went out to view the construction and perhaps get an advance glimpse of the Iowa Building.

As he roamed the grounds, Frank bumped into the Reverend

C. B. Larrabee, a Methodist minister whom he knew from Creston. The two men visited at length. Larrabee told Frank about his recent tour of duty as a missionary in Indian Territory. Frank was spellbound by the tales of cowboys and Indians, outlaws, and other colorful characters. Larrabee's stories of the lively little towns fascinated Frank.

So did the reverend's vivid descriptions of a black substance oozing out of the prairies not far from burgs with names such as Pawhuska and Bartlesville. Larrabee said the black stuff was crude oil. Folks down there in the Indian Nations called it "black gold," Larrabee said — and some of those folks had become very rich.

CHAPTER TWELVE

BLACK GOLD

·WP·

By the spring of 1905, while the remaining
equipment was being sold off from the defunct Hawkeye Coal
Company, Waite, impulsive as always, quickly took to the road.
Vowing to keep in touch with Genevieve, he departed Knoxville.
Tucked away in his suit-coat pocket was a letter of introduction
written on Hawkeye stationery.

> To whom this may come:
>
> This will introduce the bearer Waite Phillips who has
> been in our employ more than two years during which
> time he was advanced from bookkeeper to salesman and
> ass't supt. He has left our employ owing to our closing
> down our mines at this place.
>
> Mr. Phillips is attentive to business details, and in every
> way worthy of confidence. And it is with pleasure we rec-
> ommend him to anyone to whom he should offer his ser-
> vices.
>
> Very truly yours,
> L. E. Phillips

L. E. enclosed with the letter a newspaper clipping about a
Des Moines businessman who had outlined some rules for a successful life. Next to several of the guidelines, L. E. had inked an *X*

just to make sure Waite saw them. But two of the rules were underlined for even greater emphasis. The first was, "Keep the body in good condition. Do not abuse it with drink or lust," and the other, "If you have lost an opportunity, find or make another."

Waite was amused by his brother's advice, but he had no intention of overdoing when it came to drink or lust. And as far as lost opportunities, he remained optimistic about the future.

When mine deal was completed in April he departed Knoxville to St. Louis, Mo. and secured a pass from there on the Frisco railroad for construction work at Catoosa, Okla. [Indian Territory] near Tulsa. From Catoosa he journeyed to Guthrie, Okla. [Oklahoma Territory] for an extended visit with his Uncle John Phillips and in June he returned to St. Louis. In June contracted with firm in St. Louis to go to Chicago to work as teamster.
~ WAITE PHILLIPS DIARY, 1905

In the midst of his travels among Indian Territory, Saint Louis, and Chicago, Waite received more letters from L. E. and Frank, offering their opinions about what he should be doing with his life. Weary of getting so much unsolicited brotherly counsel, Waite was especially angry at what he considered to be harsh reprimands from Frank. As usual, L. E. acted as mediator and tried to resolve the conflict between his brothers.

Just before he moved to Chicago, Waite received a letter from L. E. scolding him for his attitude about Frank. Instead of offering his normal pleasantries, L. E. went straight to the heart of the matter.

Your letter made me both glad and sad. The part you mentioned about sending Frank's letter back to him and also in not acknowledging receipt of it before. Frank feels very much hurt about it and I feel so too. . . .

You must write him an apology. Frank has had your welfare at heart all the time and has now. And you must learn to mellow your disposition, not only in this case, but in all. I know it is not pleasant to be constantly reminded of one's faults but as I have often told you, your greatest one is to misjudge people and their motives too quickly and by carrying an air of mystery which causes you to be misjudged. I think you have misjudged our motives toward you at all times and we have been ready and tried to be your confidential advisors but you have not seemed to want to allow us to get close to you. . . .

I believe in you, my boy, and know there is good stuff in you. Keep in mind you have a good family and then set your head to push and I know you will win out.

To drive home his point, L. E. carefully cut out paragraphs from a letter Frank had sent to him, fastened them on with a straight pin, and included them in his epistle to Waite. In the excerpts from his letter to L. E., Frank's displeasure with Waite was obvious.

He has had a fair chance to demonstrate his tendencies and beyond the affection which I shall always hold for him, he has not shown himself worthy of further financial favors. . . . If as a brother one third older than he, I cannot offer suggestions to him at a time when he is asking for money without indicating that I am worthy of this confidence then he can apply elsewhere where he will find that before he can establish credit he must make a confident [sic] of his banker regarding all his business besides demonstrating his ability to make and save money.

I do not mean to be hard on the lad but after waiting so long to receive an acknowledgement from him, his letter did not sit well with me. In fact it hurt me. He is under no obligations whatever. . . . I only am anxious to see him get started right for that means everything at his age now with the experiences he has had.

L. E.'s strategy of using a straightforward approach with Waite and including portions of Frank's angry letter worked. Although during the years there were many more disputes among the Phillips brothers, especially between Frank and Waite, at least the current dispute was put to rest. By early June 1905, L. E. and Frank sent cordial greetings to Waite at his Chicago address, a rented room on Desplaines Street.

In his letter, Frank even went so far as to assure Waite, "You need not pay me the money which you owe me until you get a position. I hope you succeed in finding one." Frank signed off with, "You always have my best wishes." In a handwritten postscript, he added, "If you can keep me posted I might have something for you after while. I have an oil well doing 50 barrels per day."

On June 3, L. E. sent a birth announcement to herald the arrival of his and Node's second son. They named the seven-and-a-half-pound baby Lee Eldas Jr. But of more importance to Waite, L. E. also made mention of Frank's fifty-barrel oil well. Still hanging on in Iowa and cleaning up odds and ends with George Rex, L. E. added an important note — "Think I will leave." To Waite, that meant only one thing — L. E. was ready to join Frank.

By that time Frank was settled in Indian Territory. He had started making scouting trips to Bartlesville shortly after hearing the Reverend Larrabee's stories of oil discoveries there. With the backing and blessing of his father-in-law, John Gibson, Frank started to purchase oil leases in the area. Early in 1905, he established a small office, hired a driller, and started to develop his first oil well. Now it had begun to pay off.

Buoyed by Frank's good news from Indian Territory and the

fact that L. E. was moving there also, Waite quit his teamster job in Chicago and went back to Iowa. He realized he had to bide his time and hang on a little longer before he could join his brothers in the oil fields.

Returned to Knoxville, Iowa in early September for a visit with Genevieve and told her of future plans. Then visited parents at Gravity, Iowa. In late September accepted position as traveling salesman for Rex Coal & Mining Co. of Creston, Iowa. ~ WAITE
PHILLIPS DIARY, 1905

George Rex, still solvent even though his Hawkeye Mine was kaput, was happy to welcome Waite back. He gladly provided lodging for the young salesman at his home. But Waite spent very little time in Creston. His work kept him on the road, calling on coal customers scattered throughout Iowa, eastern Nebraska, and northern Missouri. He stayed in ramshackle hotels and boarding-houses, and dispatched orders for coal to the Rex Building in downtown Creston.

In his written responses to Waite on the road, Rex included praise such as, "You have made a good start this week. I hope you will keep up the clip," and words of encouragement such as, "Keep your courage up and do your work thoroughly" or "Hope you will meet with better success next week."

After a month back on the job peddling coal for Rex, Waite was happy to get good news from his brothers in Indian Territory. During the summer and autumn, Frank and L. E. had organized their own bank — Citizens Bank & Trust Company. With a capitalization of fifty thousand dollars and with Frank as president and L. E. as treasurer, the bank would not officially open for business until December 5, 1905. Those "Iowa upstarts," as some of the locals called the brothers, were making waves.

Frank wrote to Waite on October 17.

I can appreciate in a very large measure just the experience you are having," "There is not a day that Elda [L. E.] and I do not speak of you and wonder how you are getting along. I want to see you make good up to January 1st and then if George [Rex] does not offer you sufficient inducements to remain, it is barely possible something might develop here. I would like for you to plan to spend the holidays with us here. I think it will be of value to you and I am sure there is no one who will enjoy you more. I purchased a new house last week and hope to be located in it just as soon as Jane arrives from the West. She is now in California and writes me that she is having a very delightful time . . . and expects to be in Bartlesville early in November.

I moved my office today from the hotel and paid my bill to date. . . . I will now room and board with Elda [L. E.] until Jane arrives. . . . We expect our bank building to be completed in about three weeks.

Waite's confidence also was boosted significantly because of a steady stream of correspondence from Genevieve Elliott. Veva, as she often signed her letters, was enrolled at the Stevan School on Drexel Boulevard in Chicago. Genevieve's marks for the fall term of 1905 in all her courses — art history, English composition, psychology, German, and spelling — were exceptionally high. She was proud of her perfect scores for deportment.

"My dearest Waite," she wrote in early October, "Just received your letter as it was sent home and mamma forwarded it to me. I was sure glad to hear from you for I had begun to think you had forgotten me. . . . Waite, you don't know how good it seemed to hear from you and I hope you will write me often & soon. With lots of love remember I remain yours as ever."

Waite did exactly what Veva had asked of him. He quickly responded, and enclosed a prized photograph of himself and

Wiate. Sending her a photo of himself and his dead twin was a sure sign that this young woman was special, maybe even extra special. Genevieve instantly sent off a thank-you note.

"My dear Waite," she wrote, "I received your letter this Sunday and the picture today and was certainly glad to get both of them, especially the latter as you know I have always wanted it & it was surely kind of you to give it to me. I showed it to the girls and they will not believe but what it is the same fellow. Wish you would tell me which one is you, for I really cannot tell which is which."

While Genevieve busied herself in Chicago with schoolwork, downtown matinées, and sorority activities, Waite continued to sell coal. But not a day went by that he did not dream of the "black gold" that waited for him, not in the midwestern coal mines but in the oil fields developing in Indian Territory.

As 1905 wound to a close, Waite thought it was time to visit and take a closer look. Three of his brothers lived in Indian Territory by then. Ed Phillips and his family resided in Okmulgee, a bustling town and cultural center for the Creek Indians, due south of Tulsa. Ed had found a position there at the Okmulgee Loan & Trust Company. And the two oldest brothers, Frank and L. E., were going full steam ahead with their banking and oil ventures in Bartlesville.

Waite sent Genevieve a box of flowers for Christmas and his best greetings. Instead of visiting her in Knoxville, he spent the holidays with his brothers in the Indian Nations. He was back in Iowa just after New Year's 1906, but his days as a coal peddler were fast coming to an end.

In mid-January, L. E. got word to Waite that the Phillips brothers were drilling yet another oil well. L. E. also mentioned that he had noticed in the newspapers that "the coal operators and miners seem to be fortifying themselves for the struggle that will no doubt be a serious one . . . .

"I have had no opportunity to talk with Frank since receiving your letter, but I have no doubt we can arrange to make a place for you, if you decide you wish to come here and take up the oil business. I would suggest, however, that before you come, you have a definite arrangement with Frank, and then as soon as you have, to notify George that after a certain date you will want to be released. You understand that Frank is in control of the oil business, so that any arrangements you make in that line, will have to be made with him directly."

Waite reacted immediately. A little more than a week later, he got the assurances he wanted from his oldest brother.

"I note what you say about the coal business," wrote Frank. "Of course, there are ups and downs in all lines of business, and you will experience your share of depressed times . . . .

"In regard to your coming down here, of course, we will do what we can for you, in case you decide to come, but I can not say just what we might open up. Just the thing you would want might not be available on short notice, but probably everything would work out right in time.

"You will, to be sure, have to learn a new business and work up to the top rounds, but that is always the best thing to do, and the fellow who commences at the top of the ladder, usually falls back a few notches, so it is best to commence at the bottom and be sure of your ground as you make progress."

Continued as salesman with Rex Coal & Mining Co. until it became insolvent in February on account of lack of business volume. ~ WAITE PHILLIPS DIARY, 1906

By March 1906, Waite Phillips, hopeful and brash as ever, was gone from his native Iowa. He headed straight to Indian Territory. His game plan was bold but simple. He intended to strike it rich — very rich.

CHAPTER THIRTEEN

BARTLESVILLE, I.T.

Waite, wary of his sometimes stormy relationship with Frank, did not go directly to Bartlesville. Instead, he took the train to Okmulgee and stayed for a couple of weeks with his brother Ed. That is where Frank caught up with Waite in early April 1906.

"I am pleased to hear that you are in Indian Territory again," wrote Frank. "I wish it were convenient for me to run down and see you, but I have been away so much lately that I think it is best for me not to leave for awhile now.

"We will expect to see you up this way in a few days unless you should find some opening down there, to which you want to apply yourself. Look into conditions carefully in that section so that you can make a good comparison after you have been with us for awhile. . . . Hoping to have you with us before long. . . ."

That was all Waite needed to hear. Within days, he was standing tall in Bartlesville, ready and willing to learn the mysteries of the oil business.

When Waite first arrived, he found a vacancy in a boarding-house across the street from Citizens Bank. He shared his sparsely furnished third floor room with Fred J. Spies, a young man originally from Creston. He once had worked for John Gibson, and came to Indian Territory to serve as an assistant cashier at Citizens. Waite and Spies became good pals and had some high times together, even though Waite did not stay at the boarding-house very long.

Frank had other plans for Waite. He soon sent his kid brother out into the wilds of the oil patch. Waite worked on the Anna Parady lease, a well site maintained by Phillips & Company, one of the many independent oil companies that the brothers formed during their early years in the area. Frank also sent Waite to the Anna Anderson lease, site of the Phillipses' first big gusher — the Anna Anderson No. 1.

Named after the eight-year-old Delaware Indian girl on whose eighty-acre allotment the Phillips brothers controlled all the drilling rights, the No. 1 well came blowing in on September 6, 1905. The gushing well not only made Anna Anderson the rich-est Indian girl in the territory, it also was the first big winner for the Phillipses and the rest of their stockholders in their Anchor Oil and Gas Company, another of their many independent oper-ations.

Putting in hard time on oil leases such as the Anderson, Parady, and Needham was the best possible training any oil-patch rookie could get. Frank told Waite if he was going to learn the business, he needed to stay close to his work. So instead of com-muting back and forth to Bartlesville, Waite moved into an oil-field shack on one of the leases in the wild Caney River bottoms just north of the town of Dewey.

He stayed on the grimy oil lease six-and-a-half days a week, working day and night right alongside his crusty roustabouts and eating out of tin cans. He put up with mud, snakes, chiggers, and ticks, and listened to the mournful songs of coyotes every evening. But on Sunday afternoons, Waite got a reprieve when he hightailed it to Bartlesville to get a hot bath, clean clothes, and a hot dinner at L. E.'s home.

Waite proved to be a quick study. He learned the ins and outs of the oil business by what he said was the "doing" method — going into the field and doing the work until the job was done and done right. As the old-time drillers would have put it, when it came to his oil-field education, Waite was "as serious as a heart attack."

While Frank and L. E. dabbled in oil deals and took gambles that paid off by lending money to two high-risk types — oil operators and outlaws — Waite diligently served as his brothers' most capable and conscientious "field man." He had spent much of his young life wandering around the country, going from place to place and job to job, but at last it appeared that Waite Phillips was settling on an occupation. He had a nose for oil. At the ripe old age of twenty-three years, Waite had found his niche.

Having learned practical features of oil development by working and living on leased premises, Waite progressed to position of Field Sup't. as new oil properties were developed under Frank's management and promotions.

Under the expert and benevolent supervision of Frank, his younger brother Waite began to take life and business affairs seriously. He will never, during his lifetime, forget or cease to be grateful to these two older brothers — Frank and L. E. — for the help they gave him. ~ WAITE PHILLIPS DIARY, 1906

In December 1906, Waite gave up his rustic digs in the oil field and moved back into town. He moved in with Frank and Jane and their son, John, and worked out of the Bartlesville office. Every day, Waite took a buckboard pulled by a team of horses out to the field to check on various oil properties.

Although he was mastering the oil business as fast as anyone, sometimes there were reminders that he still had some learning to do.

For instance, there was an incident on an unseasonably hot afternoon on the Emmet Longbone lease, a fifty-acre tract near Blue Mound. Anxious to get more oil flowing, Waite went out to oversee the drilling of a wildcat well. Never content to just sit and watch or bark orders, Waite pulled off his suit coat and necktie and pitched right in with the crew to help lay pipe.

While the others sweated away as they wrestled with the heavy pipe, they did not notice that Waite was overexerting himself in the glaring heat. Finally he collapsed from sunstroke and was unconscious until someone looked back and saw him lying on the ground. Some of the roustabouts splashed water on his face and whisked him back to Bartlesville in the buckboard.

After a few days under a doctor's watchful eye, along with some loving care from Jane Phillips, his sister-in-law, Waite recovered. He returned to his duties a tad sunburned and slightly embarrassed, but a whole lot wiser.

Throughout the rest of 1906 and 1907 — the year Oklahoma was admitted to the Union — Waite continued to work closely with Frank and L. E. as the Phillips brothers expanded their companies and oil developments. The Lewcinda Oil & Gas Company, a name taken from a combination of their parents' first names, Lewis and Lucinda, was organized to develop new oil leases while more properties were being acquired constantly.

Shortly after the brothers formed this newest company, another incident took place that Waite never forgot. During drilling operations at their Barnes lease, the brothers discovered that some casing pipe had disappeared from the site. Waite investigated and eventually found all the missing pipe in a local junkyard. Although the pipe was stenciled clearly with the Phillips name and the name of the brothers' newest company, the owner of the junkyard refused to give it up without being paid. Ultimately, the matter of the stolen casing went to court, where the judge ruled against the Phillipses. Angry beyond belief at the time, Waite was able to joke years later that he had had to pay twice for the pipe because he had been such a poor witness that the brothers lost their suit. Thankfully, there was little else being lost by the trio of Phillips brothers of Bartlesville.

About this time Waite began to take full charge of the oil office, lease purchases, as well as the field operations. These offices were located in the rear of the Citizens Bank Bldg.

No particular incident is recalled of unusual nature in this year except plenty of hard work and attention to duty on about a 15-hour daily basis, 6 ½ days a week.

Occasional trips were made to Knoxville and Gravity, Iowa.
~ WAITE PHILLIPS DIARY, 1907

The visits to Iowa were essential. Not only did Waite need to stay in touch with his parents on the farm at Gravity, but he was compelled to see his Veva, the enchanting Genevieve Elliott.

Matured into a comely young woman of twenty years, Genevieve no longer attended Stevan School but resided at her family home in Knoxville. Always busy with a wide range of activities, she flitted from card parties and dances to sleigh rides and road-show performances at the local opera house. She also took trips to Kansas, Arkansas, New Orleans, and many other destinations, and lots of holiday excursions with family and friends.

From Knoxville, Genevieve sent a constant barrage of letters to Waite. Addressed simply, "Waite Phillips, Bartlesville, Indian Territory," almost every one of them was filled with harmless gossip and sprinkled with offhand insinuations about eligible young men and frisky suitors sniffing around the Elliott household.

Waite read detailed descriptions of bridal showers and weddings. It became quite clear that practically all of Genevieve's friends were marching down the matrimonial aisle or at least had made definite plans for their wedded bliss. Sometimes Genevieve had to wonder if her beau down in the oil fields would ever take the hint.

Back in Bartlesville, the handsome Waite, whose personal account at Citizens Bank was growing larger every day, was considered to be one of the most eligible bachelors in Indian Territory. Waite made the most of his coveted status. He and his best running pal, Fred Spies, escorted Elsie Shea, Reba Baldwin, and a bevy of other local belles to dances and parties. Sometimes they splurged and took their favorite dates to theatrical events staged at the Oklah Theater at the corner of Third and Johnstone.

A few of Waite's lady friends might have been called exotic, at least by Iowa standards. He was seen around town with a young lady with Cherokee blood said to be related to the famous Texas patriot, Sam Houston. One of his preferred partners for Elks Lodge dances was Greta Stokes, granddaughter of Governor Montfort Stokes of North Carolina. Greta's sister was Olive Stokes, sometimes known as Princess Theotoway. She ended up as one of the many wives of Tom Mix, the 101 Ranch cowboy, Dewey town marshal, and cement-plant worker who went on to become a famous silent-movie star.

With such a rich social life, further spiced by visits with such local characters as Emmett Dalton — a survivor of the infamous Dalton gang and the Coffeyville bank raid — and a plethora of profitable work in the oil patch, Waite had little time to worry about Genevieve's escapades in Iowa.

Nonetheless, Waite was becoming very concerned about his relationship with Miss Elliott. And well he should have been. By 1908, he and Genevieve had been courting, at least off and on, for five very long and sometimes turbulent years. The boxes of fancy candy, books, and bouquets of flowers Waite sent to Genevieve and his infrequent visits to Knoxville could no longer ensure that the charming Veva would remain his special sweetheart.

Waite knew that the competition for Genevieve's affections was definitely increasing. According to the best intelligence reports Waite could gather and from what he could glean from between the lines in Genevieve's letters, a young man named

Henry Cross — chuck-full of potential and promise and member of a respected local family — was leading the pack of spoilers. Action was called for; the rivals had to be outmaneuvered.

During the dog days of 1908, Waite Phillips, the bold wildcatter feeling as confident as a roustabout on payday, made his move. It would go down as one of the most important negotiations of his life.

> *About this time a most important deal was made in securing an agreement with Genevieve for marriage.* ~ WAITE PHILLIPS DIARY, 1908

CHAPTER FOURTEEN

GAMBLERS'
NUMBERS

In later years, well-publicized stories circulated about the marriage of Waite and Genevieve. Some were baseless claims that the Elliott family, especially Genevieve's protective father and mother, vehemently opposed the union because they did not consider Waite good enough for their daughter. Some of the more malicious stories even made their way into print. None of those stories — not a single one — was true.

Even though Waite was a diehard Republican and J. B. Elliott was a staunch Democrat and had served a couple of terms in the Iowa legislature, the distinguished banker gave the couple his blessing. He even put it in writing after he received an official request for his daughter's hand from young Phillips.

On October 19, 1908 — a little more than two weeks before Elliott's choice for president, William Jennings Bryan, lost to Waite's candidate, William Howard Taft — J. B. Elliott wrote to Waite, "It is with regret — and pleasure — I give my consent to your marriage with my daughter Genevieve. I regret to lose her yet am pleased that her choice is one who I have every reason to believe will treat her kindly and do all in his powers under all circumstances to make her happy. . . ."

The following month, Genevieve's mother, Nora Elliott, added her more tentative endorsement to the marriage. "My dear

Waite, when could I say nay, when the rest say yea. It is impossible for a mother to think there is any man quite good enough for her daughter. I suppose mothers of sons think the same. . . .

"While it will leave our home so desolate (the one in which she has been so carefully shielded) we strive to think only of her happiness. May she be to you all you could wish and I feel she will do her part as best she can. She is not very strong and has never had any responsibility, so if you don't feel suited just send her back. That she is a true, pure, and good girl I know. . . . I want you to know that we welcome you as one of the family and trust it may ever be a pleasure to us all."

Except for some dejected young men in Knoxville, no one was really opposed to the marriage. Still, the timing of the proposal and engagement announcement was critical. Waite later found out that he had arrived in Knoxville just in time. Henry Cross, Genevieve's other vehement pursuer, was also knocking on the Elliotts' door with marriage on his mind. In a letter of congratulations to Genevieve, her close friend, Ruth Woodruff Maher, commented on the difficult choice that had to be made.

"How strange for he [Waite] and Henry Cross to both come at the same time," wrote Ruth. "Aren't you glad that you have really made up your mind? It seems to me you have the happiest & brightest future anyone could wish for and I know you will never regret it. He idolizes you and will always be good to you. You know I have always been an ardent admirer of Waite and I don't think the world has very many just like him. One thing I know, he ought to be the happiest fellow in the world to win a prize like you!"

Ruth wrote nothing but the gospel truth as far as Waite was concerned. He was indeed happy. He told Fred Spies and his other Oklahoma chums that he felt better than he had since those long-ago days when he was on the scout with his twin.

In Bartlesville, Waite prepared for married life by tending to his business. He, Frank, and L. E. organized yet another company

— Meredith Oil — to develop the Butler lease near the old trading-post town of Copan. Waite was now in a financial position to pull money from his salary and invest in the stock of many of the oil-field ventures. In the autumn of 1908, he also shelled out a hefty $850 to purchase a new Ford Model T, fresh off the assembly line. Instead of making the rounds of the oil leases in a buckboard, Waite arrived in a cloud of dust in his shiny automobile.

Next, Waite sent for his younger brother, Fred, an eager nineteen-year-old still living on the family farm at Gravity. Waite convinced his older brothers that they needed to give young Fred a chance. They concurred and sent the youngster to work on the oil leases at Dewey. With Ed down in Okmulgee, all five Phillips brothers lived in Oklahoma.

W. P. invited him [Fred] to come in order to give a younger brother the same opportunities in the oil business that his older brothers, Frank & L. E., had given him. ~ WAITE PHILLIPS DIARY, 1908

Most days out on the oil leases, where he showed his kid brother the ropes, Waite found a few spare minutes to read the regular stream of letters from Genevieve. She bubbled over with news about wedding preparations, and was filled with questions about the plans for the dream house Waite wanted to build in Bartlesville. The young couple worried over the size of their future home, what kind of woodwork to install, and scores of other details.

Often after finishing one of his financée's letters, the resourceful Waite used the envelope as a driller's log. He dug a stub of pencil from his suit-coat pocket and carefully charted the figures at the well site. The rough log he fashioned listed the various depths where cable tools reached sand or water and, sometimes, where the crew struck pay dirt — a show of gas or a vein of crude oil.

The new year, 1909, began with the Phillips brothers still rolling the dice in the oil patch and coming up big winners. As they started to prospect for oil near the town of Vera, they launched the Janeora Land & Development Company, its name taken from a combination of the first names of Frank and L. E.'s wives. Other oil firms owned or controlled by the Phillipses soon came with further expansion — Phillips and King, Phillips & Company, Luddington Oil, and Standish Oil, as in Miles Standish. The half owner of Standish was H. V. Foster, the oil tycoon often called "the richest man west of the Mississippi."

When local investors, including Frank, L. E. and Waite, acquired Lot 67 from Douglas Oil Company of California, they organized Creston Oil Company. Lot 67 was located just west of Ramona in the oil-rich Osage Indian lands. L. E. and Waite were given minor interest in Creston Oil, and Waite was made the company's president.

All the time Waite bustled about the oil patch, adding to his knowledge of the industry and helping his brothers create new businesses, his bride-to-be prepared for their wedding. At last they picked a date in March.

Genevieve was plagued by a bout of measles that February, but still managed to beset Waite with concerns about the wedding ceremony and reception. She also had questions about the new home under construction on a lot Waite had purchased from Frank on Cherokee Avenue in Pemberton Heights, a newly developed residential section of Bartlesville. Genevieve fussed about the colors and shades of paint for various walls, the furniture placement, and all the other details she had anguished over ever since their engagement had been announced.

"This is the last letter I will write you until after we are married," Genevieve wrote on March 24, just six days before the wedding. "How long the time has seemed to me so far away from you and I can scarcely realize that we shall soon be together for always. I know we will both be very happy."

Scores of folks from all across Iowa, Oklahoma, and other parts of the country soon learned of the big event.

MR. AND MRS. JOHN BROWN ELLIOTT

ANNOUNCE THE MARRIAGE OF THEIR DAUGHTER

GENEVIEVE

TO

MR. WAITE PHILLIPS

ON TUESDAY, MARCH THE THIRTIETH

ONE THOUSAND NINE HUNDRED AND NINE

KNOXVILLE, IOWA

The wedding was everything Genevieve had wanted. Her married sister, Helen, came from her home in Arkansas to help with the last-minute preparations. Many other members of Genevieve's family and several of her closest friends were in attendance. The Phillips family also was well represented. They arrived by train and took rooms, along with the other out-of-town guests, at the Parsons House, one of the better hotels in Knoxville. Besides his brand-new wedding suit, Waite brought along a large trunk, at Genevieve's request, to accommodate some of her clothing.

The simple nuptial ceremony was held in the parlor at the Elliott residence. Various aunts and uncles, cousins and friends turned out in their Sunday best. Waite's two oldest brothers and their spouses were there, with L. E. acting as best man. Genevieve's close friends, Ruth Woodruff Maher and Bertha Stewart, served as bridesmaids. The Reverend Charles Pace, a local Methodist minister, did the honors. The groom had just turned twenty-six, and his bride was twenty-one.

Dressed in his somber banker's suit, J. B. Elliott proudly walked arm and arm with his younger daughter through the parlor, crowded with flowers and guests, and presented her to Waite. There were reports that the mothers of the bride and groom cried

— supposedly tears of joy — as Waite and Genevieve were pronounced husband and wife.

After the ceremony, the minister signed the marriage license, and cake and punch were served. Waite and his bride went to see kinfolk at Omaha and Gravity, and then they went to Kansas City. But their honeymoon was cut short. Frank wired Waite, ordering him back to Oklahoma because of a threatened lawsuit over the title to the Lot 67 property. Genevieve quickly learned that being married to a man in the oil business made its demands on a relationship. Sometimes a new wife and breakfast in bed in a fancy Kansas City hotel had to wait.

Waite and Genevieve settled into life in Bartlesville. Until their own place was finished, they stayed at Frank and Jane's recently completed home — a splendid Greek Revival residence — at 1107 Cherokee Avenue.

Although their own house was not nearly as grand or fancy as Frank's, Waite and Genevieve were pleased with their charming bungalow, complete with dormer windows, a porch facing the avenue, and a large paneled oak front door. It was up the street a short distance from Frank's fine house.

The first of many homes they would live in during their long life together, this bungalow was Waite's wedding gift to his sweet Genevieve. By the first week of May, everything was completed; the house was ready for them.

Waite especially was taken with their assigned street address, which he noticed right away. Like the 1107 address given to his big brother Frank's nearby home, Waite and Genevieve's house also sported those three lucky digits. Their address was 711 Cherokee Avenue — "seven come eleven" — like the winning numbers in a dice game. Waite thought it was all quite fitting — 711 — gamblers' numbers.

1910-1924

III
THE LONG
TRAIL

*There's a long,
long trail
a-winding/ Into
the land of my
dreams,/ Where
the nightingales
are singing/ And
a white moon
beams.*

Stoddard King, 1913

*Genevieve and Waite Phillips with
Helen Jane, Bartlesville, Oklahoma,
1912. A Waite Phillips Company
service station in the early 1920s.
The Phillips family gathering in
Gravity, Iowa, July 1917. Waite
and Genevieve are at the top left.*

Interior of the receiving house at Waite Phillips Company refinery, Okmulgee, Oklahoma, in the 1920s. Below, a tank truck and a panoramic view of one of the Phillips oil leases in early 1920s Oklahoma.

Headquarters of Hawkeye Ranch, 1922. Above, Elliott Phillips astride a Shetland pony inside the main house of Highland Ranch, 1921.

Waite Phillips Ranches
Hawkeye Ranch.
Cimarron New Mexico

The Phillips home at 1621 South Owasso Avenue, Tulsa, early 1920s. The Phillips family in Egypt during a Mediterranean cruise in 1924. Waite is on the camel second from the left. Beside him are Genevieve, Helen Jane, and Elliott. At lower right, Waite holds Helen Jane and Elliott at their Owasso Avenue home.

M.A. HAMAM
PYRAMID

CHAPTER FIFTEEN

AGAINST THE WIND

·WP·

Waite remained as impatient as the wind which blew across the Osage prairie. His restless nature never disappeared, but age and experience taught him how to establish priorities and set long-term goals. After the close of the first decade of the twentieth century, Waite persisted in the oil patch and at least appeared to be a man who knew how to bide his time.

During the next four years, still working out of Bartlesville with his brothers, Waite went on to hone his natural and acquired talents. He improved his management skills and expanded his oil-field experience. He learned how to assert his authority and maintain control amid chaos. These were lessons Waite could not have learned at the finest universities or in the fanciest boardrooms. His education came from direct contact in the field. It came from, as he continually said, relying on the "doing" method.

His classrooms were scattered across Oklahoma and Texas and Arkansas. His classrooms were at the muddy spudder sites and in the shadows of cable-tool drilling rigs and beneath the wooden derricks in the Osage Hills. His classrooms were the oil boom-towns, the rag towns, the machine shops, the supply stores, the tank farms, the hotel lobbies, the saloons, and the front porch of his home.

His teachers were profane and surly roustabouts and unforget-table characters. His teachers were eccentrics in greasy overalls who believed they could smell crude oil flowing beneath the earth. His teachers were brokers and shooters and drillers and rig builders and tool pushers and machinists and pipeliners. His teachers were wildcatters who searched for oil in unproved areas and were willing to risk everything for one more gusher. His teachers were Frank and L. E. Phillips and Josh Cosden and Harry F. Sinclair and Tom Slick and E. W. Marland and Burdette Blue and old man H. V. Foster and the other pioneers of the oil patch whom Waite worked with or competed against. His teachers were the best, the very best.

If there would have been some sort of official schooling program in those rough-and-tumble oil fields and whoever was running the show had handed out degrees, Waite Phillips would have earned his Ph.D. — a doctorate in oil, summa cum laude.

The oil business continued to develop for Waite and his brothers. Much of Waite's energy went into their Creston Oil property at Lot 67, near Vera in Washington County. The lease foreman was Clyde Alexander, a first-rate oil man. He was also an eternal optimist. Despite the many dry holes drilled there, Alexander and the crews kept drilling until Lot 67 became one of the most prolific of the Phillipses' properties.

In 1910, Creston Oil Company sold Lot 67 for $325,000 to Gypsy Oil Company of Tulsa, later a subsidiary of Gulf Oil Company. C. E. Crawley, a Bartlesville representative of Gypsy Oil, was a good friend of Waite's and became a frequent visitor at the family home on Cherokee Avenue.

At about this time a new project was launched in the oil business under the title of "Waite Phillips Special." Oil leases were taken in his name but the ownership carried as follows: F. P. 1/2, L. E. P. 1/4, and W. P. 1/4. An outstanding venture in this account was the Teehee Block of leases in the Delaware Extension for which profitable offer was made in spring, but when drilled in summer was abandoned. ~ WAITE PHILLIPS DIARY, 1910

When Waite appraised some oil property north of Tulsa for Gypsy, the company presented him with a handsome silver tea service which the Phillipses gave a place of prominence in their family residence.

The bungalow with the lucky address pleased Genevieve. She made it into a comfortable refuge for herself and her busy husband. In the evenings and sometimes at high noon, Waite was greeted with meals fit for J. P. Morgan. Genevieve and any cook or housekeeper who ever worked for the Phillipses remembered that Waite liked his coffee strong and black, his beefsteak well done, and his bacon crispy. They also knew he was fond of apricot preserves and mustard greens, and he had a special place in his heart for tart and tangy gooseberry pie.

Even though she was becoming better acquainted with life as a married woman in Oklahoma and developed lasting friendships with her sisters-in-law and other ladies in the community, Genevieve still got homesick. She made many trips back home to Iowa. Like the wives of other oil-field executives, she tended to spend holiday vacations and most of the hot summer months out of town. In Genevieve's case, that meant going to her parents' home in Knoxville.

Waite tried to find some time for travel as well. For instance, in 1910 after he purchased a new automobile, Waite and Genevieve took L. E. and Node on a motor excursion through the Midwest. L. E. and his wife quickly grew tired of the bouncy ride and abandoned the journey at Saint Joseph, Missouri, but Waite and Genevieve pressed on. They continued to Gravity and Knoxville for the necessary parental visits, and returned to Oklahoma by way of Omaha, accompanied by Genevieve's good friend Ruth Woodruff Maher.

Later that autumn, Waite and Genevieve were given the good news that they were to become parents for the first time. Their baby was due the following summer, and they immediately set about to prepare a home nursery. Waite hoped they would have a son, but he was not disappointed when Genevieve bore him a daughter.

The baby was born at the Phillips home at 711 Cherokee Avenue. She arrived on a Saturday — July 1, 1911. On that day, San Francisco was rocked by the severest shock since the deadly earthquake of 1906.

Family and friends knew that if the baby was a girl she was going to be called Virginia, because it was one of Genevieve's favorite female names. In fact, several of the congratulatory cards and letters sent to Waite and Genevieve greeted the infant as Virginia. When L. E. Phillips called at his brother's home that hot July afternoon, he brought a gift for his new niece. It was a gold necklace and locket with the name Virginia inscribed on it. But much to L. E.'s chagrin, Virginia was not the name Waite and Genevieve ultimately gave their baby.

Instead, they named her Helen Jane, after two of the infant's aunts — Genevieve's sister, Helen, and Jane Phillips, the wife of Waite's oldest brother.

The new father, bursting with pride, phoned everyone he knew who owned a telephone with news of his daughter's birth. When he reached Genevieve's sister, Helen, at her home in Eureka Springs, Arkansas, she was in the midst of a bath but leaped from the tub to hear all about her namesake. Waite reached the L. E. Phillips family on extended holiday in Colorado Springs. Besides their two sons, L. E. and Node now had a daughter, born in 1906, named Martha Jane. When she heard that the Phillips clan had another girl, Martha Jane complained about not being in Bartlesville to see the stork arrive at her Uncle Waite's house.

Waite also called Genevieve's parents in Knoxville. As he hung up the telephone, a deliriously happy J. B. Elliott immediately sat down and poured out his heart to his daughter. "You can never know the pride I feel at this moment over having a granddaughter," Elliott wrote. "You have now reached the highest point in womanhood, that of a mother. Just think you are now the mother of a dear little girl baby all your own. There is nothing sweeter or more precious on earth then a girl baby. I know where of I speak. My two girls have been a source of great pleasure and satisfaction to me all through life. Just as soon as you are able to travel all of you come home and we will have a jubilee."

By the end of the month, Genevieve and her baby daughter had taken up Elliott's invitation, and they spent the next few months in Knoxville. Waite missed his wife and infant daughter, but was pleased that they both were gone for a while and in good hands. He faced more work than he could say grace over, as oil-field activity increased. The great Cushing oil field — destined to be one of Oklahoma's largest — was less than a year away from being opened by Tom Slick, a former Pennsylvanian known as the "king of the wildcatters." Waite had a gut feeling that Cushing was the place for the Phillips boys to go next. He implored Frank to strike early and make a move in that direction.

W. P. advised taking leases there but F. P. decided to confine operations north of Tulsa. Agreement, however, was made to investigate the new Burkburnett Field near Wichita Falls, Texas, and W. P. spent most of the summer there for that purpose. ~ WAITE PHILLIPS DIARY, 1911

Waite took a room at Westland Hotel in Wichita Falls. He looked forward to updates from Genevieve in Knoxville about their baby daughter ("Helen Jane is getting so sweet & just like her Dad isn't still a minute"). Out in the Burkburnett Field, Waite was able only to negotiate for a single four-hundred-acre lease, but because of that deal he became acquainted with W. G. Skelly. Another Pennsylvania native, William Grove Skelly became a leading Tulsa oil man and one of the principal developers of the Osage oil fields. Waite admired his straightforward style and determination.

Back in Bartlesville, Waite's brothers were expanding their financial grip by buying out rival banks and absorbing them into Bartlesville National Bank. Besides enlarging their banking enterprises, they were developing even more oil companies.

Yet Frank did not take Waite's advice. Instead of venturing into the distant oil fields, Frank insisted on staying close to home. Waite disagreed with that strategy. He knew Frank was a proved gambler, so he did not understand Frank's reluctance to take a few more chances. Waite believed his brother was playing it safe — too safe.

After all, Waite reasoned, all that is at stake is money. And what good does it do anyone to hoard a bunch of money? Even in those days, years before he made his vast fortune, Waite Phillips found no pleasure in possessing money. What he enjoyed, pure and simple, was the hunt.

The Phillips brothers trio and their duties, responsibilities, and functions remained the same. ~ WAITE PHILLIPS DIARY, 1912

Before long, Waite found that his restless feeling was creeping back again. It was the same sensation that kept him on the move throughout most of his life. It drove Waite crazy, just like a permanent thirst or an itch that cannot be scratched.

That feeling was a constant in Waite's life, as familiar to him as the eternal wind.

CHAPTER SIXTEEN

SOLO

For two more years, Waite kept his sanity and hung on in Bartlesville. During 1912 and 1913, he remained committed to doing his job to the best of his ability, helping to manage the eleven oil interests which he and his two older brothers operated.

Waite spared some time for his family, but for little else. He did help his younger brother, Fred, acquire an interest in B. M. Wells & Co. when Wells retired. And in July 1912, Waite was forced to leave the piles of work in his office and rest when he was stricken with a case of what doctors diagnosed as malaria. He convalesced and received treatments and medical care at Manitou Springs, Colorado, near Pike's Peak, where Genevieve and little Helen Jane joined him. Later that August, he made a trip alone to a remote section of Colorado for a much needed fishing vacation. For continued good fortune, he carried with him a four-leaf clover which his daughter had picked from her grandfather's lawn in Knoxville.

But the lucky clover leaf, the Rocky Mountain hideouts, and a mess of plump rainbow trout did not cure what really ailed Waite Phillips. With each passing day, he was more discontented with the existing business arrangements in Bartlesville. His brothers, especially Frank, largely ignored his ideas for expansion into new oil fields. Waite sensed that some of that intense fire and passion that once had raged in Frank's belly was starting to burn out when it came to pursuits in the oil patch. Frank acted more like a banker instead of a seasoned wildcatter who, Waite recalled, used to throw all caution to the winds so he could pursue the pools of first-class crude oil hidden belowground.

Waite's instincts about the situation in Bartlesville were not far off the mark. By 1913, Frank indeed was seriously contemplating quitting the oil business. The plan he formulated called for him to sell all of the oil interests and to relocate to Kansas City with L. E. There they would engage solely in banking. L. E. was overjoyed with the prospects of such a move.

Never truly enamored with the oil business as were his other brothers, L. E. most loved his job at the bank. His main ambition was to leave Oklahoma and establish a banking empire, but he knew he needed Frank with him to make it all work.

But this did not materialize. The reason it did not materialize was on account of the depressed conditions in the oil industry in the mid-continent fields. Therefore, without new flush production the various Phillips oil companies were almost impossible to dispose of.

So the oil and banking operations continued without spectacular advancement, except the drilling of leases in the Squirrel Pool east of Bartlesville, owned by the W. P. Special. These were prolific and offset to a considerable extent the losses sustained in other operations, such as the block of leases southeast of Dewey. ~ WAITE PHILLIPS DIARY, 1913

After all the commotion caused by Frank and L. E.'s Kansas City bank scheme subsided, everyone involved tried to get things back to normal. Journeys always seemed to help the Phillips family gain perspective. Waite and Genevieve met Frank and Jane at Atlantic City, New Jersey, and then made their first visit to New York. It was a pleasant trip, particularly the time they spent in

Manhattan, but the brothers mostly avoided discussing their differences of opinion, and nothing was resolved.

Waite, feeling as though he were carrying the burden, saw the future as clear as a mountain stream. He had no interest in moving to Kansas City and living a banker's life — not when there were oil fields to discover and wells to drill. He also knew that although his brothers had put their banking scheme on hold because of market conditions, they were still determined to make drastic changes. The concept of building a bank empire was still alive. Frank and L. E. were biding their time, just as Waite had done for so long. The problem, however, was they did not have a common goal in mind. All of the Phillips brothers had different agendas, and at least two of them — Frank and Waite — were as obstinate as old plow mules.

Waite realized he had to beat his brothers to the punch. He needed to control his own destiny, and no longer could rely on Frank and L. E. It was time to make his move. It was time to go.

In May 1914, Waite summoned his two older brothers for a meeting. He told them he had something important to discuss. No doubt Frank and L. E. figured their kid brother was going to try once again to talk them into probing some new oil fields in unexplored territory. If they did think that, they were mistaken.

When everyone was seated, Waite rose to speak. He looked straight at his brothers and told them he appreciated everything they had done for him, ever since he was a boy, including paying his salary at Coan's store in Iowa and picking up the tuition at business college. He said he would never forget how they had taken him in to learn the oil business. He offered them his undying gratitude for being there for him in those black times when Wiate had died.

Then Waite indicated that he had something more to say. Without pausing or mincing any words, he told his brothers that he had formed other plans. He said he was ready to move on by himself to new ventures in the oil field. He explained to Frank and L. E. that he wished to sell them all his interests in the various oil companies.

Startled by Waite's announcement, Frank and L. E. tried in vain to talk him out of leaving. Their arguments had no effect. Waite's mind was made up firmly. Frank knew his younger brother was just like him and would not be swayed. They had no choice but to submit to Waite's request. Lawyers and accountants were summoned to Frank's office to start dividing up the Phillips brothers' pie.

> *Some difference of opinion arose between F. P. and W. P., in an otherwise agreeable association, regarding the policy of oil company operations. Waite held to the opinion of proceeding with Phillips brothers' own capital, and Frank to the contrary. Therefore W. P. sold his interest to F. P. and L. E. P. in May of this year. His total assets at that time amounted to approximately $25,000. Another reason, of more importance, was Frank's disinclination to operate south of Tulsa and as a result they did not get into the Glenn or Cushing Pools.* ~ WAITE PHILLIPS DIARY, 1914

Almost forty-four years later, when he was seventy-five years old, Waite shed more light on his parting of the ways with Frank and L. E. In a detailed internal memorandum written on April 1, 1958, a mellower Waite reflected on those times so long before. He wrote:

> With Frank's duties as a promoter and financier and L. E. running the bank there naturally developed a situation where I became office manager, lease buyer, and manager of oil operations. This association continued, as already recorded, until the year 1914 and it was altogether a pleasant and cooperative one because under such able tutors as my older brothers I was rapidly learning the fundamental

principles of business and was doing quite well in a financial way although I never received a larger salary than $150 per month. Only one incident occurred, according to my memory, that could have marred this pleasant association and it was caused by some petty complaints issued to Frank about operating matters on the Anderson lease and he patiently replied by offering to accept my resignation. That settled the matter by my apology and I never forgot it. In fact I successfully used the same policy on my older brother Ed when he was employed by the Waite Phillips Company many years thereafter.

In 1914 business conditions, particularly oil, were more or less static in Oklahoma and according to my recollection Frank and L. E. were considering the idea of getting into a big banking situation in Kansas City. With the record Frank made in business affairs during his lifetime it is not required that anyone recommend him for his ability and judgment in such matters. However, he had become rather provincial in his viewpoint by confining his oil operations to the general Bartlesville district during this time when a vast amount of oil was being produced in El Dorado, Kansas, Burkburnett, Texas, Glenn and Cushing pools of Oklahoma, which created a glut of over-supply and a low price per barrel yield to oil producers.

Therefore he took a rather pessimistic view of that line of business for the future. On the other hand, being ten years younger and with a record yet to be made, I was more optimistic about the oil business at that time than he was. The situation resulted in the sale of my small interest in most of these eleven oil companies to Frank and L. E. and they later on, in a year or two, sold all the properties to the Tidal Oil Company.

Despite Waite's decision to break away, he and his brothers remained civil and respected one another's positions, and their families stayed close. In later years when he was asked about the stories of sibling rivalry, Frank's pat response was, "We Phillipses just can't get along with each other when it comes to business." No one who knew the brothers disagreed.

Most of the Phillips family decided the main reason for the split was because Frank and Waite were just too much alike. Waite's son, Elliott, who was born in 1918, explained the relationship between his uncle and father by saying, "If two men are riding the same trail, one has to be in front."

Once the announcement about Waite leaving Bartlesville and selling out to his brothers became public, he and Genevieve quickly sold their house at 711 Cherokee to Frank Larkin and put their belongings in storage. They decided to take a long trip so they could clear their heads. Waite also needed a little more time to finalize his plans and weigh all options.

By the late spring of 1914, as war clouds brewed in Europe, the Waite Phillips family bade Bartlesville farewell. Once again, Waite found himself where he felt his best — out on the road.

He was thirty-one years old, had good health, some money in his pocket, and the promise of more in payoffs from his brothers. He had a devoted wife and a little girl who adored him. The only thing missing was Wiate. If his lost twin were there, Waite told Genevieve as they drove out of town, the picture would be complete.

CHAPTER SEVENTEEN

BUBBLING WATER

An extended tour of old haunts and new places was the best way for Waite to clear his head before jumping back into the fray.

He and Genevieve headed first to Harrison, Arkansas, to visit Genevieve's sister and her husband, Helen and R. S. Granger. From there the Phillipses made a beeline to New York. They were taking in the best the city offered that August when World War I erupted in Europe. They next traveled to Boston, followed by a voyage up the Saint Lawrence River to Québec and Montréal before finally traveling to Knoxville by train.

A letter from L. E. written on August 5 was waiting for Waite at his in-laws' home. Much of it was devoted to news about the war and speculation about the effect it would have on business conditions. L. E. expressed his concerns for the future of oil because pipeline companies just had announced they were going to cut back and take only 60 percent of the production. There were some serious hints, L. E. lamented, that the pipeliners might even discontinue receiving any oil production.

"I don't think I am given to being pessimistic or an unusual optimist either," wrote L. E., "but I do rather feel pessimistic on the outlook of oil in the future. I feel today as though I would like to have a good 160 acres of land in Iowa where I would like to raise chickens and pigs and corn, and have down in the cow pasture a few greens where I could play golf, and I would then let the oil business and the European situation take care of themselves. The outlook is that we will have to sit pretty tight on the lid in the banking business as well as the oil, in order to keep our heads above water.

"I wrote you the other day that we will have the first payment ready for you on the 15th, as you asked. . . . It will be necessary to borrow to meet the contract, as under unsettled conditions we will not be able to make it out of business."

Late in the summer, Waite left his family in Iowa and went by himself to Idaho to inspect a copper mine on behalf of his father-in-law, J. B. Elliott, one of the mine stockholders. As a reward for Waite's assistance, Elliott, a gentleman horse breeder in addition to being a banker, named his prize studhorse for the 1914 season after Waite. A handsome bay standing sixteen hands high and weighing twelve hundred pounds, the horse was billed as "magnificently bred" and "the equal of any stallion living." Elliott's gesture flattered Waite who, like the horse named for him, was ready to race against all contenders.

When his survey of the mine was completed, Waite filed his report with Elliott and continued on to Montana and Fish Creek. He camped all alone next to the stream and beneath the stars, in that familiar high country he still knew so well from his days spent there with his twin brother. It was almost as though he were checking in with Wiate before Waite started the next chapter of his own life. Many years later, Waite noted in a memorandum, "This interlude was taken to double check my plans for the future."

In September, as the nation eagerly read news of German troops being halted at the Marne, Waite carried out his own quiet advance into new territory. He purchased the North Arkansas Oil Company, marketers of wholesale and retail refined oil products, from his brother-in-law, R. S. Granger.

Waite and Genevieve shipped their belongings to Arkansas

and established the family's new residence at Fayetteville, in the rolling hill country in the northwestern corner of the state. Their home was on a quiet avenue in the gracious university town that had been a stop on the Butterfield Stage Route.

This business consisted of refined oil sales to merchants as oil fill-ing stations were not yet established in this country. The business extended, as indicated, over the entire portion of north Arkansas.
~ WAITE PHILLIPS DIARY, 1914

After they moved into their new home, Waite and Genevieve made sure their lines of communication remained open with fam-ily and friends in Bartlesville. In a brief note to Waite on October 12, 1914, Jane Phillips thanked him for sending a box of candy. She also mentioned, "Bartlesville seems a little different this year, so few of us left here, and even yet I cannot feel right that you are not coming back. You know Waite, I think so much of you and I am sure you never will realize how much I miss you."

Waite missed his family in Bartlesville too, but he was satisfied with his decision to embark on his own course. Besides, Waite's oil-marketing firm in Arkansas made him a little more money to stash away for the future. And as a bonus, the work permitted him to learn another branch of the oil business.

A master of timing, Waite knew exactly when to make his next move. After less than a year of running North Arkansas Oil, he felt he was ready to reenter the oil-producing business. In July 1915, he sold his company to Kansas Refining Company of Coffeyville, Kansas.

In August, Waite moved back to Oklahoma. He went to the town of Okmulgee, an old settlement which means "bubbling water" in Creek. Waite was already quite familiar with Okmulgee. He had made several visits there in the past to the home of Ed Phillips, his brother. Ed had since left but was not too far away. He was president of Okemah Abstract & Title Company, a firm

Frank and Waite had helped him establish in the nearby town of Okemah.

Started to buy oil and gas leases as a nucleus to establish a wholly owned oil producing business. After dissolving association with brothers at Bartlesville, Waite visualized plan of building an oil business without the aid of public financing. The marketing experience in Arkansas and these ventures were to test this policy.
~ WAITE PHILLIPS DIARY, 1915

Waite sent Genevieve to Knoxville along with four-year-old Helen Jane who, only a short time before leaving Arkansas, had endured having her tonsils removed at Sparks Memorial Hospital in Fort Smith. Plans called for Genevieve and their daughter to join Waite once he made sure he was going to make a go of it and could find a home.

While he searched for a suitable abode in Okmulgee, Waite took up residence in one of the one hundred comfortable rooms at the Parkinson Hotel, at Seventh Street and Morton Avenue.

The pride of the community, the Parkinson's upper rooms each featured a comfortable bed, spacious wardrobe, hot and cold running water, and a panoramic view of the city. A second-floor parlor was furnished elaborately in mahogany with a plush carpet and a grand piano that was never quiet. Waite and his fellow diners feasted on top-drawer cuisine prepared by chefs, cooks, and bakers hired straight from Kansas City's best kitchens. All the dishes were served beautifully by polished waitresses brought to Oklahoma from Saint Louis, every one of them as dexterous as brain surgeons when it came to their dining-room duties.

Waite liked the bustling town of Okmulgee and the robust men and women who lived and worked there. Most of all, he was glad to be back in the producing end of the business in the oil patch. He knew it was exactly where he belonged — at least for that time.

Early every morning after he had downed his breakfast and a pot of stout coffee at the Parkinson, he walked outside and breathed in the smell of crude oil riding the winds. For a true independent such as Waite, that aroma was sweeter than Genevieve's fanciest perfume. It was the smell of success.

CHAPTER EIGHTEEN

WILDCATTER DELUXE

Waite Phillips was a hard man to get to know.
Unquestionably much more subdued than gregarious, when mixing with folks in a social setting, Waite tended to withdraw to the sidelines and leave the party early. Often, he was labeled mistakenly as a cold fish by some of those who tried to penetrate the protective barrier he had built around himself. They mistook his shy nature and dislike of public posturing for aloofness. Genevieve and those few others within his inner circle knew Waite's loving and tender side, but also understood his need for privacy.

Even though he did not openly express his love or dish out compliments and lavish praise, Waite was no slouch when it came to showing his passion for hard work. Out on the job was where his energy burst forth. Waite's eyes sparkled with life when he put in a long day in the oil field or negotiated a difficult deal. He may have been erratic in his early years when he wandered the countryside with his twin brother, but even back then, Waite was never opposed to toil.

If it is really true that other than love, the most sacred gift a person can give is labor, whoever came up with that axiom must have known Waite Phillips.

When it came to work, Waite gave his all to everyone involved with whatever the job was. Out in the oil patch while his unwashed crews drilled for precious crude was where Waite, at least now and then, showed his true colors. When the work reached a fever pitch was precisely when, if only for a fleeting moment, Waite removed that shell and let his love shine.

In Okmulgee, Oklahoma, in those hectic war years when he was flexing his wildcatter muscles, Waite's eyes shone like gemstones.

Those eyes were shining bright in late 1915 when he traded some ranch land near Dighton in western Kansas. He had purchased the land from his father the year before, but when Waite saw he could not operate the ranch or rent it, he made the swap. In exchange, he ended up with what was said to be a parcel of excellent oil and gas property not far from Bald Hill in Okmulgee County, Waite's new home territory.

Waite was attracted by what he believed were the almost unlimited possibilities the Oklahoma oil industry offered to those able to take advantage of the opportunity. He realized that in general, the conditions in the oil industry were far less favorable than they had been in previous years. Nonetheless, he pushed forward with what he later described as "more imagination and courage than wisdom and experience." He started out with limited capital — approximately twenty-five thousand dollars — to invest in well-selected leases at cheap prices. That formed the foundation of Waite's later operations.

In December began drilling wells on Starr leases on Bald Hill.
~ WAITE PHILLIPS DIARY, 1915

Besides drilling wells, Waite added to the town's growing population of more than ten thousand citizens when he brought his family to Okmulgee. Late in the year, Waite gave up his room at the busy Parkinson Hotel, where streetcars clanged outside, and moved Genevieve and Helen Jane into a five-room cottage he had purchased at 219 North Morton Avenue, not far from the busy downtown square. Genevieve made many new friends, including the W. A. Stewart family just across the street. Before long, she found herself liking Okmulgee as much as her husband did.

The Phillipses did some restrained socializing with certain of Waite's business associates. An impressive team was assembled in Okmulgee, including a salesman Waite had recruited from his former company in Arkansas. Waite hired Jay C. Parks, who lived with his wife, Ada, next door to the Phillipses, as office manager and cashier. The firm of Levan and Munsen was the brokerage Waite selected to assemble many of the oil leases. Frank King and E. W. Kimbley, working from their offices in the Arlington Building, served as his oil-well drilling contractors. Waite's law firm of choice was Moore & Noble, headed by Edward H. Moore and Edgar T. Noble.

With payrolls to meet and salaries to pay, Waite now only needed to drill a few gushers. But those initial efforts in the Bald Hill pool were busts. The wells the Phillips crews first drilled were close to being nothing but "dusters" — the one word any true wildcatter loathed more than any other.

> *From January continued acquiring oil and gas leases and to drill Starr acreage at Bald Hill. The wells there were not successful, so sold pipe and equipment to Morris Sanditen in late spring.*
> ~ WAITE PHILLIPS DIARY, 1916

In the detailed memorandum drafted in 1958 which explained some personal details of his long career, Waite wrote of the disappointments of his initial drilling efforts in Okmulgee County. "The first venture in actual drilling operations was on the Starr leases at Bald Hill northeast of Okmulgee and in that I learned a lesson that served me well later on. The two or three wells drilled there were such small producers as to make them less than commercial ones. This lesson taught me it's necessary to combine good judgment with persistence and not to be like a stubborn mule so I sold the material connected with the wells to a junk man and moved on to a more favorable location, where oil in paying quantities might be found, south of Okmulgee."

In August 1916, while Brigadier General John J. Pershing led his troops on a fruitless search for Pancho Villa and his guerrillas in the Mexican mountains south of the border, Waite took a break by heading north. He and the family went to Yellowstone Park and to a few of his old stomping grounds in Montana. Genevieve, Helen Jane, and her nursemaid continued the journey to Washington, Oregon, and California, but Waite went home to Okmulgee.

It was time to get back to the task of finding some crude. Waite recognized that searching for oil was not for sissies. Like a macho bronc rider who gets pitched from his bucking horse and climbs right back on for another try, he shook off the defeats from earlier in the year and went to work. Unfortunately, the situation did not improve.

> *In October acquired block of leases south of Okmulgee from John Bell of Pittsburgh — one small oil well and some gas wells on them. Did further drilling without increasing production of either oil or gas. This was the low period of W. P.'s experience in the oil business as an independent oil producer.* ~ WAITE
> PHILLIPS DIARY, 1916

Shaken but not defeated, wildcatter Waite refused to give up. He ordered his brokers to keep looking for more oil properties. The nation was edging closer to entering the world war, but Waite's instinct told him that 1917 was going to be his pivotal year. He was correct. His moxie paid off in huge dividends.

In February 1917, he purchased the Lou Robinson lease, one mile south of Okmulgee near a graveyard, as an offset to a well being drilled by E. W. Kimbley. All the wells, especially the Number 2 Lou Robinson, came in big — very big. The rest of the fifty acres on the lease soon was developed into good production.

The so-called "graveyard lease" was a good investment which gave Waite his first big money. Heads in the oil industry started to turn toward Okmulgee. Waite did not slow down as he and his men brought in several other wells on the graveyard property. Then just when he had managed to build up a superior production, the terrible fate of proration, including government assessment regulations, descended on the industry. Without flinching, Waite sold his graveyard lease to the Atlantic Petroleum Company for $200,000. He took a series of vacations, interspersed with returns home so he could check on his oil properties and take the industry's pulse.

First, in April, just as Congress voted for the United States to enter the war, Waite and his family ensconced themselves in a hotel at Mineral Wells, Texas. Among the matters they discussed while they relaxed in the Lone Star State was the fact that Genevieve was pregnant with their second child. According to his pleased wife, Waite could expect to become a father again shortly after New Year's 1918.

The next vacation came in July. Along with all the other Phillips brothers and sisters and their families, Waite and Genevieve attended the golden wedding anniversary celebration, complete with a roast pig, for their parents, Lew and Josie Phillips, in Gravity.

Finally, in August, there was one more big trip for the year. This time Waite rented an apartment for the family in Denver. He and Genevieve took L. E. and Nora to Estes Park. From there, the two brothers traversed the continental divide to try their luck at fishing in Trappers Lake, near Yampa, Colorado.

With traveling out of his system for at least a few months, Waite returned to Okmulgee. Satisfied that the oil industry had recovered from the effects of the proration, he turned to new fields of exploration.

While Waite busied himself with drilling oil wells and with traveling, his brothers in Bartlesville were far from idle. Although Frank and L. E. had sold almost all their oil-field properties to Tidal Oil Company, they held onto one Anchor Oil and Gas Company lease. Tidal could not accept title on that property because of the restriction imposed on any one interest owning more than forty-eight hundred acres of Indian leases.

Confronted with this situation, the Phillips brothers purchased Lot 185 in the Osage oil fields to liquidate the Anchor Company. They decided they might as well drill on the property to see if they could find any production. They found a bona fide gusher.

In early 1917 after having drilled six dry holes, they brought in what was described as "a wonder well," one of the most prolific producers in the field. Any lingering hopes and plans for a Phillips banking empire in Kansas City were dashed. Oil had won out.

With this successful property as a foundation asset — and when oil skyrocketed from forty cents to more than a dollar a barrel because of the war — Frank and L. E. wisely decided to stay in the oil business, only in a bigger way. They founded Phillips Petroleum Company on June 13, 1917, with assets of $3 million and twenty-seven employees. Within seven years, those assets would jump to $303 million.

Waite had to smile when he found out about the new firm his brothers had founded in Bartlesville. He fondly recalled that he was the one who had bought the Lot 185 property for two thousand dollars after having negotiated with Ed Reeser from the Barnsdall Oil Company office in Pittsburgh. Now Lot 185 was responsible for spawning Phillips Petroleum Company.

Pleased with his brothers' success but not at all envious, Waite had absolutely no regrets that he was on his own. He was making plenty of money — more than he had ever seen. Not every well Waite drilled was a gusher, but enough of them came in big to provide him with a substantial income. He hired more personnel, and sold the cottage on Morton Avenue to move into a larger two-story residence at 320 South Seminole. Working from his Okmulgee office in the Parkinson-Trent Building, Waite remained focused on his personal projects but did not neglect his brothers.

After Waite began to strike it rich, he turned to the third-oldest Phillips brother, Ed, who resided with his family in a new home on North Grand Avenue. By 1917, Fred, the youngest of the Phillips boys, had also moved to Okmulgee. At first he lived at the Hotel Melton on East Main Street, but late in the year he married Alma Stine, from Texas, and they took up residence on North Taft. Like Waite in his younger days, Fred had bounced around different jobs, mostly in the oil industry. Included among Fred's experiences was a hitch as treasurer of Geronimo Film Company, producers of "True to Nature Western Films," with headquarters in Lawton, Oklahoma.

It looked as though Fred was ready to settle down. Marrying Alma, whose brother Phil Stine ran an abstract company in Okmulgee, was a definite step in that direction. Within five years of their marriage, Fred and Alma would have three children — Jacqueline, Geraldine, and Bill Dwight, all born in Okmulgee.

But in 1917, Waite was concerned about his brothers' financial future. He offered Ed and Fred, along with Johnson D. Hill, the husband of Waite's younger sister, Lura, an opportunity to snatch some of the money that was up for grabs in the oil fields. After giving the three men some of his own property, Waite assisted them in organizing Iowa Oil Company. As time soon would tell, it seemed that not all of the Phillips boys had the Midas touch when it came to oil. As Waite noted in his diary, only a few years after its founding he was also involved in the liquidation of the oil company "at a loss because they did not succeed."

The ill-fated Iowa Oil Company was the exception, however. Wherever Waite turned, success followed. That was the case with

Central National Bank, an Okmulgee financial institution with a capital of $100,000 that Waite and other local citizens helped to organize in August 1917. Billed as "A home bank owned by home people" where "Every dollar's worth of stock . . . is held by successful business men of Okmulgee," Central National elected Waite Phillips to its board of directors shortly after the beginning of 1918. Still, Waite did not believe his own publicity.

Asked to join the Okmulgee Rotary Club, Waite, attending his first meeting, listened intently as the chairman made a very glowing and complimentary speech about a certain individual without mentioning the name until the end of his talk. Then the chairman turned toward Waite and introduced him. As the applause died down, Waite managed to rise from his chair, but he remained so shocked he was unable to utter a single word.

But Waite and everyone else in that room knew he was standing in tall cotton.

In a very short time and with only a little operating capital, Waite had made some gutsy moves and had become a wealthy man. But besides the income and all that the money bought, Waite Phillips — a wildcatter of the first order — was confident that the best was yet to come.

CHAPTER NINETEEN

LUCKY STRIKES

Elliott Waite Phillips was born on January 11, 1918, at the family residence on Seminole Avenue in Okmulgee. The very Friday the baby arrived, family and friends came calling and observed that the boy was frail and delicate. Waite did not notice. He was so proud of having a son at long last that when he offered his colleagues expensive Havana cigars and accepted their congratulations, he would say, "Yes, he's a fine big robust boy!"

The baby was to have been named John Elliott after his maternal grandfather, but just as they did when their daughter was born, Genevieve and Waite changed their minds at the last minute and slightly altered the name. They dropped the John but kept the Elliott and inserted Waite for a middle name.

Folks said it was a "substantial name." Both sides of the family were appeased. Helen Jane, a dainty six-and-a-half-year-old who would have preferred a little sister, told Waite she was willing to give Elliott a chance. Besides, she confessed, even a boy was better to play with than her lifeless baby dolls.

Approving letters poured in from Iowa, Arkansas, Oklahoma, and many other places. "The expected telegram came today," wrote J. B. Elliott on January 12. "I need not say it was a great relief to know it is over. We hope both are doing well. Just think: we now have a boy in the Elliott family!"

A note to Genevieve dated January 14 from her sister-in-law

Jane Phillips in Bartlesville was as warm and loving as any sent. Jane and Frank's son, John, was grown, and in 1918 they became the legal guardians of two young orphaned sisters, Mary Frank and Sara Jane Phillips. "I was so happy to hear that you have a son," wrote Jane. "I feel it is the greatest blessing that can come into anyone's life." Frank sent a tribute of his own to Waite, as did Fred Spies, Waite's old pal who still served as cashier for Bartlesville National Bank.

As exhilarated as he was with all the praise about his baby son, Waite had to turn back to the oil field and the business that allowed him to pay for fancy automobiles, family trips, and his children's nurses. Of equal importance, it was a business that provided the funds Waite needed for chasing after more pools of untapped oil. And in 1918, the chase was definitely on for Waite Phillips.

Acquired Youngstown leases — Lou Murell and others — in another deal with E. W. Kimbley. M. C. French had 1/8 interest in one of them. These leases were good producers. ~ WAITE PHILLIPS DIARY, 1918

The lease partner whom Waite mentioned in his diary entry was Merritt Chester French. A former newspaper publisher twenty years Waite's senior, French had come to Okmulgee in 1908 to enter the oil game. He was a master at it. After he had paid his dues through a long string of dry holes, French's fortunes improved. He was one of the lucky ones in the Youngstown Pool and Beggs districts. In 1914, he founded Jayne Oil and Gas Company, named after his granddaughter.

French, also successful in the mining of gold, lead, and zinc, had a seat on the Chicago Stock Exchange. A strong Democrat cited by President Woodrow Wilson for extraordinary service on behalf of the Red Cross during the world war, French was yet one more from the oil industry who set a good example for Waite.

The distinguished gentleman, in smart suit and high collar with a monocle in place, enjoyed his daily strolls downtown to the Parkinson Hotel lobby, a favorite gathering place for oilmen. French looked forward to his long visits with Waite, and even forgave his younger friend for being a Republican.

Up in Iowa another forgiving Democrat, J. B. Elliott, burst with pride throughout the spring of 1918 when the Knoxville newspaper boasted in bold headlines "IOWAN STRIKES OIL" and "PHILLIPS MAKES OIL STRIKE" and "WAITE PHILLIPS HAS BIG OIL WELL." In a March 7 report, the newspaper spoke of Waite as being "remarkably fortunate in his ventures." Then it quoted a firsthand report from an Oklahoma reporter.

"Gushing from 55 feet of solid pay sand at the rate of 130 barrels per hour — more than 3,000 barrels per day — the Waite Phillips-Okmulgee Producing & Refining company and M. C. French well in the northwest location of the Mary Jane Foster allotment . . . proved the Youngstown pool, the greatest new oil pool in the mid-continent field and put Okmulgee in the spotlight yesterday.

"There were times during the day when the well was flowing at close to 4,000 barrels per day. The figure of from 125 to 130 barrels per hour is not an estimate, but figures taken from the gauge by Waite Phillips who was on the lease from early Friday morning until last night."

The following month, there were more glowing reports from Oklahoma for Knoxville to read about. "Waite Phillips, a former Knoxville citizen, son-in-law of Mr. and Mrs. J. B. Elliott, and once interested in the old Hawkeye coal mine, east of town, has every prospect of getting into the near millionaire class in the very near future," the newspaper reported.

In May, as if for good measure following the run of big gushers, Waite, with E. W. Kimbley as his broker, sold the Lou Robinson lease south of Okmulgee to Josh Cosden for $150,000. It looked as if Waite could not make a bad deal.

Sold Tiger Flat leases to C. B. Schaffer for his Barbara Oil Company. In order to acquire the Barbara Oil Co. in the trade, Mr. Schaffer refused to make the deal unless W. P. agreed to take an additional 50 acres. Rather than have the deal fall through W. P. agreed to do this and the property purchased proved to be very productive. ~ WAITE PHILLIPS DIARY, 1918

In a notation written forty years later, Waite recalled that "from then on (the spring of 1918), by good luck, favorable conditions, and hard work, success followed in the Youngstown pool and on other leases previously purchased in Okmulgee County."

In July 1918, Waite took the family entourage, including Elliott's nurse, to Chicago for an extended summer holiday. As he often did on certain dates, including his birthday, Waite became reflective on July 16 that year, the sixteenth anniversary of Wiate's death.

In addition to the grisly war reports from the trenches of France, the world would learn later that on that same day, July 16, the Bolsheviks had executed the former Czar Nicholas II and his family, bringing to an end the Romanov dynasty that had ruled for three centuries.

Waite, secure in the grand apartment he had rented for his family, was far removed from the madness and bloodshed of Europe. On those early summer mornings in Chicago, while his wife and children slept, Waite stared from the high windows of their apartment building opposite Lincoln Park. He looked far beyond the well-groomed lawns and shrubs. He looked past the statues and fountains. He watched the sun come to life over Lake Michigan.

He thought about his dead twin, still nineteen years old in Waite's mind. He thought about the hectic years since that day in Spokane when Wiate had died. Perhaps Waite wondered what might have been if his brother had lived.

But Waite knew there was no turning back. He had to move

forward and hold onto those memories for special times — the birth and death dates, the celebrations and holidays, or those quiet summer mornings when dawn came creeping and it seemed that nobody else in the whole world was awake.

CHAPTER TWENTY

OIL CAPITAL

After a summer spent on the Chicago shore and in northern Michigan, stalking the dimensions of Mackinac Island, the Waite Phillips family returned to Oklahoma in September 1918.

They did not, however, go back to their residence on Seminole Avenue in bustling Okmulgee. Although both he and Genevieve had enjoyed their time there together, Waite recognized that he had simply outgrown the town. Because of his diversified and rapidly expanding oil operations, Waite needed to relocate to a larger setting.

The Phillipses did not have to move very far. Waite chose Tulsa, the state's second-largest city, which became the self-styled "Oil Capital of the World."

Before leaving for summer vacation purchased home in Tulsa on Owasso Avenue. Moved to Tulsa in September in order to be in better location to handle all matters connected with oil business. After moving there resumed social activities which had been dormant in Fayetteville and Okmulgee. The social group consisted mainly of the Crawleys, Boles, Sinclairs, Dressers, McClintocks, Moores, et al. ⁓ WAITE PHILLIPS DIARY, 1918

Constructed on a block-long corner tract at 1621 South Owasso Avenue, the house was brand spanking new when the

Phillipses moved in. With sixteen rooms in two stories, servants' quarters, and a three-car garage, it served as the family's home for the next decade.

The new domicile was located ideally in a neighborhood of affluent homes, all of them with broad lawns and manicured flower beds. Elms and maples lined the streets, and flowering magnolias and mimosas graced the yards. Almost everyone the Phillipses knew had at least a maid and gardener, if not a cook and sometimes a driver who could act as butler if an auspicious occasion arose.

Nearby was the Maple Ridge area. Many of the big names in banking, legal, and oil circles resided there. One stretch of homes became known as "Black Gold Row." The mix of architectural styles ranged from Italianate and colonial revival to Gothic Tudor and Georgian. Many of the residents, especially those connected to oil, had come to Tulsa from the eastern United States. Few of them hailed from so-called "old money," but had made their fortunes only recently. These upper-echelon oil people were typically Protestants, especially Methodists and High Church Episcopalians. Unlike rural Oklahomans and many of their fellow Tulsans, the majority were Republicans and were conservative in business and politics — but not when it came to showing off their newly acquired wealth.

One of those who fit the profile perfectly was W. G. "Bill" Skelly. Known in Oklahoma as "Mr. Republican," Skelly lived on South Madison Avenue, not very far from the Phillipses. The founder of Skelly Oil moved into his palatial home in 1921, just a few years after Waite came to Tulsa. Skelly's twenty-one-room mansion came complete with a walk-in vault, a pair of Baccarat crystal chandeliers, and a half dozen fireplaces on three floors. Within a few years, Waite would create a much more grandiose and larger estate. But for the time being, the Phillipses were satisfied to be on South Owasso in their brick residence with its tile roof and canvas awnings.

On the threshold of the Roaring Twenties, the residents of these sprawling neighborhoods seemingly had little to worry about except what to wear to church or to the next reception. They gazed at close-by downtown Tulsa during their morning strolls and at twilight veranda parties, catered by the best bootleggers and fanciest florists.

The nearby skyline changed almost daily in this city that had grown by leaps and bounds since shortly after the turn of the century. That was when highly productive oil wells were brought in across the Arkansas River in Red Fork and later in the Glenn Pool. Petroleum played a key role in Tulsa's economy, lifestyle, and culture. The oil fields lubricated and drove the city. Such a place was made to order for Waite Phillips. It was a perfect location for Oklahoma's newest millionaire, who grew wealthier every day in the boom times that followed the end of World War I.

Near the rear of the Phillipses' new residential property, separated from the main house by terraces, a rose trellis, and shrubbery, was Waite's very own inner sanctum. It was not at all fancy or plush, but only a log cabin with a shake roof. Waite filled the small rooms with western-style furnishings he picked up on his many trips to Colorado, Montana, California, and elsewhere. He kept his personal treasures and remembrances there. The cabin became an essential haven, a genuine sanctuary for Waite when he wished to escape the tension and turmoil that were part of his business life.

On warm summer evenings he was in the cabin, usually for hours at a time. In the heart of the coldest winter, Waite went there all by himself. He stoked the stone fireplace with seasoned oak, and stared into the flames. No one disturbed him. Genevieve understood that the cabin was a time machine for her husband. It was Waite's tie to the past, to those long-ago times when he and his twin brother had roamed the West.

The restless Waite still arranged for his essential out-of-town trips, for business and personal reasons. Like his cabin retreat,

Waite found traveling the best possible therapy. Part of that itinerary included long summer holidays, such as in 1919 when he rented a house for the family on Ocean Avenue in Long Beach, California. Various visitors, including Tulsa banker and oil executive R. Otis McClintock and his wife, Gladys Belle Stebbins, came out for visits. While in the far West that summer, Waite also took his family on a motor tour of Sequoyah National Park and to San Francisco. On their return to Tulsa, they came via the Grand Canyon and the Indian lands of the Southwest.

At home, Waite still was forced to spend most of his time overseeing his growing oil operations. To help with the load, he tried to find and retain the best personnel in the oil patch. He brought along J. C. Parks, his office manager in Okmulgee, to run the Tulsa office, a five-room suite in the First National Bank Building. Waite was pleased to be with his old friends, and liked making new contacts in Tulsa and elsewhere in the oil field.

He quickly began to buy developed oil properties in the Bartlesville area, and established a field office there with Earl Beard as superintendent. Waite hired B. B. Blair, another Iowa native, to operate several farms Waite had purchased between Nowata and Henryetta. Development continued at the Youngstown Pool properties and at several gas wells west of Okmulgee. The successes Waite had enjoyed in the past paled greatly in comparison with those that came his way in the 1920s.

During the first year of his residency in Tulsa, Waite purchased a sizable block of acreage from the Berk-Greis Oil Company and the Savoy Oil Company. When the new acreage, ten miles northwest of Okmulgee, was drilled, the discovery well came in the highly productive Wilcox sand. The well's initial yield was more than one thousand barrels of oil per day — not bad for openers. Many more wells — all of them huge producers — followed. Eventually, two hundred wells dotted that field. Clearly, when the time came, there was really only one name to give Waite's newest leases — his own.

Continued to develop Jane Reed-Henry Thompson block of leases, now called Phillipsville Pool. Maximum production 20,000 barrels per day at $4.00 per barrel. ~ WAITE PHILLIPS DIARY, 1920

Waite wished to expand and diversify by getting into the refining business. He ordered two of his top men, W. E. Burke and Ralph B. Pringle, to erect a gasoline plant at Phillipsville. To make a good start in his integrated operations, Waite had a pipeline laid to Okmulgee and purchased his first refinery, just south of the town. Burke served as Waite's first refinery manager.

Waite confided to his most trusted lieutenants, such as Pringle, that sometimes he was operating mostly by instinct. He said he felt as though he were wheeling and dealing by the seat of his pants, and relied on less than perfect techniques for finding oil and gas. Even so, Waite had to admit, those methods paid off many times. He confirmed those feelings many years later when writing about the early 1920s. "In those days oil men did not employ geologists to any considerable extent and up to that time I depended on tracing the trends of old shore lines, from oil maps, as a guide to drilling operations. These Phillipsville leases were located on a shore line trend that extended from a point south of Okmulgee northwest to Bristow, Oklahoma, and my two properties were on it. Moreover, there was a well on the Phillipsville property that produced gas from the Dutcher sand so I surmised there was an anticline [an arch of stratified rock] there which, by deeper drilling, was proved."

By that time, Waite had done more than prove he knew where to find "black gold." Yet despite all the good fortune, he believed he did not have to go out of his way to demonstrate anything to anyone — except, perhaps, to himself.

Throughout 1920, as chaotic as his business calendar was, Waite continued to take as much time as possible to escape the oil patch. The Phillips family, including baby Elliott with his nurse, went on jaunts to Texas, Louisiana, and Florida, and took a train tour of New England. Waite led a party of family and friends on packhorses through the rugged high country of Montana. And, in December, Waite went to Arkansas and Iowa to grieve when his brother-in-law R. S. Granger, whom he described as "a very fine character," passed away.

Back in the log cabin on South Owasso Avenue in Tulsa, there was plenty for Waite to think about as 1920 ended. It was the year when America went on the wagon. Women, including Genevieve Phillips, had voted for the first time in a national election. Newly elected Republican Warren G. Harding, pledging a return to "normalcy," prepared to begin what turned out to be one of the most scandalous terms of office in the White House.

In his 1920 novel, *This Side of Paradise,* F. Scott Fitzgerald wrote: "Here was a new generation . . . dedicated more than the last to the fear of poverty and the worship of success; grown up to find all gods dead, all wars fought, all faiths in man shaken."

Fitzgerald did not have Waite Phillips in mind when he wrote that passage. Two-thirds of the world's oil originated in the United States in 1920. Much of that oil — barrels and barrels of it — came from beneath the Oklahoma prairie where Waite Phillips, a newly elected director of First National Bank of Tulsa, was entrenched firmly as one of the largest individual producers.

Unlike Fitzgerald's lost souls, Waite did not worship success, and his faith was not shaken. He definitely was not afraid of poverty. By the end of the year, while Waite stretched his legs before the fireplace in the cabin and thought about his approaching thirty-eighth birthday, his income was said to be in excess of forty thousand dollars a day.

Ironically, the year's greatest national celebration was the tercentenary of the Pilgrims' landing at Plymouth. If the astute Captain Miles Standish could have vaulted through three hundred years of time and space to that log cabin in Tulsa, he would have had an enjoyable visit with his young descendant. They did, after all, have so much in common.

CHAPTER TWENTY-ONE

THE WAITE PHILLIPS COMPANY

·WP·

As the second year of the new decade clicked into place, Valentino, Chaplin, Dempsey, Ruth, and Jolson kept Americans swooning, laughing, cheering, or humming. Even so, many people, including several of the nation's best young writers, did not feel so good about themselves or the country. Ernest Hemingway, Katherine Anne Porter, William Carlos Williams, and others became so disillusioned with American values that they said farewell and moved to Europe.

In 1921, overly zealous patriots caught up in the paranoia of the "Red Scare" launched their decades-long search for communists, whom they said were lurking behind every tree and bush. Other miserable souls joined in a campaign of wholesale hatred and bigotry triggered by a revival of the insidious evil known as the Ku Klux Klan. That year, in a twenty-four-hour span in Tulsa, occurred one of America's most disastrous racial conflicts. Untold numbers of innocent black citizens were left dead, wounded, homeless, or traumatized by a rampaging white mob.

Waite Phillips and the people he knew were not directly affected by the social upheavals of the time, even the racial bloodbath that exploded just a few miles from his residence. The primary dilemma most affluent whites encountered in the Tulsa tragedy was the loss or disruption of domestic service.

Waite and his associates never faced or dealt with any of the same problems of the "Lost Generation" of expatriate artists, or those perceived as social and political misfits, or the poor and people of color, especially the blacks and the Native Americans of that time. Yet even oil-field millionaires were not exempt from all pain and suffering.

On February 15, 1921, while staying with Genevieve and the children at the Eastman Hotel in Hot Springs, Arkansas, Waite received a telegram from his older brothers. The wire contained the terrible news that their father, Lewis Phillips, had died, at age seventy-seven, in a Kansas City hospital. Frank and L. E. were at his bedside. They took him home to Iowa for burial.

Waite hurried to Gravity to comfort his mother and mourn for Lew. All the children came home. They surrounded Josie in Gravity Cemetery, when their father was laid to rest near Wiate's grave.

After his father's estate was settled, Waite saw to it that the small portion of his inheritance was assigned to his sisters. He had plenty of money. All Waite asked for and wanted was a small copper button. It was from a veterans' organization called the Grand Army of the Republic. Lew Phillips had worn it proudly in his coat lapel to show his service to the Union. That old soldier's button remained in Waite's jewelry box for the rest of his life.

In spring drilled good wells on Winey Stake lease northeast of Phillipsville pool. With expanding oil production, gasoline plant, and oil refinery, W. P. started buying and establishing filling stations in Okmulgee and Tulsa.

Gave properties to help liquidate Iowa Oil Co. at par, for Ed, Fred [his brothers], and Johnson Hill [his brother-in-law].

~ WAITE PHILLIPS DIARY, 1921

After assisting with the disposal of Iowa Oil, Waite spent the entire summer in Colorado. He had purchased a ranch there just the year before, in October 1920, with advice from Genevieve and from B. B. Blair. It was named Highland Ranch.

E. G. Hayward was hired as property superintendent to boss the hired hands and look after the place. Located just south of Denver near Littleton on the Platte River, the twenty-five-thousand-acre spread was practically self-sufficient. Mile after mile of barbed-wire fence surrounded vast grazing pastures. There were stables, barns, a complete poultry operation, hog and sheep pens, vegetable gardens, and great herds of cattle and horses.

The main house looked more like a huge castle than a ranch headquarters. Made entirely of stone and surrounded by a low rock wall, the house had a flat roof studded with turrets. Almost all the rooms featured beamed ceilings, fireplaces, and massive furniture. Animal skins and Navajo rugs covered the floors, and mounted bison and elk heads peered from above some of the mantles.

Waite enjoyed his billiard room, Helen Jane and Genevieve were provided with ladylike furnishings and quarters, and little Elliott spent most of his time out-of-doors. Soon after he could walk, Elliott took to the ranch ponies. He was a born cowboy and even posed for photographs astride his favorite mount inside the house, with the pony standing on a bear rug before a fireplace.

During his summer stay at Highland, Waite arranged a trip to California for his widowed mother, his mother-in-law, and his sister Jennie. He also frequently checked in with his business headquarters in Tulsa. Once again, he was thinking about the family. Even though the oil firm he had helped organize for his brothers and brother-in-law was a bust, Waite had bigger and better plans for all three men.

Waite came back to Oklahoma in October. He was occupied the rest of the year with the expansion of his oil production and marketing departments. More filling stations and wholesale plants were built throughout Oklahoma, Kansas, Arkansas, and Missouri. The district offices stayed busy in Okmulgee, Bartlesville, and Bristow. He even helped his brothers Frank and L. E. entertain the Phillips Petroleum directors when they assembled for meetings and inspection trips.

During the first few months of 1922, Waite left Tulsa for a variety of activities. He attended a stock show in Denver, spent the late winter with his family at the Ambassador Hotel in Los Angeles, and looked, in California and New Mexico, at more ranchlands that he considered adding to his dominion. Waite passed up property at Lompoc, California, not far from Santa Barbara on the Pacific coast.

Instead, he chose New Mexico — "the Land of Enchantment."

Waite was not at all pleased with the recreational opportunities his Highland Ranch offered. Genevieve found the big stone house cold and ominous. Waite, who had become well-versed in the cattle business, was told that the best cow country, especially for raising calves, was in New Mexico.

In the spring of 1922, he learned of the proposed sale of what had been known at one time as the McCormick Ranch, in northern New Mexico's rugged Colfax County on the eastern slope of the continental divide. Once owned by Stanley R. McCormick, youngest son of famed reaper inventor Cyrus McCormick, the ranch belonged in 1922 to George H. Webster, Jr. With headquarters near the town of Cimarron, on the historic Santa Fe Trail, the ranch provided a stunning view of the peaks and canyons of the picturesque Sangre de Cristo Mountains.

Accompanied by Gene Hayward, his Highland Ranch manager, Waite visited Cimarron in March and inspected the two tracts of the ranch that were available for sale. He also investigated the surrounding territory. Waite liked what he saw. More than that — he loved it, especially the high meadows and distant snow-covered peaks.

"Dad later told me when he and George Webster rode their horses up in those mountains to have a look around that memories of his dead brother, Wiate, came back to him and he recalled their high times together," said Elliott many years later. "Dad said, 'When I thought of my brother, I made up my mind to buy the ranch.' "

On April 25, 1922, the transaction was completed. Waite handed George Webster a check for $150,000 and became the owner of forty-two thousand acres containing the Urraca and Rayado tracts. Waite called his new ranch the Hawkeye, in honor of his native state's nickname and after the coal company there that once had given him gainful employment.

The purchase of Hawkeye Ranch was just the beginning of what eventually became Waite's most beloved and greatest land-holding.

Hayward was transferred from Highland Ranch to this new ranch property, near Cimarron, as manager. Tried to get cattle brand of "W" but it was already taken in New Mexico so took "U U" — Unusually Useful — also "Double U" instead of "W".
~ WAITE PHILLIPS DIARY, 1922

Back in Tulsa, Waite saw that his oil operations and staff had grown so large that he needed a corporation to service them. Previously, he had organized and operated a series of smaller operations, including Clifton Drilling Company, Parks Producing Company, Okmulgee Refining Company, Phillips Hawkeye Oil Company, Phillips Highgrade Refining Company and, for the Highland Ranch staff, the Waite Phillips Company of Colorado.

In May 1922, he incorporated his businesses under one name — the Waite Phillips Company.

After organization of the company was completed, 120,000 shares of common stock were issued at a par value of one hundred dollars. Waite held at least 75 percent of the stock, with his vice president, Ralph Pringle, the next largest shareholder. Waite later wrote that one of the primary reasons he formed the company was to make it more convenient to issue "carried stock" to his staff. He had started his policy of profit sharing with employees at Okmulgee in 1916, and continued it throughout his active business career.

Some of Waite's employees in the new company were his brothers Ed and Fred and other family members. Ed was made manager of the marketing department, and Fred became an assistant in the leasing, or land department. A cousin by marriage, Horace L. Skinner, was made treasurer, and Waite's brother-in-law Johnson Hill became a vice president in charge of purchases.

Oil production developments by this time had extended to Beggs, Bristow, Bartlesville, and Osage areas in Oklahoma. A 160 acre lease was purchased in the Burbank pool, where oil was found, and other leases taken southwest of Burbank where prolific production was drilled. In the eastern tier of lots in the Osage, southwest of Ochelata, Oklahoma, an acreage amounting to 1,100 acres of good oil property was acquired and developed in partnership with D. B. Mason of Tulsa. In addition, leasing operations were carried on in southern Oklahoma and in north Texas and southern Arkansas where oil was found and produced. Coincident with these oil production expansions a program of buying and building oil filling stations continued. ~ WAITE PHILLIPS DIARY, 1922

The trio of Phillips brothers of the Waite Phillips Company, with headquarters in Tulsa, became increasingly competitive with the two oldest Phillips brothers, who headed Phillips Petroleum Company, based in Bartlesville.

On June 28, 1922, at the colorful oil-lease auction staged beneath the so-called "million-dollar elm" at the Osage Indian agency in Pawhuska, the Phillips brothers took each other on in their mutual quest for drilling rights on Osage land. Phillips Petroleum and its allied interests were the largest bidders that day, but the Waite Phillips Company outmaneuvered and outbid Frank for at least one desirable Osage tract.

"Waite Phillips is Frank Phillips's brother, but does not operate with him," understated a *Kansas City Times* news story published the next day. "The Waite Phillips $665,000 purchase was one lease that he took away from Frank after spirited bidding."

On June 30, in a confidential interoffice memo, Frank vented some of his frustrations to L. E.

> Permit me to say as a memorandum that I regret exceedingly the situation which arose at the Osage Sale as between Waite Phillips Company and our own.
>
> You understand that our maximum price on Tract No. 44 was $1,020,000.00. We finally bid it in at $805,000.00. Waite was the runner-up on this for the last one to two hundred thousand, all of the other bidders having dropped out. Considering it from an ethical standpoint, we were certainly entitled to this tract inasmuch as we had proven it up with our own well adjoining and the tract adjoined our block of acreage. I took no exception, however, to Waite's bidding against me on this tract after all others had quit.
>
> Tract No. 45 to the south was desirable for us and our maximum price on this was $560,000.00. When the bidding had reached about $400,000.00 I noticed everyone else had quit except Waite. I immediately turned around and suggested that someone go and see Waite and advise him that we would drop out and he could run the bidding up to $600,000.00 and we would join him.
>
> He sent word back that he wanted all or nothing. We finally obtained the tract, as you know, for $495,000.00.
>
> In view of what happened in our purchase of Tracts

Nos. 44 and 45, and that we had extended every consideration and courtesy to Waite and inasmuch as he continued the competition on these tracts adjoining our property and the further fact that we bought them below the price anticipated, it was entirely proper that we should continue to bid on tracts adjoining us even at a little higher price as it gave us a good average and blocked up our acreage. I naturally would have been pleased for Waite to have Tract No. 46 at a lower price but in view of what transpired I felt justified in running it up near what we thought it was worth to us and would have continued bidding a little higher if anyone else except Waite had been bidding against us.

Notwithstanding all this, I cannot help but regret that we bid against each other. I hold no ill feeling, however, and hope this is also true with Waite.

Frank need not have worried. It was true with Waite. Like his oldest brother, he held no grudges and subscribed to the theory that all is fair in love and war — and at oil-lease auctions. Also like Frank and the select others in their splashy oil-field fraternity, Waite remained a regular figure beneath the big elm at Pawhuska, where flamboyant Colonel Ellsworth E. Walters conducted auctions. The siblings' love for one another and the competition among them never ceased.

In April purchased 160 acres Burbank lease at Osage sale, Pawhuska, for $1,300,000. Returned to Tulsa that evening in Harry F. Sinclair's private car. ~ WAITE PHILLIPS DIARY, 1923

That July of 1923, before departing for the summer to his ranches in Colorado and New Mexico, Waite led his senior executives — Ralph Pringle, Gillette Hill, M. M. Doan, and Oscar L. Cordell — to an important conference in Chicago. Top officials from Standard Oil of Indiana wished to meet with Waite and his men about the possible sale of the Waite Phillips Com-pany.

Although his company had been formed only fourteen months earlier, Waite saw no need to hold onto it if the right deal could be cut. A sale of the Waite Phillips Company that was satisfactory to all parties — especially Waite and his troops, spread across several oil-patch states — had to be considered seriously.

But this time, however, there was no sale. Negotiations with Standard of Indiana failed. A few other oil firms made noises about purchasing the Waite Phillips Company, but those inquiries also went nowhere. The lone exception was the sale of a portion of Waite's holdings. In September 1923, R. J. Berry of the Mid-Kansas Oil & Gas Company bought all the oil property owned by Waite north of Tulsa for $5,250,000.

Then before the end of the year, after a tour of his oil stations in Arkansas, Waite purchased more oil lands, north of Oklahoma. With help from Johnson Hill, he bought the Rainbow Bend leases near Winfield, Kansas. To commemorate the acquisition of the new leases, and to celebrate Christmas and toast the new year of 1924, Waite and the family headed to their Rocky Mountain ranches. The time in Colorado, and especially at the Hawkeye Ranch in New Mexico, gave Waite the luxury of reflecting on the future but also on past events.

During this year an office was opened in Denver with the idea of establishing an integrated provision business, similar to that of the Waite Phillips Co. operations, to include producing, packing and marketing ranch products. The plan provided for a packing plant on the Highland Ranch, and several grocery stores were purchased before it was decided to abandon the idea on account of lack of time to devote to it. A special general manager was hired for the operation and R. W. Coan, brother-in-law, operated stores in Denver and Littleton for some time prior to the abandonment of the plan. This plan was adopted by Safeway Stores and other chain grocery stores later on, except for owning land and produc-

ing their own products. ~ Waite Phillips Diary, 1923

As he rode horseback on those bitterly cold mornings at his New Mexico place, Waite knew the sun would break through and warm him. Just being out on his ranches with his children and a few pals had become increasingly important to Waite.

He knew there was something more valuable than all his riches. It was more precious than the crude oil and gasoline, the filling stations and refineries, and the fancy homes and automobiles. Not a commodity or anything tangible, but time — the gift of time — was what Waite coveted the most. Time was what he wanted more than anything else on earth.

He needed time for Helen Jane and Elliott, time to spend with Genevieve, time to be all alone with his thoughts on top of a horse high up on a mountain trail. At forty years of age, Waite knew he had to pay dearly for more time. It was in awfully short supply, but it was worth the price.

1924-1941

IV
THE GIFT
OF TIME

To every thing there is a season, and a time to every purpose under the heaven.

A time to be born, and a time to die; a time to plant, and a time to pluck up that which is planted;

A time to kill, and a time to heal; a time to mourn, and a time to dance;

A time to cast away stones, and a time to gather stones together; a time to embrace, and a time to refrain from embracing;

A time to get, and a time to lose; a time to keep, and a time to cast away;

A time to rend, and a time to sew; a time to keep silence, and a time to speak;

A time to love, and a time to hate; a time of war, and a time of peace.

ECCLESIASTES 3:1-8

Overleaf: George Rockenfield, farm foreman, harvesting oats at Philmont Ranch, 1939. The shadow in the foreground is that of Alvin Krupnick, the photographer. Above: Waite Phillips in the Territorial Room at Villa Philmonte, late 1920s. The table in the fore-ground bears the carved initials of each of the Phillips brothers and Tulsa oilman William G. Skelly. Inset: Interior of the main cabin at Fish Camp, about 1930.

Above: The Beacon Building, in Tulsa, donated by Waite Phillips to endow the Philbrook Art Center, 1938-1939. At right: Waite's library at Villa Philbrook, ca. 1939. Inset: Alvin Krupnick with Gene Hayward, manager of Philmont Ranch, taking pictures of the cattle headquarters. Waite frequently employed Krupnick for family and business photography, and many of the photos in this book were made by him.

PHILBROOK
2727
ROCKFORD ROAD

PAC 027

The south terrace (below left) and the music room (above) at Villa Philbrook, Tulsa, ca. 1939. Above left, the Phillips family on the east terrace at Philbrook, ca. 1930. Inset at right, Waite with Helen Jane.

District Office Building
TULSA

August 1925

Waite Phillips at Philmont in 1940.

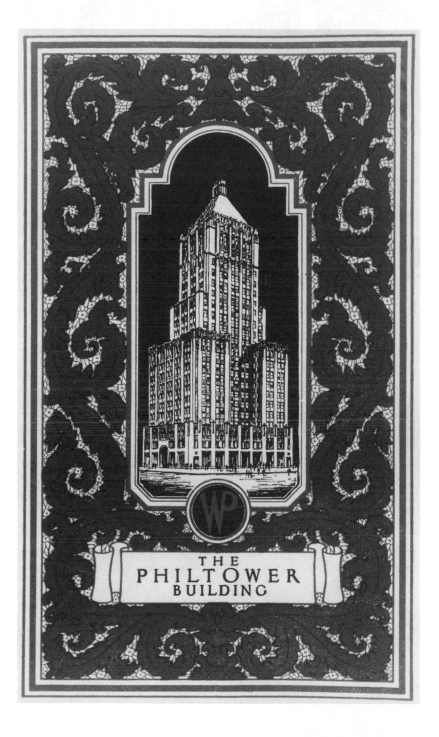

THE
PHILTOWER
BUILDING

A view of Fish
Camp, Philmont
Ranch, in the 1930s.
Above, Villa
Philmonte under
construction, 1926.
Below, the Phillips
family in about
1928 at Fish Camp.

Above: Left, the Trophy Room at Villa Philmonte and, right, the breakfast room, 1930s.
Left, Waite Phillips with Elliott and Helen Jane and the dog Fritz at the site where Philbrook would be built the following year.
Right, Waite at Villa Philmonte in 1928 wearing a costume he brought back from Spain.

TRAP SHOOTING

LOST

THE STUTZ

VILLA PHILMONTE

THE BOSS

Left, a drawing by John McCutcheon, cartoonist for the CHICAGO TRIBUNE, made as a memento of his trips with the Dawes party to Philmont Ranch in 1927 and 1928. Right, one of the last photographs made of Wiley Post and Will Rogers before their deaths in Alaska, taken in the courtyard at Philmont, July 1935. Waite holds his grandson Phillips Breckinridge. Post is at left and Rogers at right. Below, the stairway at Villa Philmonte, seen from the living room, 1930s.

A gathering of the Phillipses at Woolaroc Ranch near Bartlesville, Oklahoma, ca. 1926. Waite is seated second from the right between brothers Ed and Frank (in cowboy boots).

OVER THE RAINBOW

As his forty-first birthday approached, in January 1924, Waite's life was more than half over. Of course, he had no way of knowing that, and he really did not care. As usual, he did not have a spare moment to ponder such matters. Waite, escorted by Ralph Pringle and Oscar L. Cordell, was occupied with an inspection of his company's initial oil well at the Rainbow Bend leases in Kansas. Besides refining crude oil, he also had his first trip to Europe on his mind.

Waite had visited most of the United States and Canada, but he had never been abroad. On January 27, the day Lenin's body was laid in a marble tomb in the Kremlin, the Phillips family, with an array of steamer trunks and suitcases, went to New York. On Wednesday, January 30, 1924, they departed on a luxury cruise of the Mediterranean.

Helen Jane, a beautiful twelve-and-a-half-year-old with long curls and big dark eyes, and her little brother, Elliott, an animated boy just turned six years old, stood on their toes at the ship's railing. They waved with their parents at the crowds gathered on the docks as their ship, the SS *Scythia* — named for an ancient region in southeastern Europe and Asia — sailed for distant ports and exotic lands.

The long voyage took the family to the Madeiras, a group of five Portuguese islands off the coast of Morocco, and on to

Algeria, Spain, Rome, Athens, Egypt, and the Holy Land. While the Phillipses visited Greece, the country became a republic, which caused a holiday mood. Throngs of rejoicing Greeks waved small flags inscribed with the words "Republic and Reconciliation." At the same time the Greeks were busily celebrating their newly found governmental power, Waite scrambled to grab all of the port-of-call news he could find from back in the United States.

He learned that developments again had boiled over in the Teapot Dome Scandal, involving the leasing of federal oil reserves to private interests. Waite was engrossed by the little bit of information he picked up. Fellow oil tycoon Harry F. Sinclair, the often ruthless producer who leased Wyoming oil reserves from the federal government without competitive bidding, had been convicted already. So had the man responsible for the leasing, Secretary of the Interior Albert B. Fall, the first cabinet member in history to go to jail. Then Waite learned that Attorney General Harry M. Daugherty had been forced to resign in disgrace.

While the ship cut through the Mediterranean for new destinations, Waite thanked his lucky stars that he was far removed from the oil-patch transgressions in Wyoming.

The rest of the trip proved enjoyable. The Phillipses discovered new lands and made several friends aboard ship. They rendezvoused with American acquaintances and business associates for lavish dinners and visits in Paris and Cannes. On April 12, after almost three months, they sailed from Southampton, England, on the SS *Berengaria* bound for New York.

Visits with Waite's mother and family outings to Atlantic City with the McClintocks, of Tulsa, accounted for much of Waite's summer. But by early autumn, he was going full steam ahead in the oil field.

Production rapidly increased in Kansas — so much that in September, the Waite Phillips Company purchased another refinery, in Wichita. Once a pipeline was laid, the newest refinery serviced the oil wells in the Rainbow Bend pool. Waite's company owned half interest in those properties. The other half interest in the Rainbow Bend leases was divided equally between Marland Oil Company and Independent Oil & Gas Company.

Meanwhile, the Okmulgee refinery continued to operate at full capacity. The Waite Phillips Company's daily production increased at the hundreds of wells operating on thousands of acres controlled by the firm in Oklahoma, Kansas, and Texas. Fleets of railroad tank cars carried Phillips Higrade products to filling stations that mushroomed in the primary four-state marketing area — Oklahoma, Missouri, Kansas, and Arkansas. The first well Waite drilled at the Camden, Arkansas, lease, near Smackover and El Dorado, yielded forty-two thousand barrels per day.

There was no slowing down. Waite did not often lose his magic touch. The very few times things did not go his way left no lasting damage and did little to affect him or his organization. As another prosperous Tulsan of that time put it, "When Waite hits salt water instead of oil, it doesn't upset him any more than it would a carpenter when his nail splits a piece of wood he has carefully fitted." The best choice was to not slow down but to keep plugging away.

J. J. McGraw, president of the old Exchange National Bank in Tulsa, had his own evaluation of Waite: "He isn't a gambler. He is a shrewd investor. I don't want to say he's the best oil man on earth . . . there are lots of good oil men. But I have never seen a better."

In December to New York with Johnson D. Hill, R. B. Pringle, and G. E. P. [Genevieve], to negotiate and complete loan for the Waite Phillips Co. with E. W. Marland of the Marland Oil Co. to be liquidated from oil runs at the Rainbow Bend pool. Met Amon Carter there. Returned home with Marland in his private car from St. Louis to the American Petroleum Institute convention in Fort Worth, Texas. Returned from Fort Worth in H. F.

Sinclair's private car with party consisting of H. F. and E. W.
Sinclair, H. L. Doherty of Cities Service, Van Dyke of Atlantic
Refining, Leovy of Gulf, Pratt of Standard Oil of N. Y., J. J.
McGraw, Johnson Hill, and others. ~ WAITE PHILLIPS DIARY,
1924

By 1925, the Waite Phillips Company's seventeen departments, ranging from legal and leasing to purchasing and geologi-
cal, employed hundreds of men and women in district offices,
gasoline plants, and refineries spread across several states. A crack-
erjack executive department — with Waite in complete control
— governed the entire operation with care and precision.

As the firm grew, it needed more office space. The headquarters office was moved from its suite in First National Bank of
Tulsa to a complete floor of the Petroleum Building, at Fifth
Street and Boulder Avenue. Soon, it was necessary to take another
full floor in the building, and to acquire a large building on
North Peoria Avenue to house the accounting staff of the distrib-
ution division.

Sales of Phillips Higrade gasoline and motor oils, kerosene,
lubrication products, and grease showed substantial and constant
increases month after month. Esteem for Waite Phillips' products
was so great in Tulsa in 1925 that city officials made the Higrade
gas and oil the official fuels for the city's new fleet of 100-horse-
power Seagraves fire engines. More new customers looked for the
gas pumps displaying a Higrade crown globe at scores of filling
stations dispensing Waite Phillips Company products.

Among the cities and towns in Oklahoma with one, if not
several, of Waite's gas stations were Tulsa, Oklahoma City,
Okmulgee, Bartlesville, Pawhuska, Claremore, Wagoner, Stigler,
Tahlequah, Holdenville, Sallisaw, Muskogee, Chelsea, Guthrie,
and Norman. The locations in Missouri included Kansas City,
Springfield, Carthage, Rich Hill, Republic, Joplin, and Clinton.
In Arkansas, at least one of Waite's retail outlets could be found in

Little Rock, Fayetteville, Jonesboro, Rogers, Siloam Springs, Fort Smith, Helena, Paragould, and Eureka Springs.

A few Phillips retail locations were outside the company's true marketing territory. Some of them received a fair amount of attention. A good example was McCurnin's Service Station in Des Moines, an exclusive Higrade retailer with six busy pumps. The station was built to resemble a colonial bungalow with a porch. Inside, where cans of Higrade oil lined the shelves, patrons found all the comforts of home. The station provided customers with a coffee shop, soda fountain, and accessory store. It also had a large parlor for ladies, and a smoking room for men.

The Iowa location merited special mention in the August 1925 issue of the *Philco News,* the Waite Phillips Company's official newsletter. Despite the size of the organization, every attempt was made to help all office employees and plant workers feel that they were part of one big family. That was one of the main missions of the newsletter, which ended up being edited by R. C. Jopling, the company's advertising manager.

The *Philco News* served up generous helpings of company and employee gossip and photos from all district offices and departments. It contained technical articles, personnel briefs, and stories of the company baseball team. Managed by Fred Phillips, the team was usually locked in heated league competition against other oil firms such as the Texas Company and Skelly Oil.

Also peppered throughout the monthly *Philco News* were tidbits of wisdom and pithy sayings. Waite supplied most of the epigrams himself. He found many of them in various publications, newspapers, or books. Others he got from people such as the late Reverend Jenkin Lloyd Jones, whose descendants published the *Tulsa Tribune.* He was quoted in the newsletter as saying, "Those men who try to do something and fail, are infinitely better than those who try to do nothing and beautifully succeed."

Waite continued his practice of collecting epigrams for the rest of his life. Published sources were as varied as Abraham Lincoln,

Ralph Waldo Emerson, Mark Twain, George Bernard Shaw, Oscar Wilde, Henry Ford, and Walt Whitman. His favorites ended up on a typewritten list he carried in a suit-coat pocket. A number of them Waite composed himself, such as, "Some important human ailments still resist modern medical science and one of them is self-pity," and "When we get something for nothing it's generally not worth much to us and sometimes downright detrimental."

Another of his special epigrams was, "Nothing in this world is permanent but change." Perhaps Waite was thinking about the permanence of change in 1925 when he decided the time had come for him to get out of the oil business.

> *In February at New York with G. E. P. Started to Florida for vacation but met Henry Lockhart of Blair & Co. there and discussed sale of W. P. Company so returned home for that purpose. In March back in New York with Johnson D. Hill to negotiate with Lockhart. M. M. Doan was active as broker but deal was abandoned.* ~ WAITE PHILLIPS DIARY, 1925

Waite was not about to let the deal die, however. Rumors of the contemplated sale of the Waite Phillips Company bounced around financial circles and boardrooms. Many industry insiders put their money on Standard Oil Company of Indiana as the best bet to buy out Waite.

Throughout the summer of 1925 the newspapers, inundated with oil-patch gossip, kept Waite and his firm in the limelight. Most of the newspapers and trade magazines speculated about just what Waite would do after he left the oil industry. Some of the stories had the ring of a business obituary as reporters summed up Waite's colorful career so far. On June 13, the *Bartlesville Enterprise* reported on Waite's dealings.

> Waite Phillips went to Okmulgee in the pioneer days of Okmulgee County about eleven years ago and opened up a

pool with nothing to go on but a shoestring. He rapidly developed to be the most remarkable individual operator in the Mid Continent field and was unusually successful in bringing in producers and developing new fields in outside or wildcat territory. His long string of successes led to a reputation of having been born under a lucky star and being a favored child of fortune. Those who know him best and have been closest to him attribute his success to his ability and daring without discounting the great part chance plays in so venturesome a business as the oil industry. He is a producer, a refiner and a distributor and has been successful in all these lines of the industry.

Mr. Phillips is in the early forties. A man who has made a host of friends since he became one of the wealthiest men in Oklahoma and who has the warm friendship and esteem and good will of those who knew him when he was merely a pumper on a lease.

Should he sell to the Mid-Kansas, or to any other company, any or all of his holdings it is contended that Waite Phillips is always to be logically counted as an important factor in the oil game in this territory and sure to play a prominent part if he does sell out and reengage.

This much is clear. He hasn't sold and, despite the rumors, may have no intention of selling. He has always been a speculator, though not erratic figure and many groundless rumors of sales of his properties have been made in recent years. He is popular with his employees and with the oil fraternity and great personal interest is attached to his rumored activities.

On July 25, 1925, all the rumors and gossip about the possibility of Waite's selling out came to an end. The deal was done.

On that date, Waite sold the Waite Phillips Company and all its properties to a syndicate headed by New York investment bankers Blair & Company, Inc., which included the Barnsdall Corporation and Chase Securities Corporation. The sale was made for the astounding price of $25 million, at the time one of the largest oil transactions ever made. Waite had found his pot of gold at the end of the rainbow — and the pot was overflowing.

> *In July went to New York and on July 25th completed the sale of the Waite Phillips Co. for $25-million. R. O. McClintock was in New York trying to sell to Dominic & Dunn, and Ed Moore to Durant interest. After the sale was made Lockhart of Blair & Co. paid Doan a commission and W. P. was under the impression that 1/2 went to R. O. McClintock. At the time of the sale Rainbow Bend oil pool near Winfield, Kansas, and Licke Wilson leases, Archer County, Texas, were producing prolifically. Blair & Co. wanted W. P. to take presidency of Barnsdall Oil Co., but it was declined. Bob Law, president of Barnsdall, conferred with W. P. about it in New York.*

> *Returned to Tulsa and told L. E. and Frank of deal.*
> ~ WAITE PHILLIPS DIARY, 1925

That summer, Frank and L. E. were enjoying themselves at Waite's ranch near Cimarron, New Mexico. Many years later, Waite wrote about their reaction to the sale of his company, and provided more insight into his relationship with Frank.

"This was indeed an unusual situation," Waite wrote. "Particularly when I state that no young man was ever furnished a better opportunity to learn business principles than I was under the guidance of my two older brothers and no one I can think of, at the moment, so eagerly embraced that opportunity as I did. Yet from 1914 to 1925 we were more or less competitors in the same type of business and in the same territory. . . . I have every reason to believe that both of my older brothers were proud of my success and yet, being human, I feel sure that at the same time the elder of the two resented it.

"In that summer of 1925 while I was in New York trading with the bankers, these brothers were vacationing . . . and when I returned to Tulsa and they from their vacation it was with considerable surprise that they learned of the deal I had made. Before leaving New York, Henry Lockhart, of Blair & Company, had told me to contact Frank because he wanted the Phillips Petroleum Company to join in the big merger of the oil companies he had arranged to consolidate. When I talked to him [Frank] in Bartlesville about it he was in another periodical mood to sell but after negotiating with Lockhart in New York something happened to cause him to change his mind."

Once all the paperwork was completed, in early 1926, and the Blair & Company bankers merged Waite's properties with those of Barnsdall Oil Company, a new batch of rumors surfaced. Most of them were about Waite's plans and the future of his employees and top executives. There was no need to worry about anyone who worked for Waite, however. Many were rewarded substantially for their services when their stock was sold. Others, who had the resources, marked time while Waite chose his next move. Every person who had been part of Waite's team was well cared for; none was left high and dry.

Almost sixty years after the Waite Phillips Company merged with Barnsdall, Dale R. Snow, Waite's chief geologist from 1919 to 1926, recalled his impressions of his former boss. Snow admitted that Waite was a hard man to work for, but he was always fair and did not ask anyone to do anything that he was not willing to do himself. A story in the *Tulsa Tribune* on January 29, 1984, quoted Snow.

I saw a parade of vice presidents while I was there. Phillips was an autocrat and was concerned with every aspect of the business. Nobody crossed him or disagreed with him and stayed on. But he had the true oil man's gambling spirit. He believed in buying leases every place he even thought there might be oil.

We worked six days a week and had a conference on Sunday morning to talk over what leases to buy. He was very exacting but generous. Four years before Phillips sold out to Blair & Company for $25 million, he signed over $1.5 million worth of stock to about ten key employees.

Snow said the contract specified that Waite would receive a predetermined price, but when the stock was sold it turned out that the employees got the dividends and all the profit. "It multiplied in value about five times before it was sold in 1926," Snow recalled.

The financial writers and petroleum journalists tried to guess just why Waite had sold out and what he would do next. When asked, Waite told the public and all inquiring reporters that he simply wished to free himself from the duties of managing a big company. He did not volunteer anything about his immediate plans.

The *Oil Industry*, in its continued coverage of Waite Phillips, reported on October 23, 1925, that its best sources believed he would not stay away from the oil business forever. "Naturally a big question," posed the trade publication, "in the wake of the transaction is what will Waite Phillips do next? He has not said.

"His friends expect him to get back into the oil game. But they think he will get back as an individual. His love for the oil game stops when he can not know what his wells are doing."

One of the most cogent summations of Waite's colorful career appeared that September in an *Oil and Gas Journal* feature story written by J. L. Dwyer.

The passing of Waite Phillips, even temporarily, ends a chapter of one of the most interesting careers the oil business has ever witnessed. Contrary to a popular fallacy, he brought money with him when he came to Oklahoma to enter the oil business 18 years ago. He has seen periods of adversity, but Waite Phillips was never "broke" as many are prone to allege. His career is not of the sensational "Horatio Alger" variety, but marks the slow, painful, methodical success of a life spent in various phases of the petroleum industry. For him, indeed, like many others there was no short cut to success and time and again failure greeted his efforts. In meeting these failures he proved his genius, and he attacked trouble tirelessly, fearlessly, intelligently, and critically, and this is science of the highest order.

In the opinion of one who has watched him for seven years, Waite Phillips is a perfect example of how the man with money should act and there is no one who has come into such money as he who has changed less. He is the same Waite Phillips today as he was in 1919. Tulsa and the oil industry will surely miss him, but let us hope he will not long remain away.

CHAPTER TWENTY-THREE

PHILMONT

Despite a phalanx of the finest lieutenants of commerce he could recruit and money could buy, Waite stood alone at the corporate helm. The demands were great for anyone, and they required total attention. There was no margin for error, and often only a little time in which to respond to a situation, let alone think it through. Slugging it out in boardrooms thick with tension and cigar smoke, Waite was as busy as a one-armed roustabout trying to tame a runaway gusher by himself.

In the heat of the most furious negotiation or after still another complex agreement was forged, he surely must have wondered how things might have turned out if his beloved twin had been there to help him.

Ultimately, there was no bringing Wiate back from the dead, so it was all pure conjecture. To Waite, most hypothetical questions were a waste of time, and wasting time was not his favorite activity. By the time he was an old man in the early 1960s, living out the last days of his life and reflecting on his many achievements, Waite told his son, Elliott, that he probably would not have accomplished all that he had if his twin brother had lived.

His reasoning made sense. Wiate was the natural leader and more of a gambler than Waite. No doubt the lost twin would have maintained that dominant role and taken on most of the risks for the two of them. Wiate's passing at only nineteen years of age left a great void that never was filled in Waite's life. On the other hand, his brother's death also allowed Waite to become a person in his own right and to emerge as an adroit entrepreneur, willing to play for high stakes and wager the whole pot.

"My father never minded taking a risk when I knew him," said Elliott Phillips thirty years after Waite's death. "He didn't really gamble much at cards or such, except for a bit of poker now and then, but still he was always very much a risk taker. He took risks in everything he did."

Back in the lively 1920s, when Elliott was just a boy watching his father wheel and deal through precarious business transactions of staggering proportions, Waite's titanic stockpile of assets made the most seasoned speculators and daredevil gamblers as envious as orphans on Christmas Day. Waite, with millions of dollars in cash from oil and stock earnings and royalties tucked away, could afford to lose — at least a little bit. The thing was, he hardly ever did lose — not in the oil patch or in anything else he tried.

And as the first quarter of the century ended, Waite was trying all sorts of things. For him, there obviously was life beyond the oil fields. He simply would not allow himself to become wed solely to any one aspect of his busy life.

Waite remained a first-class oilman — a true wildcatter deluxe — but he also excelled at so much more, including the management of banks and herds of beef cattle. He also was especially capable in the multifaceted business of real estate. Waite liked it all. His ability to sniff out, purchase, and fully develop choice properties — whether for commercial buildings, ranches, residences, or just as investments — was uncanny.

In 1925, with his Waite Phillips Company sold off for the staggering sum of $25 million in cold cash, Waite moved into a span of years devoted principally to the stewardship of monumental tracts of land and the erection of stunning architecture. To make it all the more exciting, this surge in property acquisitions and construction occurred during the remaining years of the

Roaring Twenties and throughout the 1930s — a catastrophic decade marred by the nation's collective nightmare called the Great Depression.

It was a bittersweet period for the nation and for Waite. As was expressed so well in the book of Ecclesiastes, those years became, for him, "a time to build up." Despite the many difficulties, that was exactly what Waite did. And as was his style, he did it with restrained passion, determination, and to the utmost of his ability. He also did it with flair.

That was evident just before Waite sold his company. In a carefully worded message from his Tulsa office, he gave his more than one thousand employees a glimpse of the personal philosophy that would guide him through the coming years. Waite said in part:

> Let us not be confused by false prophets; the really worthwhile things of life are the ones we should seek, including the thrill and satisfaction of doing our best. . . . There is greater honor in being the best ditch digger in a gang than being a mediocre president of a company, because the man has done something outstanding by means of his own effort, while the latter is content to let the dignity of his position bear him along. Every job is important and should be done in a thorough manner if we wish to accomplish that perfection that sets us apart as experts in any line.
>
> The price of success is work with a purpose and a vision beyond the task at hand; however, work, which is foremost among beneficial habits, is often an unappreciated blessing. Our ultimate success is determined in a large degree by our attitude toward our tasks, for we should grow as we overcome the difficulties which are presented to us day by day. The really successful man is the one who has worked to develop the talents with which he has been

equipped, making them contribute to the upbuilding of his character and the service of mankind.

Rumors about Waite's plans continued to creep into the press. At the time the deal was cut with Blair & Company, a story in the *Tulsa World* suggested that Waite had sold out "due to his antipathy of having a business that was so big he could not direct and manage its every ramification. In this respect the task preyed upon Mr. Phillips somewhat, his friends say, and many of his ablest advisers have left his service because they were too zealous in trying to take off the shoulders of their chief, some of the burden. Mr. Phillips is known as a man who brooks no interference with his policy of running his oil company.

"Whatever Waite Phillips does he tries to do on a bigger scale than any other. His oil company has had a reputation of building not just well, but too well. More money has been spent at the Okmulgee and the Wichita refineries than most other major companies would have spent. The Waite Phillips filling stations are things of beauty, wherever located."

The *Oil and Gas Journal* noted that Waite was "on his ranch in New Mexico, and has announced no plans for the future. It is believed that he will take a long rest and reenter the oil business, as in the opinion of his intimates he has been engaged in the oil business too long to attempt any other form of business."

That report was partially correct. Waite would, indeed, get back into the oil game, as it often was called. However, the *Oil and Gas Journal* was absolutely wrong about Waite's not trying any other business pursuits.

By late in the year, Waite knew exactly what he wanted to delve into next. But before he could begin to execute his new plans, family obligations once again beckoned. This time, the problem was not with one of his brothers or some other member of the Phillips family, but with his wife's father, J. B. Elliott.

In December to Des Moines, Iowa, to meet Mr. & Mrs. J. B.
Elliott regarding financial difficulties of Knoxville National
Bank. ~ WAITE PHILLIPS DIARY, 1925

Waite's perplexed in-laws greeted him in Knoxville, and quickly apprised him of the seriousness of their predicament. Whether from poor management practices, a surplus of Iowa crops, or a lending policy based too much on personal relationships, the First National Bank of Knoxville was in deep trouble. In fact, Elliott was just about ready to close the bank.

Waite listened to the explanations and then closely examined the troubled bank's books. Straightaway, the problem was apparent to Waite. He understood that by the mid-1920s, Iowa farmers, who had branched out too much during the war years, had found a glutted market for their crops. Those farmers, many of them First National customers, were unable to pay their mortgage principal, interest, or even their taxes.

A powerless J. B. Elliott watched helplessly as mortgages which had once been so sound turned into frozen credits. His eldest daughter, Helen Granger, even had sunk some of her own funds into the bank, but it did not stop the panic.

Word about the problems at First National spread faster than poison ivy. A run had just begun on the bank when Waite stepped in and saved the day.

Furnished funds to re-finance the bank for Mr. Elliott and reim-
bursed Mrs. Granger for her personal losses in attempting to make
up the bank's deficit. Placed Frank Butcher of Denver in active
charge of the bank. ~ WAITE PHILLIPS DIARY, 1925

The "funds" Waite furnished to his father-in-law's bank amounted to more than $800,000. When they learned of the huge infusion of cash at the bank, timid depositors began to put their money back into their accounts faster than they had drawn it out. Thanks entirely to Waite, the First National Bank of

Knoxville was saved. Flush with money from the recent sale of his company, Waite could afford to be generous, especially since the party in need was his Veva's father.

Waite took no credit for what he had done. He said none was deserved. When reporters or associates asked him about saving the Iowa bank, he replied that he really could not accept praise for just doing the decent thing. As he would explain later: "There would be nothing remarkable if a man with $25 put up a dollar of it to help a relative. It's all a question of proportion."

As was the case throughout his life and career, Waite was more concerned about putting his fortune to good use than hoarding it. It truly was a matter of proportion when it came to money and land.

By that time, Waite's landholdings were tremendous — more than 700,000 acres. Most of that acreage was in the West in several active ranches he owned, including two more big spreads he had bought before he sold his oil company. Named the H-V and H H, those cattle operations were south of the Navajo trading center of Gallup in far western New Mexico. Purchased strictly for raising cattle and never intended for his personal use, the H-V and H H ranches alone totaled well over 300,000 acres, much of that U.S. forest land, spread over New Mexico and into Arizona. Besides those investment properties, Waite continued to run registered Hereford cattle on the Highland Ranch outside Denver.

But by far, Waite's favorite place to go was his Hawkeye Ranch in northern New Mexico. Waite's greatest pleasure was taking a saddle horse to a remote fishing cabin in the high country, or galloping across one of the lush mountain meadows. He treasured the place so much that in 1925, he acquired an additional thirty thousand acres of the ranch for one-quarter of a million dollars to go with the forty-two thousand acres he had purchased in 1922. Still not content, he schemed to add even more land to the ranch holdings.

Waite also renamed the Hawkeye in 1925. He wanted something more personal, so he used part of his surname, *Phil,* and combined it with *monte,* a common New Mexican Spanish word for mountain. *Philmont* was the name that resulted. This enormous ranch, with its abundant grazing fields, droves of stock and wildlife, and a history as rich and spicy as enchilada sauce, became known far and wide as the Philmont Ranch.

Ironically, for those who did not know Waite, the first part of the ranch name could have been interpreted to stand for the Greek word *philo,* meaning "having a predilection for" or "loving." That was fitting, because Waite did love this ranch about as much as anything he ever owned. For Waite Phillips, the Philmont, nestled in the foothills of the Sangre de Cristo range, was heaven come to earth.

CHAPTER TWENTY-FOUR

A TIME TO BUILD

·WP·

In 1926, as work was about to gear up on the newly christened U.S. Route 66, Waite Phillips launched his own formidable construction spree. It soon turned into a building marathon that kept architects, designers, carpenters, masons, craftsmen, and laborers on a whirlwind pace for years to come.

Financing for such ambitious undertakings was not a major concern because Waite Phillips' personal net worth, at the ripe old age of forty-three, was estimated to be at least $40 million — in 1926 dollars.

The cornerstones of Waite's many construction projects were two palatial estates that were created simultaneously. After more than two years of planning and preparation, both of them were ready for occupancy in 1927. One of the opulent homes was erected on the Philmont Ranch in New Mexico. Called Villa Philmonte, with the addition of the letter *e* to set it apart from the name of the ranch, this residence was the family's holiday and vacation oasis and a summer home from the beginning of June to the beginning of October. The other mansion was built in Tulsa, and was intended to accommodate the Phillipses as their primary abode during the rest of the year.

Waite purchased the property, located about two miles from the downtown Tulsa business district and one mile south of the family's home on South Owasso Avenue on what had been Creek

Indian land, in 1920. For about thirty-two thousand dollars, he first bought an eleven-acre parcel, then acquired an additional tract of twelve acres. Waite amassed more than seventy acres, but later sold about fifty for a residential development.

Formerly known as the Shuler and Cline farms, the remaining twenty-three acres of hilly land on the far south side of town were transected by a stream with gentle twists and bends called Crow Creek. Sycamores and flowering trees lined the banks of the narrow stream. Beavers were seen on the brook, and a wide variety of native birds and animals, such as red foxes and raccoons, made their homes in nearby thickets. Along with the property came a white frame farmhouse, barns, and other outbuildings. There were small fields and a fruit orchard, where white-tailed deer were known to steal twilight nibbles if a gate was forgotten. Much of the property was studded with oaks, hickories, redbuds, black haws, and cedars.

Even before the farmhouse and other buildings were razed and the earth was broken for his new home, Waite knew what he would call the Tulsa estate. In keeping with his penchant for naming his properties with part of his surname, Waite chose *Philbrook* — combining his name and the word *brook,* after the picturesque creek that gurgled through the acreage.

In January started building new residence in Tulsa, to be called Philbrook. ~ WAITE PHILLIPS DIARY, 1926

To create his pair of elegant estates, by late 1925 Waite had assembled an impressive design and construction team. At night in his small log cabin behind the family residence on South Owasso or in his downtown Tulsa office in the Atlas Building, Waite pored over an assortment of recommendations for architects. He carefully scrutinized every one of them and weighed the advice and suggestions of friends and associates.

The one person who gave Waite the best counsel concerning

the hiring of a lead architect was his friend Jesse Claude Nichols, known best as J. C. Nichols. A leading Kansas City builder and developer, Nichols was also a prominent Democrat and a civic leader during those colorful years when Kansas City was controlled by the political machine of Tom Pendergast.

J. C. Nichols was known far and wide as the person responsible for the creation of the internationally known Country Club district, Kansas City's first planned residential section. Located south of Forty-seventh Street and west of Rockhill Road, the area contained the city's finest homes. Nichols launched the development in 1908, transforming abandoned rock quarries, trash dumps, and shanties into a sprawling neighborhood of noteworthy homes with broad lawns and landscaped gardens.

Waite admired the residential neighborhoods his friend had created, but he was more interested in Nichols' Country Club Plaza, the business section of the district and the nation's first suburban shopping center catering to the motoring public. Located on fifty-five acres at Forty-seventh Street and Mill Creek Parkway, the upscale plaza, an eclectic blend of Spanish architecture, was built on the site of an old hog farm.

Country Club Plaza opened for business in the early 1920s, featuring outdoor statues and fountains as well as Moorish-style retail buildings, specialty shops, and restaurants, all constructed with cream-colored bricks and stucco, red tile roofs, ornate ironwork, and mosaic towers. Nichols, inspired by the architecture of Spain in his world travels, conceived the theme of the district's buildings and acquired the services of the one architect he believed could best execute his ambitious dreams. That architect was Edward Buehler "Ned" Delk.

Born September 21, 1885, in Schoharie, New York, Delk had received a thorough education in architecture and art. He graduated from Mercersberg Academy in Pennsylvania in 1903, and earned a bachelor's degree in architecture from the University of Pennsylvania in 1907. Delk went on to take additional art and life-drawing courses at the Pennsylvania Academy of Fine Arts, and became part of an atelier administered by the Beaux-Arts Society of New York in 1909. The following year, the society awarded Delk a prestigious prize which enabled him to go on an eight-month tour through Italy and Greece under the direction of sculptor Lorado Taft.

After Delk completed his schooling and travel abroad, he started his career in Philadelphia as a draftsman. By 1913, he had paid all his dues and was busily working as an architect. But in 1917, his hectic work schedule was interrupted by the United States' entry into World War I. Delk left his design board and answered the call to military service by serving with honor as a lieutenant in the Army Air Corps in Europe. After the armistice, Delk remained in Europe until 1919 to pursue graduate studies in town planning at the University of London.

By 1920, John Taylor of the J. C. Nichols Company, at the request of his boss, enticed Ned Delk to visit Kansas City. Once there, Nichols quickly convinced Delk to serve as the consulting architect on the design team for the master plan of Country Club Plaza. Others on the team included George E. Kessler and the associates of Hare & Hare Company, landscape architects and city planners based in Kansas City.

To prepare for the task ahead of him, Delk traveled to Spain, Mexico, and South America, where he closely observed buildings appropriate to the design envisioned by Nichols. In 1922, Delk's brilliant master plan for the plaza was completed.

Ecstatic with the architect's innovative designs, Nichols encouraged Delk to open a practice in Kansas City. Delk agreed, and was provided with ample space in an office at Ward Parkway and Meyer Boulevard. Nichols also guaranteed the ambitious architect plenty of future projects, such as designing two of the early plaza structures — the Mill Creek Building, completed in 1923, and the Tower Building, in 1924.

J. C. Nichols was only too pleased to recommend that Delk

serve as architect for the pair of villas Waite Phillips wished to build in Oklahoma and New Mexico. Many years later, a major feature story about Waite in the October 22, 1939, edition of the *Kansas City Star* referred to J. C. Nichols talking to his friend Waite Phillips about building his palatial homes at Tulsa and Cimarron.

"I know an architect that I induced to come to Kansas City from Pennsylvania several years ago," Nichols was quoted as telling Waite. "Get in touch with Ned Delk and get Sid Hare and his son, Herbert, to do your landscaping. You can't go wrong."

Waite did not go wrong. He took Nichols' advice. Before the close of 1925, Delk was commissioned to design Villa Philmonte and guest houses at Waite's New Mexican ranch. Later, a contract was negotiated for Villa Philbrook. Besides those two stunning projects, Waite also awarded Ned Delk another major design contract, in association with the firm of Keene and Simpson, for a proposed downtown Tulsa office headquarters. Work on this structure, to be called the Philtower Building, began in 1927 as construction was winding down on the two villas.

Besides Waite, another solid Oklahoma contact for Delk turned out to be John Kane, a Bartlesville banker and an associate of Frank Phillips. Kane and J. C. Nichols had been roommates at the University of Kansas and had married sisters. Delk's first completed architectural venture in Oklahoma was the Hillcrest County Club clubhouse in Bartlesville, a Spanish mission-style design completed in 1926, just as he was getting under way with Waite Phillips' projects.

During the early 1930s, after the completion of Waite's villas and office building, Delk designed several significant Bartlesville residences. First came the 1930 addition to Frank Phillips' town house on Cherokee Avenue. Among other Delk designs in Bartlesville were the John Kane family's Georgian-style home in 1931, and in 1932, oil tycoon H. V. Foster's magnificent residence, known as La Quinta.

But in 1926, the main buzz in social circles in nouveau riche Oklahoma was the Waite Phillips residence under construction in Tulsa.

Philbrook certainly was not the first or the last oil baron's palace to be built in Oklahoma, where oceans of crude oil created many showy estates. Ponca City, for example, had the Marland Mansion, home of the fabulously wealthy oil tycoon Ernest Whitworth Marland, another man with the Midas touch who by the mid-1920s was one of the nation's half dozen great oil producers. Marland, who said he wished to "live in a castle," hired master architect John Duncan Forsyth to build the thirty thousand-square-foot mansion spread over three floors, at a cost of $5.5 million. During three years, from 1925 to 1928, local citizens watched the construction of the showplace estate, which included a leather-lined elevator, a dozen bathrooms, three kitchens, a handball court, game sanctuary, nine-hole golf course, polo field, gigantic swimming pool, and boathouse to accommodate a chain of five lakes.

Tulsa alone was the site of many other awesome residences. A few of them included the fancy domicile of Bill Skelly; the Tudor Gothic McBirney mansion overlooking the Arkansas River; the mansion built in 1921 by real estate entrepreneur and oil company president James Max Gillette; and, by 1929, the breathtaking Westhope, an architectural masterpiece designed by Frank Lloyd Wright for his cousin Richard Lloyd Jones, publisher of the *Tulsa Tribune* and one of Waite's good friends.

Still, despite the abundance of grandiose homes and colossal mansions, few Tulsans or architectural critics could deny that one of the most unusual and memorable residences was Villa Philbrook.

Besides signing contracts with Delk as architect for Villa Philbrook and Villa Philmonte, Waite followed Nichols' advice and procured the services of Hare & Hare as landscape architects for the two estates.

This firm, based in the Huntzinger Building in Kansas City, was headed by Sid J. Hare and his son S. Herbert Hare, fellows with the American Society of Landscape Architects. After high school graduation in 1906, the younger Hare started work as a draftsman for his father's firm. He studied landscape architecture and city planning at Harvard University from 1908 to 1910, and then returned to Kansas City to become a partner with his father. Hare & Hare was active in projects and park designs for several cities, including Kansas City, Oklahoma City, Houston, and Dallas.

At Waite's Tulsa estate, the Hare & Hare associates were engaged to design and develop complementary formal gardens as well as several other outdoor projects. Their first task, however, was to collaborate with Delk in siting the gardens and the proposed villa structure. All vestiges of the farm buildings, including coops and pens, and the orchard were torn down and removed. Careful consideration was given in locating Villa Philbrook on the high ground, or bluff, overlooking picturesque Crow Creek. Eventually, to create more gardens and a knoll for a small outdoor temple, the architects and builders moved the Crow Creek channel two hundred yards to the east, built up the banks, and lined the creek bed with blocks of cut sandstone.

The construction team for both of the villas consisted of the John Long Company of Kansas City as general contractor, Henry Lohman of Tulsa as building contractor, and Phillip Thomas of Thomas Landscape & Nursery Company of Tulsa as landscape contractor. The furnishings for the residences were handled primarily by Percy W. French, a New York interior designer.

Much has been written about Ned Delk's accompanying Waite and Genevieve Phillips on a Mediterranean cruise during the summer of 1925 to gather architectural ideas for Villa Philmonte and Villa Philbrook. Mention of such a journey was included in many published stories and even in some of the official publications associated with Villas Philmonte and Philbrook.

Despite those references to a 1925 European cruise, it appears that no such trip took place — at least in the summer of that particular year. According to his own records and diary, Waite spent part of June 1925 in California and Tulsa, and the month of July preparing for the sale of his Waite Phillips Company or carrying out the transaction in New York. By August, he was relaxing at Philmont Ranch.

However, the following year — in the summer of 1926 — the Phillipses embarked on their second European voyage. Young Elliott did not go with his parents on the 1926 cruise, but stayed at the ranch in New Mexico along with some friends and the housekeeper. A small party of family and friends, including Otis and Gladys McClintock, made the trip with the Phillipses, but Waite makes no mention in his diary of Ned Delk being part of the entourage.

June 12th sailed on S.S. Homeric with G. E. P., Mrs. McClintock, Helen Jane, and Ruth Pringle for a tour of France, Spain, Italy, Switzerland, Austria, Germany, England and other European countries. Landed Cherbourg. Had dinner at Ciro's in Paris with Robert Stewart, Harry Blackmer, and Fred Wickett.

On July 12th W. P. returned from Europe. Visited Philmont Ranch. Mrs. Ruth Maher visited ranch with her boys. July 16th Mr. McClintock left for Europe to join the touring party. On August 16th G. E. P. and party sailed from Cherbourg on S.S. Leviathan for New York. W. P. visited Sinclairs, East Hampton, L. I. and met G. E. P. and McClintocks in New York.

~ Waite Phillips Diary, 1926

If Delk did go to Europe with the Phillips party, he may have stayed for one month and returned to the United States with Waite. In the many letters Genevieve sent from various European cities to Waite at his office in the Atlas Building on Boston Avenue in Tulsa, there were no references to Delk. Genevieve wrote of goods purchased in Spain and other lands, and of future conferences with Percy French, the interior designer, when she returned to New York. Most of her letters were filled with personal thoughts about her husband.

"I wish you were here to see Venice tonight," Genevieve wrote Waite from the Grand Hotel on July 15, 1926. "Our rooms face the canal and we are going out for a ride in a gondola. The water with the gondolas and the lights on the water with the stars and moon above make it a beautiful sight. We have decided to leave in the morning for Lake Como as we have bought our Venetian glassware and I feel we want to spend more time in Switzerland. I am enclosing bill for glass, which is paid in full, and some lace. . . . This is a most romantic spot and I wish you were here."

Waite would have enjoyed staying on with Genevieve and the others in Europe, but he came back to Tulsa so Otis McClintock could take a much-deserved vacation. Waite wanted his friend to be rested and fresh. Besides, only one of them could be gone from Tulsa for very long, because only a few days before the European trip started, Waite and McClintock had entered into a business agreement together. Someone needed to watch over the infant firm they had created.

Waite, anxious as always to keep things stirred up and in motion, had organized yet another oil company. Industry observers and speculative reporters who had bemoaned his disappearance from the oil patch apparently did not know the restless Waite as well as they thought.

Earlier that year, before he started the new company, Waite had examined other opportunities before him. He even seriously flirted with entering the political arena. Along with his family, Waite spent almost five months — from February 4 to June 1, 1926 — in Washington, D.C. The Phillipses resided at Wardman Park Hotel.

While quietly making high-level rounds and establishing new contacts in the nation's capital, Waite became acquainted with

Andrew W. Mellon, a foremost industrialist, financier, and public official. One of the wealthiest men in the nation, Mellon had become a symbol of the prosperity and "business-minded" government of that era. He did not look the part. The frail and shy figure who shook hands only with his fingertips was described by a reporter as looking like "a double-entry bookkeeper who is afraid of losing his job." Another reporter wrote that Mellon reminded him of "a dried up dollar bill that any wind might whisk away."

Regardless of his looks and demeanor, Mellon wielded enormous power as he faithfully served for a dozen years as secretary of treasury under Presidents Harding, Coolidge, and Hoover. In 1926, Congress passed a bill advocated by Mellon that reduced taxes on incomes of $1 million or more from 66 to 20 percent. By the time Waite went to Washington, Secretary Mellon and the rest of the Coolidge administration were very familiar with the incredible success story of the Iowa farm boy turned oil tycoon who had risen from modest means to great wealth in a relatively brief period of time.

Was offered Under-Secretary of Treasury job by A. W. Mellon. Had conference with him by appointment made by Col. J. W. McIntosh, Comptroller of Currency. This position was afterwards offered to and accepted by Ogden Mills and he later succeeded to Secretaryship. ~ WAITE PHILLIPS DIARY, 1926

When another candidate got the nod for the cabinet job, Waite did not fall to pieces. Ogden Mills certainly had the inside track. A Harvard graduate and career politician, Mills had served in both the New York legislature and U.S. House of Representatives before losing a bid for governor of New York to Alfred E. Smith in 1926. And just as Waite noted in his diary, Mills did become secretary of the treasury under Hoover in 1932, when Mellon resigned to become ambassador to Great Britain.

Like the good Republican soldier he was, Waite did not question the decision, but marched on. With no other reason to linger in Washington, as soon as he learned that Mills was to be awarded the cabinet post, Waite went straight home to Oklahoma to check other options. There were many more opportunities ahead.

Back in Tulsa, as he planned his second European trip, Waite and Otis McClintock announced the formation of their company. He had convinced McClintock to resign his position as vice president of Gypsy Oil Company and join in the new venture. McClintock was given a "carried" interest in the firm. Waite persuaded a few of his old associates from the Waite Phillips Company and other executives from Gypsy Oil to come aboard. They named the new operation the Philmack Company. Its primary purpose was to purchase royalties and a few proved oil properties for future investments.

In June returned to Tulsa and made deal with R. Otis McClintock and organized the Philmack Co. Stockholders — W. P., R. Otis McClintock, Gillette Hill - WAITE PHILLIPS DIARY, 1926

Although Waite and McClintock generally received wise counsel, some business recommendations were off the mark.

For instance, in 1926 they had an opportunity to purchase a working cattle spread called the McElroy Ranch, in Texas, consisting of twenty-four hundred head of cattle on 20,800 acres. The asking price was $600,000. The word was that there might be more to the ranch than good grazing land. Some folks said they smelled oil. But based on the advice of a close associate, McClintock turned down the offer. In time, the property became worth more than $25 million, and by 1957, it had produced sixty-four million barrels of oil from more than seven hundred wells.

Waite could afford to let a few big ones slip away, however. He also wanted to rid himself of some of the obligations he had been keeping up, and to trim his business inventory.

Late in the summer of 1926, Waite was back at his beloved Philmont Ranch, where he spent most of the rest of the year except for a quick trip to Iowa to dispose of his father-in-law's bank. Waite also sold his Colorado property — the Highland Ranch. It had some appealing aspects, but mostly the Phillipses found the residence not to their liking. Besides, a brand-new residence was under way at their ranch near Cimarron in the mountains of northern New Mexico.

Aug.-Sept. on Philmont Ranch. Started building new ranch residence, Villa Philmonte. Delk architect and Long Construction Co. the builders.

In October to Knoxville, Iowa, then to Denver and from there to Cimarron, New Mexico. Sold Knoxville National Bank to local Knoxville interests. Also sold Highland Ranch to Frank Kistler.

In November on Philmont Ranch with family. Bob and Helen King visited and John Long and Delk attended Thanksgiving party. ~ WAITE PHILLIPS DIARY, 1926

The stunning New Mexican landscape — the remote lodges and camps, the lively ranch, and the mountain streams — provided the ideal place for Waite to recharge his batteries and collect his wits. His life always had been a whirlwind of activity, but the pace was about to accelerate even more.

Throughout the rest of the decade and well into the 1930s, Waite faced challenge after challenge. He met them all with a roustabout's tenacity and bronc buster's resiliency. He stood up to each crisis and obstacle.

Somehow, through all of it, Waite maintained his distinctive spirit of restlessness, never settling for what the present offered as long as the future — no matter how uncertain — beckoned.

CHAPTER TWENTY-FIVE

VILLA PHILBROOK

In 1927, the decade was still roaring away as strong as a slug of bootleg booze. There were few hints that just ahead waited the cold, hard truth of the Wall Street crash and economic distress and decline for most of the nation.

That carefree time just prior to the Great Depression seemed to last forever. In 1927, there were hip flasks and talking motion pictures, and a bar of soap cost only eight cents. Ford Model A's with rumble seats rolled off the assembly lines in record numbers. That was a year that proved to be as raucous as a Tom Mix matinée, as distinctive as Al Jolson's voice in *The Jazz Singer,* as colorful as a Flo Zeigfeld show. That was the year that witnessed Charles Lindbergh's solo flight across the Atlantic, the deathwatch for Sacco and Vanzetti, Babe Ruth swatting a record sixty homers, the Teapot Dome lease invalidated by the Supreme Court, and Dempsey down for the "long count" before 104,943 fight fans as he lost to Tunney in Chicago.

In 1927, Waite Phillips — wheeling and dealing like a heavyweight champ of the boardroom — flexed his financial muscles without ruffling his impeccable tweed suits and expensive neckties. It was a time for Waite to shell out big bucks for the villas in Tulsa and New Mexico, as he oversaw major business deals, wined and dined with presidents and power brokers, and erected a corporate palace in the heart of downtown Tulsa.

In January started to build Philtower Building in Tulsa.
Employed Frank Walker as building manager. ~ WAITE PHILLIPS
DIARY, 1927

The twenty-three-story Philtower Building, another monu-
ment to Waite's surname, was located on the northeast corner of
Fifth Street and Boston Avenue. The ornately Gothic office tower
was designed by the firm of Keene and Simpson in collaboration
with Waite's most trusted architect, Edward Buehler Delk.
Besides Delk, the John Long Company — another key player on
the Villas Philbrook and Philmonte team — acted as the
Philtower's builders.

But the Philtower Building was not ready for occupancy until
1928. In the meantime, there were many other activities to occupy Waite's time and keep his interest. He stayed in perpetual
motion. There were jaunts to California to watch polo games, visits with family and friends in Iowa and at Philmont Ranch, and
business trips to New York. His new homes in Tulsa and near
Cimarron, in planning and development since late 1925, were
also taking shape fast.

Moved into new Philbrook residence this spring. . . . Before build-
ing Philbrook residence had assembled about 70 acres. After
retaining about 23 acres for residence grounds the balance was
plotted as Rockbridge Park Addition and lots sold. Frank Walker,
building manager, also handled this work. ~ WAITE PHILLIPS
DIARY, 1927

Although in the spring of 1927 much work still needed to be
done at Villa Philbrook, the estate turned out to be a masterpiece.
This came about despite continual design changes ordered by
Waite. True to form, he and Genevieve changed their minds on
the spur of the moment to incorporate various style ideas and furnishings they had found during their European sojourns. Besides
the interior changes, they also "radically adjusted the landscape

plans to retain existing trees," according to a later guidebook to the villa and gardens.

Many years after Waite's death, Elliott Phillips recalled how his father became quite involved in the design and construction of all his homes and commercial buildings. Elliott explained that one of Waite's favorite epigrams was, "The man who never makes mistakes never makes much of anything." According to Elliott, his father was not afraid of making a mistake or ordering a change, no matter the cost involved. If Waite saw something that concerned him, whether it was in some aspect of business or a shrub he did not like, he "didn't mind making changes, even radical changes."

Certainly if Ned Delk had any doubts about who was running the show when it came to designing the Phillipses' villas, those concerns were soon laid to rest. "My father would not follow anybody verbatim," explained Elliott. "He might not have done his own dental work but he told the dentist how to do it." The same held true for architects. Delk lost several battles, but the work was accomplished, and to much acclaim.

Architectural inspiration for Villa Philbrook came from a wide range of sources, including places the Phillipses and Delk had visited during their European and world travels, such as the great Mediterranean ports of call, ancient Italian Renaissance cities, French nightclubs, and baroque villas. The result was not just another massive family home for an Oklahoma oil baron, but an Italian Renaissance revival "country" house.

Closely resembling a classic Florentine villa in both architecture and landscaping, the Phillipses' new residence was topped by an Italianate tile roof with a broad overhang. According to Herbert Hare, the surrounding gardens, exquisite in every way, were patterned after fifteenth- and sixteenth-century examples such as the Villa Lante in Bagnaia, a village north of Viterbo, Italy.

Inspired by other Italian palaces such as the Villa Guilia with similar facades and columns around the portico, the Villa Philbrook structure had exterior walls that glittered white because of ground white marble in the stucco. Kasota limestone from Minnesota, similar in color and texture to Italian travertine marble, surrounded the entrance and was used at wall junctions and throughout the villa for walls, doorways, floors, and windows.

There were marble fountains and fireplaces, and marble was used for some of the floors, as well as planks of teak, walnut, and oak for the general flooring. The fine-quality silken fabrics that Genevieve had purchased during the 1926 European jaunt were used for curtains, draperies, and wall coverings. Much of the furniture had been acquired by the Phillipses in Italy.

Villa Philbrook contained a multitude of rooms on three levels. On the main floor was the Great Hall, a huge central room with a fireplace and an organ for entertaining guests. There was a living room with a coffered stucco ceiling of large octagonal panels and wall-to-wall carpet over the teak floor.

Also on that level were a formal dining room and a breakfast room, where a pair of cupids cavorted in a fountain before large windows that caught the earliest light of day. Across the wide hallway was one of the family's favorite spots — the library and study. This cozy room, with a fine I. E. Couse painting over the fireplace, had red oak flooring and walnut paneling. A focal point was the globe light hanging from the ceiling, made of select gum timbers.

Down the long hall in the music room, the wall panorama, created by Philadelphia mural painter George Gibbs, depicted a flock of dancing maidens clad in flimsy tunics. They seemed to move according to the four musical tempi whose names were inscribed below the murals — andante, rondo, allegro, and scherzo. Originally the ladies in the mural appeared totally nude, but when Waite wondered what his mother would think of such a display when she visited, it was decided to have the artist paint frocks on the dancing figures.

Upstairs were the family's sleeping quarters as well as guest bedrooms and servants' quarters, including a room for Waite's valet. Both Waite and Genevieve had their own bedrooms, but they shared a spacious sleeping porch. Waite's room, which featured Spanish-style furniture and a fireplace copied after one in the home of the painter El Greco, was much plainer. It was only about half the size of his wife's blue-and-white bedroom, fashionably decorated in a French style with four goatskin rugs on the floor. Waite ordered a Magnolia grandiflora to be planted outside Genevieve's bedroom so she could enjoy its fragrant flowers.

Helen Jane, almost sixteen years old when the family moved in, and Elliott, a spunky nine-year-old, had their own bedrooms and sleeping porches, also on the upper floor. Young Elliott, who from the time he was a toddler shunned city life, would just as soon have been out on the ranch in a bunkhouse. His sister, however, adored her room. It was all done up in pink and tan, with French doors which opened to a balcony over the terrace where Helen Jane could whisper to her young beaux on summer evenings — if they managed to get over the wrought-iron fence or slip by the night watchman.

Although Genevieve's touch and appreciation of sophisticated European style were evident everywhere inside the villa, not all of the spacious rooms were decorated or furnished in that manner. On the lower level of the villa, with a covered automobile entrance, were the rooms Waite loved best.

This suite of southwestern-style rooms in the basement housed the family's large Native American collections and other trophies, such as mounted buffalo and elk heads. Furnished in bright western and Indian motifs, furniture, rugs, and art, the comfortable clubrooms allowed Waite to escape the tensions of his business life and pretend he was in the far West, much as he had done in his log cabin at the Owasso Avenue residence.

It was because of the lower rooms that Philbrook truly achieved a balance between Genevieve's love of ancient and modern European styles and Waite's love of the outdoors and the Southwest. Waite enjoyed the lower rooms so much that some years later, he commissioned famed Taos artist Oscar Berninghaus to paint a striking view of Villa Philmonte and the surrounding New Mexican countryside on the wall of the Santa Fe Room at Philbrook.

By the time Villa Philbrook was completed, the cost for the residence alone was $597,000. The gardens and extensive landscaping came to an additional $129,000. Those sums, added to the cost of the furnishings, came to a grand total of $1,191,000.

Writing for a national publication, best-selling novelist and playwright Edna Ferber, an early guest at Philbrook, characterized the new villa as a $2 million mansion fitted with gold-plated plumbing. Ferber's ridiculing descriptions of ostentatious oilmen made Waite physically ill for several days.

A few years after her visit to Philbrook, Ferber's novel about Oklahoma was published. In *Cimarron* appeared a colorful description of the residence of one of her fictional characters who happened to be an oilman. Although Ferber's depiction applied more to E. W. Marland's mansion at Ponca City, the book troubled Waite.

"As for the Wyatt house — it wasn't a house at all, but a combination of the palace of Versailles and the Grand Central Station in New York," wrote Ferber. "It occupied grounds about the size of the duchy of Luxembourg, and on the grounds, the once barren plain, had been set great trees brought from England.

"A mile of avenue, planted in elms led up to the mansion. . . . There were rare plants, farms, forests, lakes, tennis courts, golf links, polo fields, race tracks, airdromes, swimming pools. Whole paneled rooms had been brought from France. . . . Sixty gardeners manned the grounds. The house servants would have peopled a village."

But not everyone was critical of Villa Philbrook. When famed humorist and Oklahoma native son Will Rogers, a friend of the

Phillipses, first visited the new villa and stepped into the Great Hall, he glanced around and his well-known grin melted over his face. "Well, I've been to Buckingham Palace," drawled Rogers, "but it hasn't anything on Waite Phillips' house."

Will Rogers' assessment was also the consensus of the hundreds of guests invited to the extravagant dinner party commemorating the grand opening of Villa Philbrook. Anxious as always to get on with business, Waite pushed for the housewarming to take place even though there were many uncompleted projects at the villa. It was a glorious bash that Tulsa would not soon forget.

About that time, most of the nation stayed glued to the radio to catch the latest reports about floodwaters ravaging the Midwest. Others gossiped about Mae West, about to be found guilty of indecency when her Broadway production called *Sex* was deemed to be too lewd, even for the sheikhs and shebas of the Roaring Twenties. But in Tulsa, the main topic of conversation among the wealthier citizens and even the hoi polloi was Waite and Genevieve Phillips' new residence under development at 2727 South Rockford Road.

That evening, more than five hundred guests, all of them bearing their coveted invitations, arrived at Villa Philbrook dressed to the nines. They were there for a party that was said to be unmatched in elegance, thanks to Genevieve, who oversaw every detail.

The Phillipses were anxious to unveil their new home even though much work still needed to be done at the villa, including interior details, much of the landscaping, and the erection of iron fencing and walls. Later, with the addition of the main gates, Waite's distinctive monograms were incorporated discreetly into the ironwork, just as they were in the masonry walls of the villa.

The uniformed deliverymen from Mrs. De Haven's Flower Shop, the downtown Tulsa florist that had been operated by a widow since 1905, had no gates to deal with as they began to arrive at the villa shortly after dawn the day of the party.

Throughout the day, big service trucks, bursting with loads of fresh chrysanthemums and roses, rumbled up the driveway.

Outside the villa, a small army of groundsmen made sure the fledgling gardens, courtyards, and wide lawns were impeccable. The crews policed the shaded terraces and breezy loggias. They made sure not a single leaf or speck of debris floated in the water stair and garden basins, stone fountains, reflecting pool, or swimming pool bordered by freshly planted willows, evergreens, poplars, and flowering shrubs.

At about seven o'clock that evening, a steady procession of chauffeur-driven limousines turned off Rockford Road and pulled up to the main entrance. The guest list read like a *Who's Who* of Oklahoma society. E. W. Marland, who begrudgingly admitted that Waite's home was more spectacular than his own, was an early arrival. Another visitor that night claimed to be a member of the Hohenzollern dynasty which once had ruled Brandenburg and Prussia. There was an assortment of statesmen, oil barons, and dowagers. Patrick J. Hurley, famed for his military and political exploits, who eventually was secretary of war under Herbert Hoover, also appeared.

Many of the guests congregated on the loggia overlooking the gardens. They lifted their glasses in salutes to the villa as they gazed beyond the east terrace toward the site of the Temple of Love, a classical tempietto guarded by matched blue spruces on a knoll which concealed the changing rooms for the swimming pool. As darkness slowly arrived, Waite ordered some of the vestiges of oil and gas wells on the property to be flared. This provided decorative light and reminded the gathering of the origins of the fortune responsible for the creation of the estate.

Inside the villa, waiters in crisp tuxedos hovered over round tables covered with blue, yellow, and white linen, and set with the finest china, crystal, and silver that money could buy. The formal sit-down dinner had taken nearly three weeks to prepare. The menu featured breast of chicken, new potatoes, broccoli with hollandaise sauce, sunburst salad, and rainbow parfait. The dinner and wines alone cost more than twenty-five thousand dollars.

Imported French wines and expensive champagne flowed like a runaway oil well. Orchestral music poured from the villa and echoed through the starry night. In the sunroom, a large Angora goatskin rug was removed to reveal a glass floor with alternating colored lights of red, white, blue, green, and amber. When the lamps were dimmed, the lights in the glass floor lit up. It was just like a floor Genevieve had admired in a Paris nightclub. The Harriet Frismuth sculpture in the room, called *Joy of Waters,* appeared to be poised for eternal dance, just like the maidens with bobbed hair in the music-room mural. The heartiest revelers danced until the wee hours.

But the most memorable moment of the entire gala was much earlier. For years to come, those in attendance clearly recalled that it happened before dinner, as many of the guests gathered for a toast inside the Great Hall.

Julius Williams, for many years a waiter at the Tulsa Club, remembered that unforgettable moment at Philbrook quite well. He was right there. Williams, only twenty years old at the time, had worked at the villa for three days prior to the opening party, at which he served as a busboy.

In 1977, when he was an old man, Williams told the *Tulsa Tribune* about his life. He spoke of the horrors of the 1921 Tulsa race riot, of his combat service in the South Pacific during World War II, and of the years he had served Tulsa's prosperous and the elite of the oil patch. Williams also told the reporter about that April evening at Philbrook and what he witnessed there.

"The women were beautifully gowned and the men wore white ties and tails," recalled Williams. "The waiters were in tuxes and were quite stern with us busboys, who flew around the place picking up empty glasses and snack trays.

"About 8:30 a hush fell over the crowd. I looked up on the first stairway landing and there was Mrs. Genevieve Phillips. She had been descending the stairs and stopped for a moment to look at the party going on below. She had a faint smile and carried some flowers. She wore a gown of fine material. I think it was the most dramatic moment I ever saw in Tulsa society. Those in the party applauded as she came down the stairs to join them. Then they cheered."

CHAPTER TWENTY-SIX

VILLA PHILMONTE

·WP·

No place on earth was as pleasurable to Waite Phillips as his Philmont Ranch. He was intrigued by the rich heritage of the three cultures of the region — Native American, Hispanic, and Anglo. He sought out old-timers in Cimarron who regaled him with colorful stories about Kit Carson, Lucien Maxwell, Ceran St. Vrain, Jedediah Smith, and all the other lusty characters who had passed through the land that became Philmont.

Waite reveled in the rich New Mexican history and the lore of the Utes, Comanches, and Jicarillas, the stories of ironclad Spanish soldiers, trappers, miners, outlaws, and the endless caravans of merchants and traders who had made the arduous trek down the nearby Santa Fe Trail. But most of all, Waite simply liked to get out to his ranch, change into comfortable clothes, and ride Dalhart or Gus or another of his favorite mounts to one of his mountains camps or lodges.

Anxious to move out of the old ranch house of former owner George Webster and into what most folks would come to call the Big House, Waite closely followed every step of the villa's construction. Finally, the Phillipses' dream home in New Mexico was completed. He and Genevieve did not host a fancy gala as they did at Philbrook. There were not many city folks or high-society types hanging around Cimarron. Instead, they invited all four of

Waite's brothers and their families and a few of their closest friends to enjoy the many pleasures of life on a high-country ranch in northern New Mexico.

June-July-Aug-Sept. on Philmont Ranch. For opening of Villa Philmonte entertained brothers Frank, L. E., Ed, and Fred. Also Pat Hurley, Bill Skelly, et al. ~ WAITE PHILLIPS DIARY, 1927

Like Waite's Tulsa mansion, Villa Philmonte had been in the making for several years. It was in late October 1925 when Ned Delk first visited Philmont Ranch to draw the initial floor plans for the residence. Landscaping sketches were prepared for the surrounding grounds. Both Delk and Hare finished the final plans and drawings early the following year. Soon, work crews under the direction of the John Long Company were hard at work beneath the gentle New Mexican sun.

Villa Philmonte was built on the site of the old Urraca Ranch's apple orchard. It was a spectacular location that gave the Phillipses and their guests a panoramic view of Philmont Ranch's mountain scenery to the west, especially the awesome ridge known as the Tooth of Time, rising 9,003 feet into the brilliant sky.

Although both of the Phillipses' villas were similar in appearance, there were big differences. Rather than use an Italian Renaissance design as he had at the larger Tulsa residence, Delk employed a Spanish Mediterranean theme in creating the house at Philmont Ranch. Roofed with red mission tiles, the twenty-two-room villa was constructed of stuccoed solid masonry. Painted a light buff, the villa was trimmed in an appropriate New Mexican color — bright turquoise blue.

Outside the villa was a fishpond encircled by willows, and there were gushing fountains, a rose arbor, and flower beds thick with colorful seasonal plantings. Just east of the courtyard, the more robust visitors plunged into a green tiled swimming pool brimming with water so icy it could have come straight from a mountain stream. An octagonal gazebo with a fireplace was added in 1929. It became a place where the family could cook hamburgers and watch the sunsets.

At the two-story guesthouse built for visiting family members and business associates, a balcony overlooked the south patio. Arched doorways led into open arcades and interior patios decorated with painted European tiles. Lilac bushes bloomed each spring just outside the villa windows. Waite took great pride in overseeing much of the landscaping.

"My father could be meticulous to a fault, even when it came to the plantings in the yard," said Elliott Phillips many years later. "I recall there was a certain tree growing near the villa that he had one of the hired men transplant. Dad told the man to dig up the tree and move it. But he didn't like that place so he had the guy move the tree again. That went on and for what seemed like a long time. The fellow ended up moving that tree four different times.

"At the last spot, my father looked at the tree and announced that finally he was satisfied. Then he noticed the hired hand was grinning, so he asked him what was so funny. The man looked up at Dad and grinned. 'Mr. Phillips,' he said, 'the tree is planted exactly where we started.' Dad broke out laughing. He loved to tell that story on himself."

In addition to taking an active role in tree planting and shrub placement, Waite was intensely concerned with every single aspect of the development and maintenance of his ranch retreat. Besides Waite's personal attention to all the details, the reliable design, landscape, and construction team of Delk, Hare, and Long put as much hard work into Villa Philmonte as they did at Philbrook.

Waite again engaged Percy French, the Madison Avenue interior designer he had engaged for Philbrook, to oversee the design and arrangement of all the furnishings at the Phillipses' New

Mexican oasis. French mostly used the artworks, decorative objects, and furniture that the Phillips family had acquired in Spain and from throughout the Mediterranean during their 1926 voyage.

In the foyer, some of Waite's Indian artifacts hung on the walls above an *horno,* a small native-style fireplace shaped like a bee-hive. Beyond the foyer, a spacious living room dominated the residence. The main features included massive hand-painted ceiling beams and silk-screened drapes with the ranch's cattle brand, the U U Bar, in the design. Portuguese carpets covered the floor, and the Phillipses added a handsome Navajo rug to honor the villa's southwestern connection. They also laid out a mountain-lion skin, complete with head, in front of the large fireplace, a grizzly bear turned rug stretched out in an eternal nap.

Piñon-scented fires, fed from tinder and kindling kept in a sixteenth-century hand-carved wooden chest from Spain, seemed to constantly blaze, even on summer evenings when high-country temperatures dipped to cooler levels. Above the fireplace, with the familiar W P initials emblazoned in the mantle, hung some of the old armor and weaponry Waite had picked up during his travels in Europe.

For reading and relaxing, Waite preferred the big living room. He was especially fond of a comfortable green chair near a round table which held an ornate lamp. A polished Knabe piano, custom built for the room, was equipped to serve as an electric player piano. The family kept rolls and rolls of music in a nearby cabinet. When the villa was crowded with people, all sorts of songs poured from the piano — "Bye, Bye Blackbird," "My Wild Irish Rose," "The Arkansas Traveler," "Gypsy Love Song," "The Merry Widow," "Indian Love Call," "Talking to the Moon," "Shaking the Blues Away," "There's a Long, Long Trail," "Rio Rita," and many others.

In the dining room, a mantelpiece bore the initials V P, for Villa Philmonte. The fireplace screen, andirons, and all the other ironwork in the room were designed and made by Waite's own ranch blacksmith. Sixteen guests could be seated around the long dining-room table at chairs covered in hand-tooled Moroccan leather. On the walls were portraits of Don Carlos Beaubien and his wife, Maria Paulita. Waite was fascinated with the history of his ranch. He had purchased the portraits because Beaubien and Guadalupe Miranda were the recipients of an 1841 Mexican land grant which included the area which ultimately became Waite's Philmont Ranch. Beaubien's son-in-law, Lucien Maxwell, with help from his friend Kit Carson, colonized the grant at Rayado in 1848, and eventually came to own the entire tract of almost two million acres.

Double doors off the dining room opened onto a patio for outside dining, and another door led to the kitchen, pantry, and servants' quarters. Later, the main entrance to the villa was converted to a breakfast room which eventually served as the family's private dining area when there were no guests at the ranch.

Above the landing on the stairs to the upper floors and the family's bedrooms, a leaded window in three sections depicted Santa Fe Trail traders near Tinaja Mountain, a trail landmark northeast of Philmont. At the head of the stairs, a porthole window in the library, originally a sewing room, looked out on the mountains.

In the north upstairs wing were the bedrooms of Elliott and Helen Jane. Down the hall to the south was the master bedroom suite, with separate dressing rooms for Waite and Genevieve. Their pink tile bathroom was equipped with heat lamps, a tub, and a shower with seven nozzles and a temperature gauge.

On most days, Waite withdrew to the lower level of the villa, where the main entrance opened to an auto court. Located off the downstairs hallway was the New Mexico Room, decorated with Indian artifacts and a variety of southwestern objects. Nearby was another chamber known as the Trophy Room. Animal heads were mounted on the walls of the room, which served as Waite's office and den. A door on the west wall opened into the trapper's closet, which was always kept well stocked with hunting rifles, trap guns, ammunition, fishing gear, riding clothing, and other items used by guests. As far as Waite was concerned, those rooms were perfect for entertaining.

When the Phillipses unveiled their villa for family and friends in the summer of 1927, they held frequent parties in the lower rooms. On the evening of July Fourth that year, after a particularly exciting poker game in the New Mexico Room, all the Phillips brothers carved their initials into the table, just as they had done as boys many years before on a barn door in Iowa. This time, the only brother missing was Wiate. When Tulsan Bill Skelly and a few other notable ranch visitors spied the Phillips boys' handiwork, they followed suit and left their own marks on the tabletop.

Besides his family and some Oklahoma oil-patch pals, Waite entertained another noteworthy group in that summer of 1927. The party was headed by Charles Gates Dawes, elected in 1924 as vice president under Calvin Coolidge, and one of the most colorful public figures during the years between the world wars.

Dawes, winner of the 1925 Nobel peace prize for his German reparations plan, brought several other notables to Philmont that July, including famed novelists Ben Ames Williams and Kenneth L. Roberts. Another guest was well-known *Chicago Tribune* cartoonist John T. McCutcheon who, on a subsequent visit, sketched caricatures on the walls of the Trophy Room. Roberts, later known for his novels featuring episodes in American history and the winner of a posthumous Pulitzer citation, recounted the group's high adventures at Philmont in a story entitled, "Hardships in New Mexico," published in the December 10, 1927, issue of the *Saturday Evening Post.* In fact, Dawes and the others liked their first visit to Philmont so much that they returned again in the summer of 1928, with a larger group.

The highlight of both visits of the Dawes parties was their fishing trips to Rayado Lodge, at the confluence of the Rayado and Agua Fria rivers. As always, before he and his guests departed from the villa on horseback, Waite rode to the head of the mounted procession. He also brought a cook and a helper with enough provisions for gourmet meals to supplement the trout suppers supplied from nearby streams. Known by the ranch hands as Fish Camp, this was Waite's favorite of his four back-country retreats at Philmont.

The largest of Waite's four log cabins built in the rugged mountains west of the ranch's headquarters, Rayado Lodge was fashioned of huge timbers and had four stone fireplaces in the main cabin. Before the largest fireplace was a screen with the iron-work silhouette of Waite riding his gray horse called Gus. The smoke from the rider's pipe curled into Waite's initials — W P. Another fireplace screen depicted Waite catching a trout.

There were plenty of cabinets for liquor, guns, and china built right into the walls, one of the first battery-powered radios ever manufactured, dining-room furniture made of Douglas fir and juniper pine, and sofas covered with buffalo hide. By the early 1930s, the last grizzly bear shot in Colfax County, New Mexico, ended up as a rug on the lodge floor.

Besides the main lodge, there were guest cabins, sturdy stables with wooden shingles, and a permanent house for Bob and Gladys Peoples, the caretakers who packed in supplies on the backs of four strong mules.

Visitors to the camp at Rayado usually started up the mountain trail at Waite's Crater Lake Lodge, a dogtrot cabin that faced the Tooth of Time. Once they arrived at Fish Camp, trail riders stabled their weary mounts and took to the rocking chairs on the front porch before trying some fly-fishing. With tall drinks and fresh oatmeal cookies in hand, they listened to the rush of the river and the wind through the pines. On the shady porch, hummingbirds danced in the sunlight, and brazen chipmunks darted about searching for dropped morsels to steal.

As much as Waite loved his big New Mexican ranch with all

its mountain trails, fishing streams, rustic lodges, cow camps, and high meadows where vast herds of livestock grazed, another member of the Phillips family — Waite's only son — came to cherish Philmont just as much, if not more.

Elliott Phillips was just a small boy when his father acquired Philmont. The youngster had learned to ride horseback long before, when he was only a toddler at the old Highland Ranch that the family owned in Colorado. Soon after the Phillipses started to spend significant amounts of time at their ranch near Cimarron, Elliott realized he had found the place he liked best. About this time, the boy also was pegged with a nickname that would stay with him the rest of his life.

"I got my name from an old cowboy and from some of my cousins — my Uncle L. E.'s boys," recalled Elliott when he was an old man. "Dad had bought up what became the Philmont, and I was about seven or eight years old and my cousins were out for the summer, helping to bring in the cherries and trying their hand at cowboying and such.

"Well, there was a cowboy on the place who was very bow-legged and had a great big black mustache. His name was Melaquias Espinosa and he was not very big. Guess he stood about five foot five inches tall at the most. He was a damn good cowboy and a real good man. The boys just loved him and they went up and stayed at the camp and Dad had them building trails. Once in a while they'd come down to headquarters and I'd be there with the folks, and I tried to get in with them. They were all pretty good to me, even though I was real small.

"Old Melaquias started referring to me as Chopo. Now in New Mexican Spanish, that means short in stature, and Lee Phillips and those cousins of mine got ahold of that and the name got changed to Chope, which really doesn't mean a thing. I never particularly liked the name Elliott anyway, so I decided Chope was as good a name as any, and I kept it."

Philmont was special for Chope Phillips. As far as the boy was concerned, his folks could give away their fancy place in Tulsa and all the other property they owned. As long as he had Philmont to go to, he knew he would be happy. It was not the big villa there that he liked as much as the land. Whenever he was away, Chope's heart and soul ached for those high pastures and dusty corrals.

He knew sure as shooting that he belonged where there were horses named Monkey or Buster or Headlight to ride, where there were plenty of calves to chase, rope, and brand, where there were game to be hunted and fish to catch, and where a boy could hunker by a campfire under the night heavens and listen to the harmless lies and outrageous yarns of bowlegged cowboys.

GROWING PAINS

Waite Phillips was a dapper and distinguished baron of business in his late forties, but he conducted his life like a man still on the rise. His daily work schedule, involving real estate, oil, and banking ventures, remained as full and active as ever. There was plenty to occupy Waite's time at the tail end of the 1920s other than the unveiling of the family estates and the management of a growing empire of commercial properties.

After moving into his two villas, Waite gave a big dinner party that autumn of 1927 at Philbrook in honor of his older brother, Frank, and Art Goebel. A dashing pilot, Goebel flew the *Woolaroc,* the airplane Frank sponsored in the famous 1927 air race from California to Hawaii that was concocted by pineapple tycoon James Dole. Goebel won the race, a feat that many aviation buffs proclaimed to be just as dangerous as Charles Lindbergh's solo flight to Paris in May of that year. When Lindbergh came to Tulsa in his *Spirit of St. Louis* that September 30, Waite joined Art Goebel and other dignitaries, including Tulsa Mayor H. L. Newblock, at a dinner at the Mayo Hotel. The meeting of Lindbergh and Goebel was quickly dubbed "a gathering of eagles."

In 1927, Waite also stayed focused on his many business dealings. He underwrote a stock issue for Independent Oil & Gas Company, merging the firm with his Philmack Company, organized only the year before. Waite became chairman of the board of Independent Oil, but without the responsibility of operations. Ed Moore, who had served as one of Waite's lawyers in Okmulgee, was the president. The vice presidents included Ralph Pringle, Otis McClintock, and O. L. Cordell. Russell Riggins was secretary-treasurer.

Then in October 1927, Waite was elected chairman of the First Trust and Savings Bank, a subsidiary of First National Bank of Tulsa. By the end of the year, he had purchased additional and substantial stock interest in First National Bank from G. R. McCullough, and eventually Waite was elected chairman. The oil industry and politics also took up much of his time.

In December to Chicago for Petroleum Institute meeting. Was director of the Institute for several years. In Washington and New York with G. E. P. While in Washington visited Vice President Dawes and had dinner with President Coolidge. General Pershing, Mr. and Mrs. Dawes, Mr. and Mrs. Corlaylu, et al were guests. Attended meeting in Vice President Dawes' senate office with prominent Republicans to try to persuade Dawes to announce as candidate for Presidency but he declined on account of old pledge made to Senator Lowdon of Illinois.

About this time the H-V and H H Ranches, containing approximately 375,000 acres of deeded and leased land were sold to Orcutt of Tulsa. At one time between years 1922 and 1927, W. P. owned and operated approximately 700,000 acres located in Colorado, New Mexico, and Arizona. Raised large herds of Hereford cattle, purebred and range; also sheep to extent of 20,000 head. Also horse, draft and thoroughbred, Palomino, saddle bred (registered), dairy cattle, hogs, and raised all types of feed supples on farm land. Owned and used 12,000 acre feet of irrigation water. ~ WAITE PHILLIPS DIARY, 1927

Waite and Genevieve started off 1928 with a visit to the Nautilus Hotel in Miami. They took time for a Cuban junket and a stay in exotic and spicy Havana. From there, they traveled by ship to New York, where Henry Lockhart, of Blair & Company, introduced Waite to William Averell Harriman, son of the famed railroad magnate. A future public official and diplomat who would serve four presidents — Roosevelt, Truman, Kennedy, and Johnson — Harriman made an unsuccessful bid as the Democratic candidate for president in 1952 before serving a term as governor of New York.

When Harriman, considered a powerful figure with keen financial skills, met the Phillipses, he was acting as chairman of the board of a private bank. Following the introduction, Harriman and Lockhart accompanied Waite and Genevieve to Lexington, Kentucky, in the heart of bluegrass country, where they purchased horses.

Back in Tulsa that summer, Waite was pleased to play a role in the opening of Tulsa Municipal Airport. To get the facility established, Waite had joined forces with such leading corporate citizens as Cyrus S. Avery, a civic leader dubbed "the Father of Route 66," Harry Tyrrell, Omer K. Benedict, and many others. Spearheaded by big Bill Skelly, these captains of business organized the Tulsa Airport Corporation and vowed to purchase a 390-acre tract suitable for a major airfield if the city would guarantee reimbursement.

That July, just before Waite left for Philmont to entertain Vice President Dawes and his party once again, two crude runways were cut in a wheat field near Tulsa and a temporary terminal with a tar-paper roof was erected. A handsome terminal building would be built after the airport was functioning. Waite and the other Tulsans who underwrote the $172,000 for purchasing the airport property eventually turned it over to the city. The site was about eight miles northeast of downtown, just south of Mohawk Park. By July 3, 1928, Skelly, Waite, and the others proudly hosted national dignitaries for three days of festivities to open the fledgling airport.

Other opportunities and transactions took place during 1928. Waite, working with realtor R. M. Darnell as broker, assembled about seven hundred acres of property just south of Tulsa, later called the Southern Hills acreage. There, Waite built a rustic log lodge known as Philcreek near some retaining ponds, and it became a favorite retreat for his friends who enjoyed hunting and fishing. Ultimately, Waite donated 290 acres for the Southern Hills Country Club, which officially opened in 1935. Although he seldom visited the place, Waite also contributed twenty-five thousand dollars to help build the impressive Southern Hills clubhouse, which resembled an English country manor.

Also in 1928, the construction in downtown Tulsa of the twenty-three-story Philtower Building, then the tallest in Oklahoma, was completed. Ned Delk and the rest of Waite's hand-picked design and construction team delivered another beauty.

Waite immediately moved his office headquarters from the fifth floor of the nearby Atlas Life Building into the ornately Gothic Philtower skyscraper with its unusual polychrome tile roof, towering over the intersection of Fifth Street and Boston Avenue. Known during the oil-boom years as the "queen of the Tulsa skyline," the Philtower featured floors and walls of marble, Honduran mahogany trim, a sculpted lobby ceiling with chandeliers, and massive brass elevator doors framed in marble with the distinctive W P shield in their upper panels. The elevator cars were operated by smartly uniformed attendants and dispatched by "starters" who also were deputized to police the elegant property.

"The building of Philtower is strategic in both time and location," stated an attractive marketing brochure that Waite published to lure potential shop and office tenants. "It gives to Boston Avenue the completed touch of dignity and grace — towards which its trend has been constant — an important link in the sweep of architectural magnificence between the proposed new Union Station on the North and the Boston Avenue Methodist Church to the South.

"From the west side of the tower high above the city your gaze is lured afar to the beautiful hills that hold secure the meandering Arkansas — beneath you is the young and active shopping district of the city — looking South there is almost an unbroken view of residential Tulsa . . . the homes of many wealthy men whose successes have personified the energies and ambitions characteristic of Tulsa the Oil Capitol [sic]."

Among the homes described in the brochure were, of course, Waite's Villa Philbrook and, by 1928, the residence of Ralph B. Pringle and his family, who previously had lived near the Phillipses on South Owasso. Because Ralph, or "Pring" as some of his familiars called him, was one of Waite's closest business associates for many years, it was natural that his home should be near Philbrook.

In the early plans for the Villa Philbrook grounds, which were much larger than the final design, Ned Delk had included a caretaker's house and a large garage and barn complex. But after the size of the estate was reduced to twenty-three acres, the caretaker's house, at 27th Street and Rockford Road, became the family residence of Gillette Hill, one of Waite's executives at Independent Oil. Delk also modified the design of the stable complex in the early stages of construction to echo Villa Philbrook's design. This evolved into the Pringles' impressive Mediterranean-style residence at 1550 East 27th Street.

In September merged 1st Trust & Savings Bank into 1st National and added to name "Trust Company." At a meeting held on a Sunday at Philbrook residence with associates, it was decided to elect R. Otis McClintock as president of 1st National Bank & Trust Co., to replace R. P. Brewer. McClintock accepted, was elected the next Tuesday. W. P. and W. G. Skelly made arrange-

ments with Frank Phillips for Brewer to accept position of Vice
President of Chatham & Phoenix Bank in New York.
~ WAITE PHILLIPS DIARY, 1928

McClintock, who had served as vice president at Philmack and held the same post when it was reorganized as Independent Oil, was also a board member of First National Bank and Trust. He never forgot how he got his job as bank president. "Waite Phillips put me here as bank president," McClintock told Troy Gordon of the *Tulsa World* in a September 30, 1953, story about McClintock's twenty-fifth anniversary at the bank. "He [Waite Phillips] owned some stock and the bank needed a president."

That autumn of 1928, Waite took a much needed break from the rigors of commerce and went on a wilderness journey with Gillette Hill and a few other friends. They took to the backcountry of Montana, and later, in Idaho, they hunted goats and camped along Moose Creek. Despite being a multimillionaire, Waite still liked the high adventures of his youth, when he and his twin brother had roamed that same territory.

As the journey progressed, Waite and his fellow adventurers not only encountered a grizzly bear and a fierce early snowstorm, but also horse wranglers who imbibed corn whiskey from a five-gallon jug, a solitary and harmless bandit complete with a black hat, and finally, a "crazy sourdough" whose target-shooting demonstration took place inside the Lolo Hot Springs Hotel. Miraculously, no one was harmed during any of the escapades and, for good measure, Waite even survived a bout of near pneumonia.

That fall, while her husband and his cronies chased about looking for remnants of the Wild West, Genevieve headed in the opposite direction. She took seventeen-year-old Helen Jane back East, where she was enrolled at Miss Finch's Finishing School in New York City. Several other Tulsa young ladies, all friends of Helen Jane, also attended Miss Finch's, including Minnie

Kennedy, Elizabeth Greis, and Joan Skelly. Genevieve returned home to complete the plans for the golden wedding anniversary celebration of her parents in Iowa, held on November 27. Waite was still on the road that month, but he managed to arrive in Knoxville just in time for the celebration.

In November W. P. to Kansas City and St. Louis and then to New York with E. H. Moore and R. B. Pringle on Independent Oil & Gas Co. refinancing. While in New York, Will Rogers spoke to W. P. from stage of theatre, introducing him to Dorothy Stone and Mrs. William Randolph Hearst.

Surprised W. G. Skelly with large donation to [Herbert] Hoover campaign. Good story about this in connection with Skelly stock syndicate. Made approximately $15,000 but decided never to join syndicate again. Therefore, paid the $15,000 to Skelly for Hoover campaign of which Pat Hurley was Oklahoma manager. Helped P. J. Hurley to become Secretary of War.

~ WAITE PHILLIPS DIARY, 1928

Waite should have known that 1929 was going to be a difficult year that very first month, when the family's winter visit to Philmont was cut short after the adventurous Chope, still addressed as Elliott by his parents, broke his arm.

There were some great highs but many lows that year. Waite's friend Harry Sinclair, the oil tycoon, was jailed for contempt of Congress for refusing to answer questions about his involvement in the Teapot Dome Scandal. It also would be the year of the great Wall Street crash, causing widespread panic and the loss of billions of dollars overnight.

That summer, months before the collapse of the stock market, the Phillipses again journeyed to Europe. Waite took the entire family, including a disappointed Chope. He protested, to no avail, that he would rather be eating dust with the cowpokes at the Fourth of July rodeo in Cimarron instead of dining on rack of lamb with stuffed shirts on a polished flagship bound for France.

During their thirty-day European tour, the Phillipses visited Paris, Berlin, London, and Edinburgh before returning to New York. But while the family took in the sights of the European continent, troubles for Waite began to surface on the home front back in Tulsa.

While in Europe on this trip [E. H.] Moore and [Ralph] Pringle discharged O. L. Cordell [as vice president of Independent Oil] and that started controversy with Ed Moore. ~ WAITE PHILLIPS DIARY, 1929

Although he was fast losing confidence in Moore's business judgment, Waite tried to keep his associate afloat with a sizable loan. But the writing was on the wall, and ultimately Waite would find it necessary to ask Moore to step down as president of Independent Oil.

Even as Waite wrestled with internal woes in his company, the nation's economy began its serious downward spiral. Many people far less fortunate than Waite Phillips and his cronies needed major assistance.

On November 17, 1929, a new Children's Home was dedicated in Tulsa, created largely through the gift of seventy thousand dollars from Waite and Genevieve. At the ceremony that afternoon, Omer Benedict, an associate of Waite's and president of the Children's Home and Welfare Association, presented a glowing tribute to the Phillipses for their generous gift, which had made possible the purchase of the grounds and the construction of the building.

"We are somewhat inclined in these days of struggle for dollar supremacy, where the goal of most men is the accumulation of material wealth, to appraise their worth by success in that line," Benedict told the crowd. "In that respect, Waite Phillips ranks high; and yet money is to him but a token — an instrument of good placed in his stewardship for a purpose. Knowing him as I do personally, I know that the least of his riches is money. The uses to which he puts his worldly wealth constitute a richness greater than all the gold, of which, according to his oft-repeated statement, he is but the custodian."

Throughout the Great Depression, Waite always tried to lend support to those in need. Not wanting to be taken advantage of or "to be made a damn fool of," as he put it to those who served with him on the board of the Community Chest, Waite put twenty-five thousand dollars into a special fund to be loaned without interest to worthy persons. His sole requirement was that there be no disclosure of who had supplied the money.

W. P. was General Chairman of Tulsa Community Fund. Made radio address. During time of Community Fund campaign loaned Ed Moore one million dollars.

In December had conference at Philbrook residence with executives of Independent Oil & Gas Co. W. P. requested resignation of E. H. Moore as President on account of his physical and financial inefficiency and irresponsibility. R. C. Sharp was designated as new President. ~ WAITE PHILLIPS DIARY, 1929

Waite's dilemma with his executive staff at Independent Oil was interrupted by the death of his father-in-law, John Brown Elliott, at age seventy-seven. Although he had been ill for some time, his death left Genevieve stunned and shaken. He died at the family's home in Knoxville, Iowa, on Christmas Eve 1929. The old former banker and lawyer, who had served as a respected Democratic member of the Iowa legislature for two terms, had been retired for three years from the bank where he had worked since 1884.

Telegrams and cards of condolence poured in at Philbrook from Bill Skelly, the Pringles, and scores of friends, colleagues, and family. "We are shocked to hear of your bereavement and extend our deepest sympathy," wired Mr. and Mrs. L. E. Phillips.

"I've just learned of the sudden demise of your father. I am so sorry and extend my heartfelt sympathy to you and all the family," stated Frank Phillips in a cable to Genevieve. Jane Phillips told her sister-in-law in a separate telegram, "My heart aches for you and your sorrow."

On December 26, at three o'clock in the afternoon, the Reverend W. J. Fowler officiated at J. B. Elliott's funeral, at the family residence at 534 Montgomery Street in Knoxville. Then the casket was closed and a long line of mourners went to Graceland Cemetery for the burial.

Still grieving for his father-in-law, who once had named a thoroughbred horse for him and whom he had helped when Elliott's bank floundered, Waite hurried back to Tulsa after the funeral to check on business conditions. The new decade of the 1930s was about to dawn. After only a brief rise in the stock market, increasing despair and hardship set in. Although Waite experienced some serious financial losses, for the most part he fared considerably better than many of his cohorts.

During the late fall of 1929 and the first half of 1930 considerable adjustments and distress were experienced by most active businessmen. Fortunately W. P.'s assets — except real estate and First National Bank stock — were held in municipal bonds which were salable. The Independent Oil & Gas Co. stock investment was also salable but low in price and on account of his position as Chairman it was not advisable for W. P. to liquidate it. Almost without exception his friends and associates were financially embarrassed and as a result of real estate loans made by the First National Company, a subsidiary of the First National Bank, the bank itself required financial assistance. W. P.'s financial records disclose that his losses in connection with these situations were very heavy. One of the many instances of W. P. helping friends in distress was his willingness to personally guarantee the indebtedness of C. I. Pontius for notes he had with the First National Bank. Mr. Pontius had a securities company with real estate loans and was unable to pay the participation certificates which came due in this year of depression. In the meantime he was elected President of the University of Tulsa. W. P. asked James Chapman to join him but he refused, saying he had no responsibility to do so. Of course, W. P. had none either, but did guarantee the notes, although Mr. Pontius finally was able to make payment in full in 1941. ~ WAITE PHILLIPS DIARY, 1930

Usually Waite was successful in keeping his business transactions out of the headlines and handling his financial affairs in a discreet fashion. Even so, rumors abounded concerning his firm and pending business disasters for other companies. Even Phillips Petroleum Company, headed by Frank and L. E., was said to be in extreme jeopardy.

And as 1930 continued, with President Herbert Hoover trying to convince everyone that "we have passed the worst," the gossip among stockbrokers and analysts from Tulsa to New York was that Phillips Petroleum was due to merge with another oil firm. The best bets were that the other firm was none other than Independent Oil & Gas Company, headed by Waite Phillips. In only a short time, those who heard the stories found out that this was one case when the rumor was true.

MOVING ON

During the first six months of 1930, serious talk of a Phillips Petroleum–Independent Oil merger continued to waft through executive offices and hover over mahogany conference tables. Meanwhile, Waite plowed straight ahead. Rumors were rampant and the economy was sour, but he attempted to maintain a "business as usual" attitude in his various real estate, oil, and banking endeavors.

His newest Tulsa commercial building — dubbed the Philcade — was completed in 1930 and opened immediately for tenants at 511 South Boston Avenue, just across Fifth Street from the Philtower. Offering 259 office suites and space for twenty-eight shops, the Philcade had been under construction since January 1929.

Waite turned to Leon Senter, an architect he had met years before when operating his oil business in Okmulgee, to design and build the Philcade. Senter, who headed the Okmulgee office of Smith & Senter, a Kansas City–based architectural firm, accepted Waite's commission to build the nine-story retail-office complex. He moved to Tulsa and became the first tenant in the Philtower Building, where he kept his offices until the end of a long and successful career, in the 1960s.

Because Tulsa had a 17 percent vacancy rate in office space when Senter launched the project in 1928, Waite did not want the Philcade to become direct competition for his Philtower. To avoid the problem, Waite told Senter to design as modest a structure as possible but still maintain the highest building standards.

The result was a creation with an exterior of the same colored brick but much simpler than the ornate Philtower — simpler except for a wonderful terra-cotta panel with a floral motif and a display of whimsical animals and birds, incorporated in the best tradition of what came to be known as art deco design. Part of the building's name stemmed from a pair of wide arcades, fashioned appropriately of Saint Genevieve marble, that opened onto Boston Avenue and Fifth Street. The first part of the name, of course, was from the Phillips surname, by then so well fixed in the city's psyche.

Undoubtedly, the most difficult construction problem came when miners had to be summoned to dig the eighty-foot brick-lined tunnel connecting the Philcade to the Philtower. Although it was said that the tunnel was built to provide for ease in moving supplies from one building to the other and for additional underground storage space, there was yet another reason for a subterranean passage. Those close to Waite knew that he was security conscious in an age when the kidnappings of wealthy oilmen and their families seemed a lucrative endeavor to more than one desperate person or savvy criminal.

The tunnel was completed, elaborate filigreed light fixtures were hung, and the building's lavish interior and gleaming arcades of marble, shiny metals, and gold leaf proved that Waite's Midas touch still worked. Any worries about Tulsa being saturated with office space were proved groundless. Almost as soon as the building was completed, more than 80 percent of the offices were rented. The retail space filled even faster, and included a newsstand, barbershop, cigar store, interior designer offices, and various ladies' apparel shops.

Officials from Standard Oil of Indiana, in Tulsa for the 1930 International Petroleum Exposition, were so impressed with the city and the building that they decided to make the Philcade the site of their Southwest headquarters. Later, the big oil company hammered out the contract and before long, four floors were added, bringing the Philcade to a total of thirteen stories. News of the expansion was heralded in a Pollyanna-style *Tulsa World* story as "lifting the few remaining Depression clouds that lingered on the Tulsa business horizon."

Tulsa and the rest of the country needed all the good news that could be found. Despite the expansion project at the Philcade and the other skyscrapers that oil money were still able to erect, most Tulsans, like the rest of the nation, faced the reality of the Great Depression. Few working-class Americans found any hope or humor in Henry Ford's unintentionally ironic statement of 1930, "These really are good times but only a few know it." Only a few indeed.

Even the "Oil Capital of the World" had its share of soup lines, apple peddlers, and beggars who found their way to the back doors of the more affluent homes. New words crept into the country's vocabulary — *Hoovervilles,* for the ramshackle shanty-towns; *Hoover hogs,* road-killed armadillos that became family dinners; and *Hoover flags,* indigents' empty pockets turned inside out.

Some of the well-heeled captains of commerce, such as Waite, believed they were financially strong enough to gut out the depression. After all, much of their money was not in the stock market but in oil, or in property in downtown Tulsa, the only place where most folks in the region shopped and spent what little money they had. Nearby refineries continued to churn out products, and although oil prices dropped drastically, the best operators in the oil patch managed to make money.

Nonetheless, as the nation's number of unemployed reached four million and more and more banks closed their doors, a collective shudder rippled across the land and persistent rumors became the truth.

Even Phillips Petroleum Company was in financial difficulties
with their notes being called by the Chase National Bank in New
York, and the stock declined to a few dollars per share. At one
time it was only $2.00. To "bolster" this situation Frank Phillips
solicited a merger with the Independent Oil & Gas Company and
W. P. was willing to negotiate on account of his disinclination to
continue responsibilities of a public financed oil company and the
unsatisfactory condition of having R. C. Sharp as President.

~ WAITE PHILLIPS DIARY, 1930

In his private memorandum drafted in 1958, which for the first time discussed several of his prior business dealings, Waite revealed his true feelings on the proposed merger and the business climate during the depression. He wrote candidly about Frank's decision not to sell his oil firm in 1925, when Henry Lockhart of Blair & Company wanted Phillips Petroleum to join in the merger of several large oil companies he had arranged to consolidate.

As a result of Frank's decision not to sell he continued with remarkable success in building one of the best and largest domestic oil companies in America. There was an interlude, however, in this progress which was caused by the deep depression of 1929-33, in which he had serious troubles with his bankers in New York both in a personal way and in the affairs of his company. On the other hand when I sold out in 1925 it was with the idea of devoting my time to other matters of some semi-public nature so therefore my accumulated profits from oil investments were put into municipal bonds, a new home and two large buildings in Tulsa. That sale I made in 1925 was a sizable one during those times and I am still wondering what saved me from more foolish things than this record to follow will show.

Two unwise deals were made, however, which later caused me unusual trouble. The first was that of buying a small interest in the First National Bank of Tulsa in 1928, and allowing myself to be elected Chairman, and the second was in making an underwriting deal, about that same time, to become a large investor in the Independent Oil & Gas Company and likewise accepting, what I was told would be, an inactive Chairmanship of that as well . . . the latter situation warrants more explanation because of its subsequent connection with the Phillips Petroleum Company affairs.

Ed Moore, who served as one of my attorneys in Okmulgee, was the organizer of the Independent Oil & Gas Company and when it developed into a reasonably sized going concern he moved its headquarters to Tulsa. It was then he selected R. B. Pringle, formerly operating Vice President of the Waite Phillips Company, to head his staff. This company was in desperate need of new finances when I personally underwrote the stock issue for them in the amount of $6,000,000. Soon thereafter Moore began to speculate in the stock market and it was necessary for me to loan him large sums of money to bolster his credit with brokerage firms. However, when the stock market break came in 1929 he became completely insolvent. . . .

The principal stockholders of this company were well aware of my large stockholding interest in it and therefore began to write me to protect them. In order to do this it became my unpleasant duty to remove Ed Moore as President and appoint R. C. Sharp in his place. This necessary move, of course, created friction but there was no other alternative to it.

These were only some of the demons Waite wrestled with in 1930. No doubt the grave situation at his oil company and at the troubled First National Bank preyed on his mind as he went East. In New York that May, he attended Helen Jane's graduation at

Miss Finch's Finishing School, and on June 3 he appeared at the White House for a luncheon meeting with President Hoover and Secretary of War Pat Hurley.

July and August were spent on Philmont Ranch. Frank Phillips and Clyde Alexander visited there to discuss Independent Oil & Gas Co. merger with Phillips Petroleum Co. W. P. suggested Henry Lockhart of Blair & Co. to negotiate the deal. The merger was completed in September on the basis of an exchange of 76 shares of Phillips Petroleum for 100 shares of Independent. As a result of this deal W. P. acquired over 200,000 shares of Phillips Petroleum stock.

It was Lockhart's understanding that the merged company would use the best officials of both old companies but after the merger was completed this was not done. It was also understood by Lockhart that W. P. would become a director of Phillips Petroleum. However, on account of the breach — regarding Independent officials above mentioned — W. P. declined to accept that position. Frank Phillips had previously solicited W. P. to become President, which he declined to do. To have accepted even a directorship when all the other Independent officials had been dismissed would have been the basis for embarrassment and mis-understanding. ~ WAITE PHILLIPS DIARY, 1930

The Independent–Phillips Petroleum consolidation created huge headlines in the daily press and in financial and petroleum trade publications. "Three Phillips Brothers Unite to Form Greater Phillips Company with Total Assets of $316,00,000, 54 Gasoline Plants, 3 Refineries, 11,600 Outlets," screamed a headline in the September-October 1930 issue of the *Phillips Gas Tank,* a company publication.

"The business lives of the three Phillips brothers constitute one of the many romances in oil," wrote a reporter in the September 4, 1930, issue of *Oil and Gas Journal.* "The three

Phillips brothers are regarded as among the smartest oil men in the industry. They have extensive banking facilities in New York, Kansas City, Tulsa and Bartlesville. The combination of Phillips and Independent forms a powerful organization in the hands of men of known ability and long experience."

None of the media or many insiders from Phillips or Independent Oil was aware of the internal struggle between Waite and his older brothers, especially Frank. Fortunately, Waite's 1958 memorandum spelled out some details that were far from known at the time.

"To keep this history in somewhat proper continuity I'll now return to the troubles of my brother Frank with the Phillips Petroleum Company in the 1929-30 period," wrote Waite. Then he proceeded to explain.

Frank was able financially to take care of himself but the company needed help for rejuvenating purposes. When I learned that L. E.'s notes were called at a bank in New York, with all his Phillips Petroleum stock pledged on them, I made a special trip to Bartlesville and re-financed his situation. Shortly thereafter I made a special trip to New York with the same purpose in mind to help Frank but with his unusual nervous and distressed condition at that time he did not seem to grasp what I was talking about.

On the other hand he [Frank] got it fixed in his mind that I came there with the ulterior motive of replacing him as President of his own company. It is with hesitancy and regret that I report his distressed mental condition at that time so there was nothing for me to do but return home. As a matter of record for the youngsters of today [1958] I'll report that Phillips Petroleum stock, like that of most all other industrial companies, descended to a low value on the New York Stock Exchange. . . . I could have bought the controlling interest in that company with my 20 odd million dollars worth of municipal bonds but I did not want another oil company and certainly not one my brothers had founded and built. Besides those bond investments were being held to protect stockholders, depositors and investors in the First National Bank & Trust Company of Tulsa.

Much to his credit Frank, with the help of L. E., who was now devoting all of his time to the oil business, managed to maintain the Phillips Petroleum Company affairs but was badly in need of additional properties to encourage stockholder interest in a company which heretofore had a good record of growth. Therefore, knowing that I was not happy in being forced to operate the Independent Oil & Gas Company, he and his staff approached me for a merger during the winter and spring of 1930 and it was finally consummated by Henry Lockhart in the summer of that year. . . .

This deal had a remarkable effect in strengthening the position of Frank's company and it was pleasing to me to have that occur the same as it was being permitted to finance L. E.'s personal loans. In merging . . . I insisted that they assume all liabilities in acquiring all of Independent's assets which consisted of production, refining and marketing facilities. As already stated Henry Lockhart made the Phillips-Independent deal and I understood as a part of it that the Phillips Petroleum would take the top employees out of each company to staff the merged institution. However it soon developed that Clyde Alexander, Vice President and General Manager of Phillips Petroleum, started a program of discharging all Independent men in violation of this agreement. Therefore, it was my distressing duty to refuse to accept either the Presidency of the Phillips Petroleum Company, which Frank offered, or even be a director of it because if I had taken such positions my former associates could have considered it as a betrayal of them.

In his eye-opening memorandum, Waite also stressed that although the merger benefited Phillips Petroleum, it did not entirely cure its financial difficulties. Phillips officials had acquired valuable properties, but they still had to raise additional working capital. "Frank came to my office later on to request my cooperation in refinancing, as he stated, *our* company," Waite wrote. "Then it was again a distressing experience to call his attention to the fact that it was not *our* company. These occurrences are sad to relate because of my deep-seated feeling of gratitude to these two older brothers which has remained constant throughout all the years to date. However, with Frank's own troubles to think about he did not realize my obligation to my former employees or the fact that my assets were more or less entirely frozen to protect my position in the First National Bank & Trust Company."

By 1931, it was clear to Waite and anyone else with reasonable intelligence that the worldwide economic depression had deepened. In the United States alone, the national income had dropped 33 percent since the 1929 crash, and unemployment soon would reach 16 percent. Will Rogers, Oklahoma humorist and Waite's friend, reminded everyone, "We are the first nation in the history of the world to go to the poorhouse in an automobile."

As a result of being forced to request the resignation of E. H. Moore as president of the Independent Oil & Gas Co. in December 1929 in order to protect the stockholders of that company, there naturally continued an antagonistic attitude on his part toward W. P. and this became acute in his criticism of the terms of the Independent-Phillips merger, by his charging collu-

sion between the brothers — F. P. and W. P. — to the detriment
of the Independent stockholders. Some attempt was made by a few
individuals, biased in Moore's favor and in anticipation of unfair
profits to themselves, to insinuate irregularities by the principals
in the merger and a subsequent suit was filed in the Delaware
courts by Moore, W. L. Kistler, Gordon Clark and others.
~ WAITE PHILLIPS DIARY, 1931

In his 1958 memorandum, Waite wrote that during the early
1930s, "the deposed Ed Moore was storming the streets of Tulsa
with vindictive stories about the Phillips-Independent merger."
All the while, Waite continued his responsibilities with First
National Bank and Trust Company and, as he pointed out in his
diary, conducted business at the bank "without any assistance
from any other directors and stockholders of that institution."
Waite also noted that although he had no legal obligations concerning the merged oil companies, those troubled years "hardly
could be considered an enjoyable time of his life." Winter trips to
Philmont Ranch with the McClintocks and to southwestern
Texas with his ranch manager helped to ease some of the tension.

In the spring of 1931, Waite voluntarily agreed to personally
liquidate the First National Company, the wholly owned subsidiary of First National Bank and Trust Company. According to
Waite's personal records from that period, the assets of First
National Company were approximately $10 million. Loans were
supposed to be made on 50 percent of the values of properties,
but during the depression, they amounted to 150 percent. Waite
spent ten years and lost more than $2 million on this project.

The First National Company had been used for many years to
hold assets which were not permitted for a national bank to own,
and also for the purpose of making real estate loans against which
participating certificates were sold to investors. Similar security
companies were owned by the principal national banks through-

out the country at that time and most of them became a source of
financial trouble during the 1930 depression.

C. A. King was selected by W. P. to represent him in the liquida-
tion of the First National Company and this work constituted the
principal activity of W. P. for several years thereafter and resulted,
as anticipated, in large financial loss. Kenneth Crouch did the
work of disposing of the real estate. It was necessary to foreclose
some Kansas leases and W. P. offered to take part of them but
other directors, except F. B. Parriott, refused. These oil and gas
leases were later sold to Parriott and he organized the Leader Oil
Company to develop them. This turned into a very profitable
venture which in turn was sold by him to Carter Oil Company.
~ WAITE PHILLIPS DIARY, 1931

In the summer of 1931, Waite's family suffered another loss.
Genevieve's mother, Nora Elliott, died on July 12 at the family
residence in Knoxville. Nora, in frail health for several years, died
just eighteen months after the passing of her husband.

A tribute to Nora Elliott, written by Dixie C. Gebhardt,
appeared in the *Knoxville Journal* on July 16, the date of her
funeral. "There is real sorrow in Knoxville today," wrote Gebhardt, "for many, especially among the older families of the city,
mourn with a sincere and heartfelt grief in the passing on of Mrs.
Nora Elliott, widow of our late lamented citizen, John B. Elliott.

"On Tuesday of this week, as the bright summer day approached the evening hour, when the shadows grew cool and
longer, the sunset gates opened, 'and wandering on ahead a little
way, she found the Gate of Paradise ajar, and stepped inside to
wait'. . . . Had she known Tuesday morning she would be gone
before another day dawned, she could have looked back over the
years of her life, and would have found no self reproaches."

Flowers and telegrams for the grieving Genevieve came from
throughout the country. The Ralph Pringles sent a large spray of

red roses, and more floral arrangements arrived from Bill Skelly, Mr. and Mrs. Lee Phillips in Wichita, and the Johnson Hill family in Tulsa. Several telegrams were sent to the Elliott residence in Knoxville, including wires from Frank and Jane, L. E. and Nora, and "from the girls of Miss Jackson's Shop" and Nelle Shields Jackson, proprietor of one of Genevieve's favorite ladies' apparel stores, which was located in the Philtower for many years. "Sorry Mother dear, to hear of Grandmother's death," Chope wired from Cimarron to his mother.

Two Methodist ministers presided at the late afternoon funeral service. Then Nora Elliott was taken to Graceland Cemetery. The family laid her to rest beside her husband in the family vault erected by Helen Pine, Genevieve's sister, as a memorial to their parents.

Waite had maintained an excellent relationship with both of his in-laws during the years. Periodically, Waite had asked Mrs. De Haven's Flower Shop in Tulsa to dispatch roses to his mother-in-law in Iowa, and he sent her letters filled with news of the family's busy life in Oklahoma and New Mexico.

In his final letter to Nora Elliott, dated July 8, four days before her death, Waite had inquired after her health. He wrote of the hot weather of Oklahoma, and of Helen Jane, whom Waite described as "a daughter twenty years old who finds life most interesting when in the company of college boys." There was also news of young Elliott — Chope — busily riding the range out at Philmont Ranch.

"I get a letter every few days from the ranch manager and he reports Elliott enjoying himself and doing well," Waite wrote. "Elliott's inheritance from his Grandfather Elliott of an intense love of horses, combined with his taking on my love for the great outdoors, generally, has given him a temperament that exactly fits into this ranch proposition, and without this reason for holding the property, I imagine it would have been closed down long ago, as it has been expensive."

Expensive or not, Waite made a beeline to Philmont Ranch after the funeral. He spent much of the summer and part of the autumn at Philmont.

In December Otis McClintock suggested W. P. buy one-half interest from Mosier and Levorsen in their block of leases near Ada, Oklahoma, which W. P. promised to do for $15,000. Being delayed in contacting them, however, it was found in the meantime E. H. Moore purchased it. A week or two later it was found that Moore was unable to raise the $15,000 so W. P. was then offered one-quarter interest for that sum. He declined. This property was later developed into a prolific oil field, called the Fitts Pool. ~ WAITE PHILLIPS DIARY, 1931

Despite all the ill will that had developed between himself and Ed Moore, it seemed that Waite still did not bear a lasting grudge. "Even after all these vindictive actions by Ed Moore," Waite wrote many years afterward, "I later on personally financed for him an oil operation in the Fitts Pool of southern Oklahoma which enabled him to again become solvent and wealthy."

In 1942, Waite went so far as to help finance Moore's successful upset bid for a seat in the United States Senate, making the conservative oil millionaire the third Republican to be elected senator from Oklahoma since statehood in 1907.

Some of Waite's epigrams applied to the relationship he shared with Ed Moore. There was one that went, "To hate is to hurt — not the hated but the hater." Another favorite that fit was, "Some people never learn the art of compromise. Everything is either black or white. They do not recognize, or will not concede, that the equally important color grey is a mixture of black and white." But perhaps the best of Waite's sayings for the situation was, "No person is either entirely bad or entirely good. Therefore learn to forgive yourself for error the same as you should forgive others."

CHAPTER TWENTY-NINE

EYES WEST

One of the biggest hit tunes of 1932 was the mournful "Brother, Can You Spare a Dime?" It became a popular lament that seemed best to symbolize those dreary times. Anyone who could possibly spare a dime found it did not go very far. In the troubled years since 1929, automobile sales had plummeted 80 percent and wages had dropped more than 60 percent. By 1932, unemployment had reached 24 percent.

The time had come for a change in Washington. Hoover's insistence that prosperity was "just around the corner" and the crippling depression only a fleeting aberration contributed to his political demise. Most Americans in 1932 held Hoover and his administration responsible for the Great Depression. Some Republicans, even a few diehards, privately admitted that the inevitable was approaching in that year of a presidential election.

That spring, Waite was elected as a delegate to the Republican National Convention, but he politely declined. Instead, he remained occupied with business matters in Tulsa, and from June until early September, enjoyed the pleasures of saddle horses and trout fishing at Philmont Ranch. Helen Jane and a few of her friends were also at Philmont for the summer. So was Chope, a skinny fourteen-year-old who fought tooth and nail to spend every waking moment of his life at the big ranch.

Chope liked to ride with the seasoned Philmont cowboys and

learn about ranch ways firsthand. He was fond of the camel his Uncle Frank Phillips had shipped to him a few years before when the youngster admired one of the odd-looking critters at Woolaroc, Frank's Oklahoma ranch retreat in the Osage. The camel spent most of its life believing it was a cow pony. It chased after the herds of ranch horses, but none of them ever allowed the humped beast to come too close.

Sadly for Chope, that September his cowboy adventures were put on hold. His parents and big sister accompanied him to Culver, a resort town in northern Indiana on Lake Maxinkuckee. Waite handed over a tuition check, and Chope was enrolled at Culver Military Academy. He traded his cowboy boots and jeans for a cadet's dress uniform.

Later that autumn, the pundits' predictions about political change came true. In November, Franklin D. Roosevelt handily defeated Herbert Hoover, 472 electoral votes to 59, to win the office of president of the United States. After the election, Waite, Genevieve, and Helen Jane traveled via train to Indianapolis, and from there were chauffeured to Culver for a visit with Chope. The Phillipses soon were back in Tulsa to prepare for the holidays.

What Waite and Genevieve were not prepared for was the startling announcement that their only daughter sprang on them when they came home to Tulsa after the first of the year.

Dec. 22 — As Chairman of Board, 1st National Bank, Tulsa, W. P. asked for resignation of R. C. Sharp and received unanimous approval of directors. This came as a result of unfair demand regarding bond deal with Bank.

Dec. 22 to Jan. 2 at Philmont Ranch with G. E. P. and Elliott. Upon return Helen Jane announced her marriage to W. R. Breckinridge. ~ WAITE PHILLIPS DIARY, 1932-1933

The sudden news of Helen Jane's marriage shocked Waite and

Genevieve. During the years, their daughter had grown into a beauty, with plenty of charm and intelligence. Like many of the young daughters and sons of oil barons, Helen Jane had everything she wanted, including plenty of fancy clothes and new cars. She went to the right schools, attended the best parties and receptions, and had more than her share of suitors — always wealthy young men from Oklahoma's nouveau riche upper class.

The young man Helen Jane had chosen for her husband was William R. Breckinridge, member of a well-known Tulsa family. Although the marriage seemed rather hasty to the methodical Waite, he had to admit that for the most part, Bill Breckinridge's pedigree looked every bit as enviable as the Phillipses' proud line of descent.

According to the Breckinridge genealogy, the family history in Virginia dated to before 1700 and included a long line of lawyers. One distant relative, John Breckinridge, was elected twice to the Virginia assembly and later became a senator and then attorney general of the United States under President Thomas Jefferson. Another kinsman, John Cabell Breckinridge, served as vice president of the United States under James Buchanan, and was an unsuccessful presidential candidate of proslavery Democrats in 1860 before becoming a Confederate general.

Waite was quite familiar with Bill's father, M. A. Breckinridge, an illustrious attorney and the first county attorney in Tulsa after statehood. The elder Breckinridge, born in 1880 at Fincastle, Virginia, was a distinguished-looking gentleman with courtly manners, known around downtown Tulsa for his trimmed mustache, erect carriage, and omnipresent walking stick. His father had been a lawyer and a graduate of Virginia Military Institute. He had raised a company of soldiers for service in the Civil War and had served for two years as captain, the youngest man of that rank in the entire Confederate army.

Proud of his ancestors' Southern heritage, M. A. Breckinridge graduated from Washington and Lee University, studied for the law, and was admitted to the bar in 1903. He served with a New York firm, then returned to Virginia and established a practice in Roanoke, where he married Miss Julia Robertson. In 1905, the couple moved to Indian Territory. They made their home on Elwood Avenue in Tulsa, where a daughter, Anne, and a son, William, Waite's future son-in-law, were born. Bill's mother died in 1920 and his father, best known around town as Judge Breckinridge, remarried. He practiced law and remained an active force in Democratic politics.

It looked as though Bill Breckinridge would continue his family's long tradition of legal work and community service. Blessed with above average intelligence and good looks, Bill attended Dartmouth University, the University of Oklahoma, and eventually earned a law degree from the University of Tulsa.

Besides his academic prowess, the young man had natural athletic ability. He excelled at most sports all through school, but he was especially adept at baseball. Breckinridge was so good, in fact, that he earned a brief stint as a major leaguer.

During the 1929 season, the strong-armed Tulsan was signed as a pitcher with Connie Mack's Philadelphia Athletics, led that year by such superstars as Jimmie Foxx, Mickey Cochrane, and Robert Moses "Lefty" Grove, the premier fastballer of the age. The Athletics won not only the American League pennant that season, but also went on to defeat the Chicago Cubs four games to one in the 1929 World Series.

Although his professional baseball career was short-lived, Breckinridge was not particularly worried about his future. With a prominent lawyer for a father and Waite Phillips for a father-in-law, he had plenty of options, major-league pitcher or not. Helen Jane, a dark-haired beauty with the looks of a fashion model, fell head over heels for young Breckinridge. When they dashed off together to Bentonville, Arkansas, to tie the knot on December 22, 1932, she was twenty-one and her bridegroom was twenty-six. After their honeymoon, the newlyweds made their home in a fine Tulsa neighborhood, thanks to the generosity of Waite.

Helen Jane and Bill Breckinridge — after their marriage
situation was settled — left in her Cadillac car for Florida. . . .
Purchased home for Helen Jane on South Owasso Avenue, Tulsa.
~ WAITE PHILLIPS DIARY, 1933

The well-being of Helen Jane and Elliott was always para-
mount to Waite. Throughout the tumultuous years of the Great
Depression, Waite and his brother Frank in Bartlesville remained
very much concerned about the welfare and safety of all their
family members. Besides a faithful German shepherd dog to
patrol the Philbrook grounds, Waite's night watchman at the villa
had a stainless steel truncheon that doubled as a tear-gas gun,
capable of discharging a shell of gas that would incapacitate in-
truders.

Waite's emphasis on security was not merely the reaction of an
overly protective parent or the paranoia of a rich man with a vivid
imagination. There was real cause for concern. Sometimes Waite
worried not only about his children and wife but for his own
safety.

For example, during his career, Waite received several threats,
mostly unsigned letters from disgruntled crackpots such as the
typed epistle by a semiliterate person sent to Philbrook on March
8, 1932. The cryptic letter, filled with typographical errors and
misspelled words and lacking punctuation, alarmed Waite. The
letter read: "a gangs laying for you and want your dough and you
had better tell that woman that you had in your cafe to watch out
to cause theyre frade of her. Shes got somethin on some body and
there goin to plant her first. Theyre awful hard up desperete and
rarin to go. maybe she aint workin for you maybe she is they
think she is maybe bee a big idea you double your gard and have
a driver I meen it."

Waite took a few extra precautions, but the mysterious gang
never struck. But in July 1933, when Waite returned to Tulsa

from Philmont Ranch to attend the funeral of his associate, Omer K. Benedict, he faced more than just another menacing letter. Two of his close friends had acquired some alarming intelligence about the plans of three of Oklahoma's most notorious depression-era criminals.

> *July 12th Otis McClintock and Ray Lattner received information through friend of Omer Benedict that [George] "Machine Gun" Kelly, also Albert Bates and Harvey Bailey, were in Tulsa for the purpose of kidnapping for ransom and that W. P. was at the head of their list. (This was subsequently verified by Edgar Hoover, head of the FBI). With this advance information W. P. was able to leave town and avoid being kidnapped. A few days later [July 22, 1933] the kidnappers got Charles Urschel of Oklahoma City.*
> ~ WAITE PHILLIPS DIARY, 1933

Although Waite made no notations in his diary about where he went to escape the kidnappers, the most logical place would have been back to his ranch in New Mexico. During the 1930s, Waite spent much of his time at Philmont, with its spacious villa and camps and cabins hidden in the mountains.

Philmont was the perfect site for conducting strategic meetings about business or political races with Otis McClintock and others, or to entertain L. E. and Nora Phillips and other family members. Waite also effectively used the ranch as a launching point for frequent motor trips or train excursions to Los Angeles, Yosemite, San Francisco, Tucson, Colorado Springs, Denver, and other western destinations.

When Waite and Genevieve were back in Oklahoma, they fussed over their first grandchild, born in Tulsa in 1934. Helen Jane and Bill Breckinridge were delighted with their baby son, whom they named Phillips in honor of the young mother's illustrious family. But to offset the new family arrivals, there were more losses. Waite's mother — Lucinda Josephine Faucett Phillips

— died at age eighty-four on February 8. Unfortunately, Waite was in Hawaii when his mother passed away. He was Josie's only child not in attendance at her funeral in Iowa.

January 6 left Tulsa with G. E. P. enroute to San Francisco. Sailed February 6 on SS Monterey for Honolulu. Mother Phillips died at Gravity, Iowa, while we were enroute. As Helen Jane and Bill were in Los Angeles, she attended funeral for us. . . . Sailed from Honolulu on SS Malolo arriving San Francisco March 1, then to Los Angeles. Met with Will Rogers and Elliott Roosevelt there and Lincoln Ellsworth. Spent two weeks with L. E. and Nora at the Ambassador Hotel and visited the Hearst Ranch at San Simeon, California with Amon Carter, et al. Los Angeles to Philmont Ranch and from ranch to Culver to spend Easter with Elliott — arriving back in Tulsa April 4. ~ WAITE PHILLIPS DIARY, 1934

Much of Waite's time in 1934 was devoted to helping L. E. Phillips financially and loaning large sums of money to Ed Moore to stave off foreclosing proceedings by the Exchange National Bank and to secure Moore's interest in the Fitts Pool. There were more visits with Elliott at Culver Military Academy. Even though the teenager developed into a successful cadet, Chope was only too happy to get out of uniform and into proper cowboy duds for a summer of work at Philmont Ranch.

June— to Culver with G. E. P. via train for graduation exercises. Helen Jane, Bill and Phil Phillips[L. E.'s son] drove to Culver. Left Culver June 6 with G. E. P. and Elliott for motor trip to Knoxville and Gravity, Iowa. Drove from Gravity to Kansas City and then to Tulsa via rail, arriving June 10.

July - August - September - October - on Philmont Ranch. R. E. Lewis resigned as Ranch Manager and employed H. D. Mitchell. ~ WAITE PHILLIPS DIARY, 1935

That summer, Will Rogers and his aviator pal Wiley Post were two of the celebrity guests at Philmont. Waite always enjoyed Rogers' company and wit. So did L. E. and Frank Phillips — even after a famous newspaper column penned in 1933 by Will took a friendly poke at the founder of Phillips Petroleum. "Frank Phillips, of oil fame, was out the other day, said he was going to Washington," wrote Rogers. "The oil men were going to draw up a code of ethics. Everybody present had to laugh. If he had said the gangsters of America were drawing up a code of ethics, it wouldn't have sounded near as impossible."

On July 23, 1935, just two days after Post had received his restricted license to operate his newest airplane, the one-eyed pilot and Rogers took off on a four-day test flight through Colorado and New Mexico. One of their main stops was Waite Phillips' Cimarron ranch. Wiley and Will touched down on July 26 and were wined and dined at Villa Philmonte.

Helen Jane and Bill Breckinridge and their baby son were out from Tulsa, spending the entire summer at the ranch, living in the Carson Cottage. Just outside the villa's front-door entrance Waite held his grandson, Phillips Breckinridge, and posed with Rogers and Post flanking him. Alvin Krupnick, the noted Tulsa photographer whom Waite had hired to capture on film so many of his architectural treasures, was at the ranch and snapped a portrait of the three old friends and the little boy.

On August 15, just twenty days after their visit at Philmont, Post and Rogers, on a tour of Alaska, perished when their nose-heavy airplane faltered and crashed in the icy waters of a lagoon near Point Barrow. Waite cherished the photograph of their final visit with him. Some time later, he joined with several other oilmen, including Frank, E. H. Warren, John Mabee, Lew Wentz, and Ewing Halsell, to build Will Rogers' mausoleum at Clare-more, Oklahoma.

Sometimes Waite reflected on his last visit with Will Rogers at Philmont. He recalled that one of Rogers' sons, Will, Jr., just had graduated with the class of 1935 from Stanford University, where he majored in philosophy, was a swimmer, and captained the polo team. Young Chope Phillips was also headed to Stanford that September to continue his education, so the two fathers compared notes about their boys and the acclaimed university just outside Palo Alto, California.

Besides sending his only son to one of the best universities in California, Waite was spending much more of his own time on the West Coast. Starting in 1936, his visits to southern California greatly increased. Waite rendezvoused with Elliott for weekends of horse racing at Santa Anita. He hosted dinners at Coconut Grove for his brothers and business associates, paid courtesy calls on Will's widow, Betty Blake Rogers, at her Santa Monica ranch, hobnobbed with a few of Hollywood's stars, and conducted long meetings with Harry Sinclair and Pat Hurley at a private Ambassador Hotel apartment.

> *On February 3 moved from Biltmore Hotel to The Town House. On the 5th saw Frank Phillips and family sail from San Pedro for Honolulu on SS Mariposa. Feb. 9 had lunch with Mrs. Will Rogers at her ranch and met Fred Stone and his two daughters, Dorothy and Paula, and also Billie Burke, Mr. and Mrs. Will Hays, et al. Told Dorothy Stone about embarrassment in having Will Rogers introduce us from stage in New York in 1928. Feb. 12 attended Santa Anita races and Santa Anita Ball at Ambassador Hotel. . . .*
>
> *Met and became quite well acquainted with L. W. Craig, Vice President of the Security–First National Bank of Los Angeles and talked to him about ranches in various parts of the country. . . .*
>
> *June 1st left Tulsa for Los Angeles and Palo Alto, by train, to bring Elliott home when his school closes. To Los Angeles with Elliott on June 11 and then on to Ranch for a few days. Elliott came on to Tulsa so he could get a little training in the office handling his accounts.* ~ WAITE PHILLIPS DIARY, 1936

Waite was determined that eighteen-year-old Elliott was going to follow in his footsteps and become a successful businessman. The formal education at Stanford was important, but so was the time Elliott spent in Waite's Philtower office, learning firsthand from his father, who epitomized the Horatio Alger story.

In December 1936, before he headed to Philmont to join Genevieve and Elliott for the holidays, Waite prepared yet another of his lists. This one was important, so he had it transcribed in a lovely script, worthy of presentation to his son or any other youngster interested in making his way in the world of commerce. The list contained Waite's rules for conducting business. There were seventeen.

1. CAREFULLY EXAMINE EVERY DETAIL OF YOUR BUSINESS.
2. BE PROMPT IN EVERYTHING.
3. TAKE TIME TO CONSIDER, THEN DECIDE QUICKLY.
4. BEAR YOUR TROUBLES PATIENTLY.
5. MAINTAIN YOUR INTEGRITY AS A SACRED THING.
6. NEVER TELL BUSINESS LIES.
7. MAKE NO USELESS ACQUAINTANCES.
8. NEVER TRY TO APPEAR SOMETHING MORE THAN YOU ARE.
9. PAY YOUR DEBTS PROMPTLY.
10. LEARN HOW TO RISK YOUR MONEY AT THE RIGHT TIME.
11. SHUN STRONG LIQUOR.
12. EMPLOY YOUR TIME WELL.
13. DO NOT RECKON UPON CHANCE.
14. BE COURTEOUS TO EVERYBODY.
15. NEVER BE DISCOURAGED.
16. PRACTICE ORDERLINESS, THOROUGHNESS, CONCENTRATION AND PATIENCE.
17. THEN WORK HARD AND YOU WILL SUCCEED.

Chope Phillips thought the seventeen rules of business his father put down were good ones, but he did not believe for an instant that those rules applied only to someone who wished to become a banker or an oilman or a real-estate developer. He was not interested in doing any of those things.

Chope wanted to be a rancher. That was all he ever wanted to be, from the time he first mounted a pony at Highland Ranch in Colorado. The business of raising and marketing cattle was Chope's interest in life, and he was hell-bent that nobody was going to get him off track.

CHAPTER THIRTY

PRECIOUS GIFTS

Just ten years after he had built his pair of dream homes — Villa Philbrook and Villa Philmonte — Waite Phillips decided the time had come for him and Genevieve to pack up and move on.

It would take some time for that to happen, but even as 1937 barely started, plenty of other changes were in the making for Waite. He began the new year by resigning as director of the First National Bank and Trust during the annual meeting. He also made an announcement that two of his downtown buildings — the Philtower and Philcade — would be air-conditioned at a cost of $500,000 to $600,000.

Later that winter, Waite and Genevieve were driven out to Philmont for a few days, and then they took a train to California. By March, they were back in New Mexico to greet Chope and a few of his college friends at the ranch for their Easter break. It was obvious to everyone gathered at Villa Philmonte for the holiday that Waite was preoccupied. After he took care of the details of ranch business that constantly occupied his time, Waite looked for the right moment to discuss something with his wife that had been on his mind for a long time.

Had important conference with G. E. P. regarding plans in future of leaving Philbrook residence and moving to California which

did not at that time have her approval. Returned to Tulsa with
G. E. P. via train Easter Sunday, March 28. ~ WAITE PHILLIPS
DIARY, 1937

After living in Villa Philbrook for not quite a decade, Waite was restless and ready to move on. As usual, he looked to the west, to the golden shores of California. But even though he was more than ready to leave Tulsa behind, Genevieve was quite fond of her well-appointed residence on Rockford Road. Waite recognized that his wife was not as restless as he was and liked to put down roots. He would need to quietly convince his wife of twenty-eight years that relocating to California would be in their best interests.

Waite also realized that trouble was starting to brew within the family and that it also would demand his attention. With one ear always cocked, Waite heard much of the muffled gossip being whispered around Tulsa that Helen Jane, pregnant with her second child, and her lawyer husband, Bill Breckinridge, were having marital problems. Waite had made every effort to make Bill feel like one of the family, including taking his son-in-law on a rugged camping trip through the High Sierras of California. Following the backcountry trek, just the two of them went on a long train and car journey up the coast to Santa Barbara and San Francisco and then back to Los Angeles.

Breckinridge was trying to make a go of it as an attorney. That year, he asked Waite to loan $200,000 to Elliott Roosevelt, son of President Franklin Roosevelt, to buy a Fort Worth radio station. After some consideration, Waite declined, even though Breckinridge was to be made the company's general counsel.

On August 3, 1937, Peyton Anthony Breckinridge — the second son of Helen Jane and Bill — was born at St. John Hospital in Tulsa. Both Waite and Genevieve hoped that the new baby boy and his three-year-old brother, Phillips, would keep the young couple together. That November, Waite — never one to let his family do without — purchased a new residential property at 2602 East 28th Street in the Woody Crest addition, and presented it to his daughter and her family. The attractive two-story colonial farmhouse, designed by architect John Duncan Forsyth, was situated on an angle on a corner lot.

Shortly afterward, Waite made a dash to New Mexico for a quick stay at Philmont. He came home to Tulsa for a very important conference, held in his Philtower office just three days before Christmas.

To Ranch Dec. 6th to 10th. Had conference with Walter Head, President of the Boy Scouts of America, on Dec. 22 re: plans for donating land in New Mexico to Boy Scout organization. Left Tulsa Dec. 28 with G. E. P. to spend balance of holiday season on Ranch, returning to Tulsa on Jan. 2. ~ WAITE PHILLIPS DIARY, 1937-1938

In truth, Waite had been contemplating disposing of his New Mexican ranch for some time. As far back as 1930, just a few years after Villa Philmonte had been completed, Waite had begun to correspond with Walter W. Head, president of the Boy Scouts of America, regarding how the ranch could be used by the Boy Scouts of America. Waite had written to Head at his office on August 19, 1930, more than seven years before the two men met in Tulsa.

I own a ranch near Cimarron, New Mexico, and the village of Cimarron, as you probably know, was the headquarters of Lucien B. Maxwell, owner of the Maxwell Land Grant, which consisted of 1,800,000 acres, the largest private land holding in North America. Maxwell and Kit Carson were old beaver trapper friends and buddies. Carson lived with Maxwell, both at his residence at Cimarron and in a house adjoining him in the first settlement in that country on the Rayado.

When I purchased my ranch in 1922, the old manor house of Maxwell was still standing in Cimarron, but since that time it has burned. The residence property and ruins and a plot of ground surrounding it is now owned by Mrs. Charles Springer.

The purpose of this letter is to advise you that I have given some thought to the proposition of restoring this property for a state and national shrine for the Boy Scouts, provided the idea is received with favor by the Scout organization and the influential citizens of Colfax County, New Mexico. Adjoining this village is a wonderful mountain country, part of which might be used as recreation for the Scouts. My plans are immature but I would like to have your reactions to this proposition.

Writing again to Walter Head on December 16, 1937, Waite once more admitted, "For many years I have carried the thought in my mind a project that I hoped would be beneficial to the boy scouts."

Waite still loved the ranch and the surrounding mountains and pastures, but as was always his way, he was ready to hunt new lands. As Waite had pointed out to his mother-in-law in his last letter to her, the main reason he held onto the ranch was because it gave so much pleasure to Elliott, who spent every summer with a cow outfit, moving cattle to the mountain pastures and branding calves.

Although most of the time Waite was an absentee owner, he always kept abreast of every feature of ranch life. Every ranch manager who drew a paycheck from Waite was required to send him weekly written reports with detailed information about the livestock, weather conditions, and personnel. When Waite was at Philmont, he carried a small notebook in his breast pocket wherever he went. He was often seen reining up his favorite horse Gus or a paint horse named Zack he had bought from the Miller

Brothers' 101 Ranch in Oklahoma to jot down hasty notes which later became long memorandums to his foremen.

As Stephen Zimmer and Larry Walker noted in their fine book, *Philmont: An Illustrated History,* first published in 1988, "No aspect of the ranch's operation escaped the owner's attention. Phillips was especially concerned with the welfare of his employees. On the average, the ranch employed as many as fifty people, including ten cowboys, fifteen sheepherders, twenty farmers, plus maintenance and office personnel. Each employee with a family was supplied a house, milk cow, garden seed, poultry stock, beef and pork. . . .

"Perhaps the greatest contribution Phillips made to the success of the ranch's operation was his plan for the management of the cow herd and its efficient utilization of the available range grass. This plan involved developing springs and using fences and strategic salt distributions in pastures in order to entice cattle to graze inaccessible parts of the ranch. . . . Phillips instructed the cow and sheep employees to kill grass-eating gophers wherever they were found. He had them dig loco weed in the foothills and mountains parks each spring as it began to grow and threaten livestock."

In a 1936 dispatch to his ranch manager, Waite wrote of two new wolfhounds, one to be used by the ranch's horse department and the other by the cattle headquarters. "I think this is a good idea," Waite pointed out, "and I solicit and request the help of these two departments in caring for these dogs and training them, as by so doing it will keep down the nuisance of coyotes around headquarters. In this connection, I want to again request that all stray house cats be killed when found outside their own yards [because they would attract coyotes]."

As he rode horseback through the camps and along the mountain trails with a lever-action Winchester rifle in the saddle scabbard and a powerful pistol in his holster, nothing escaped Waite's attention. He spied every leak in the bunkhouse roof, all the downed fences, and any heifers that appeared to be neglected.

A stylish rider in his polished boots with a scarf tied around his neck, Waite made sure a tin cup for dipping from a stream, a roll of toilet tissue, a first-aid kit, and an altimeter were tucked inside his tooled leather saddlebags, trimmed in silver and turquoise nuggets. Sometimes, while pausing to smoke a Chesterfield he kept in a silver case studded with turquoise, or after nibbling at a hot lunch in a cow camp, Waite reflected on his life and his meteoric climb to the top.

In a nineteen-page single-spaced typed letter to ranch manager H. D. Mitchell, dated August 26, 1937, Waite wrote about how his early experiences in the oil patch under his big brothers' watchful eyes had helped prepare him for being a rancher. "As foreman of an oil company 30 years ago, I would not neglect an operating matter such as leaving those heifers along the road in the Narciso Abreu pasture, and later as superintendent, I would have immediately called the foreman upon reaching home as you did last Friday night. . . ."

In the same lengthy letter, Waite shared further insights with Mitchell.

> I explained to Elliott and his two friends from California, not long ago, all progress and human better-ment comes as a result of mental and physical efforts. Elliott and his boy friends admitted they were lazy and none of them had any special aim in life at this time. Rather surprising to them I replied that was normal at their age for I recall having been the same when nineteen. I really learned how to work when about 25 years old and I did that under the inspiration of an energetic and purpose-ful boss. I told the boys they would have for decision sometime in their twenties, the choice of three routes. Either the life of a Digger Indian who attempts to live without effort and subsides on a diet comparable to that of

a turkey buzzard or coyote. Second, live on the fruits of other people's labor. Third, pay your own way in the world, support your own family and be a self-respecting, self-supporting individual. This ranch for 15 years has been supported by the results of my well-managed oil operations instead of on its own merits.

That single sentence in his letter to the ranch manger said volumes about Waite's true feelings. As much as Waite loved the natural beauty of Philmont, the ranch was not paying its way. To Waite Phillips, always a man of swift and deliberate action, that meant that like any other loss, it had to be cut from his vast inventory of properties and projects and, he hoped, put to a better use.

By the late 1930s, thanks to Waite's abundant care and a generous infusion of money and resources, Philmont — with its renowned horse breeding program and extensive livestock herds — had become one of the best-developed ranching operations along the front range of the Rocky Mountains. Waite and the rest of the Phillips family, especially Elliott, had enjoyed Philmont for many years, and the ranch had become an important part of their lives.

Yet by 1938, even as Waite began to make arrangements to part with the ranch and with his property in Tulsa, he and Genevieve also had to deal with more problems created by the strained marriage of their daughter. It looked as though Helen Jane and Bill Breckinridge were ready to call it quits.

Left Tulsa January 19 with G. E. P. for San Francisco via K. C. and Denver, arriving San Francisco 22nd. Helen Jane phoned W. P. at Mark Hopkins Hotel — San Francisco — that she wanted a divorce from Bill. This was surprise to us but we agreed to cooperate. Elliott came up from Palo Alto for weekend. Numerous telephone conversations with Otis [McClintock] and

John Curran [an attorney] re: Helen Jane's divorce. Helen Jane
received divorce on Jan. 31. We left San Francisco for Santa
Barbara Biltmore Hotel arriving Feb. 1. Received call from Bill,
from Memphis on February 8, reporting reconciliation and that
Helen Jane and Bill were enroute to Florida. ~ WAITE PHILLIPS
DIARY, 1938

The problems of Helen Jane and Bill flew in the face of Waite's preference for handling personal affairs in a discreet manner and keeping all dirty laundry out of the newspapers.

Although her parents were somewhat surprised by her request for help in obtaining a divorce, Helen Jane's equally rapid reconciliation with Bill, which resulted in their divorce being set aside on Valentine's Day, was also bewildering to the Phillipses. Nevertheless, on March 30, 1938, Helen Jane and Bill and their older son, Phillips, were guests at a Philbrook dinner party to celebrate Waite and Genevieve's twenty-ninth wedding anniversary.

Waite spent that spring and summer tying up loose business ends, shopping for pinto horses in Texas and California, and taking a combination sightseeing excursion and fishing trip. It took him from Montana into Canada with stops in Calgary, Edmonton, Jasper Park, Terrace, Prince Rupert, and Vancouver. By mid-August, he was again at Philmont Ranch to greet a field party sent by the American Museum of Natural History to collect a sampling of the region's indigenous mammals.

Back in Oklahoma, on September 20 Waite and Genevieve drove to Pawhuska, the seat of Osage County, to attend the wedding of Frank Grant "Mac" McClintock and Patricia Kennedy. The groom was the son of the Phillipses' good friends Otis and Gladys McClintock. "Mac," as most people called him, had attended Choate Preparatory School, Yale University, and the University of Oklahoma before helping to organize the Zephyr Drilling Corporation in 1937. His bride, Patricia, was the daughter of Mabelle Kennedy and the late Edmund T. Kennedy. Mrs.

Kennedy was a Pawhuska banker and Democratic national committeewoman. She eventually would become assistant treasurer of the United States during the Truman and Eisenhower administrations, and Truman's special ambassador to Brazil. Typical of the Phillipses' generosity, their gift to Mac and Patricia was an expense-paid honeymoon trip to Hawaii.

On September 21, 1938, the day after the McClintock wedding, Waite released a two-page statement to the media. The carefully composed announcement stunned many Tulsans. Waite and Genevieve were giving their residence, Villa Philbrook, to the city of Tulsa. The Phillipses wished to see their home transformed into an art museum, with special emphasis on Native American art and historical materials.

"It has been the desire of Mrs. Phillips and myself for several years to donate our home and estate known as Philbrook located at 2727 Rockford Road in the City of Tulsa to be used for the benefit of the public and this written declaration of intention is made to announce and confirm that purpose," wrote Waite. "It is proposed that an Oklahoma non-profit corporation be formed bearing the name of Southwestern Art Association, with a charter authorizing activities devoted to the advancement of art, education, literature and science."

In his statement to the public, Waite spelled out that the corporation's initial trustees, or directors, would be made up of the presidents of several local institutions, including the American Indian Foundation, Tulsa Art Association, and the University of Tulsa. Also named as trustees were R. Otis McClintock, John E. Curran, Harry A. Campbell, and the president of the city of Tulsa park board. Those seven directors would name four additional members as provided by the by-laws.

"The buildings now used as residence and caretaker's cottage are to be retained and used by the Southwestern Art Association for the general purpose of housing, preserving and displaying therein works of art, literature, relics and curios including those representative of the native North American peoples and being used for such purpose shall bear the name of 'Philbrook Art Museum.'"

In addition, Waite agreed to remodel the interior of the villa at his own expense so it would be a suitable museum. He hired architect H. R. Lohman to take care of all design and renovation work. Waite also addressed the future of the landscaped acreage surrounding his residence by stating, "as a part of our proposal the Southwestern Art Association shall, by appropriate deed of conveyance, transfer to the City of Tulsa for park purposes, to be known as 'Philbrook Park' and to be administered by the Park Board, all the land contained in the Philbrook property, which approximates twenty-three acres, to be maintained by them as a public park and botanical garden containing plants indigenous to the Southwest. . . ."

Within a month, the Southwestern Art Association became a reality. On Sunday, October 30, a news release announced the issuance of a charter by the Oklahoma secretary of state and the appointment of twenty-one prominent Tulsans to the association's permanent board of trustees. The announcement was made by Dr. C. I. Pontius, president of the University of Tulsa and acting chairman of the association formed to administer and promote the development of Philbrook Art Center.

"The palatial Phillips estate, the residence of which will be remodeled for use as a museum, is one of many gifts the Tulsa financier and his wife have made to the educational, scientific and cultural life of Tulsa," stated the news release. "It was accepted more than a week ago in the name of the city and the foundation trustees who have been working with Mr. and Mrs. Phillips toward the completion of the organization since that time.

"These Tulsans are Doctor Pontius, R. Otis McClintock, E. W. Pollock, W. B. Way, N. G. Henthorne, John E. Curran and Harry A. Campbell. The resignations of Curran and Campbell have been accepted by the foundation trustees with appreciation for their services and assistance in initiating the organization. . . ."

The board of trustees listed in the release represented the elite of Tulsa's cultural, professional, and business communities. Most were prominent local people, the women identified, as was the custom of the era, only by their husbands' names. Besides Dr. Pontius, the other trustees were: R. Otis McClintock, Mrs. A. L. Farmer, E. W. Pollock, Mrs. Thomas B. Scott, Jr., Mrs. Eugene Lorton, Clark Field, Mrs. H. N. Greis, Mrs. I. C. Ritts, Mrs. Fred P. Walker, Mrs. Allmand M. Blow, Ralph O. Dietler, Mrs. Walter Ferguson, Jenkin Lloyd Jones, Mrs. E. B. Lawson, A. B. Butler, N. G. Henthorne, P. C. Lauinger, Nelson K. Moody, W. G. Skelly, and W. B. Way.

"Tulsa has assumed leadership in the southwest in almost all public improvements," Waite pointed out in the release. "We have many beautiful churches. Our city is fast becoming well known as having a fine park system. With the broad development of the University of Tulsa over the last ten years, along with other public improvements, the cycle of improvements necessary to cultural advancement will have reached its peak by the acceptance of this donation."

Waite further explained that his main wish was that Philbrook Museum of Art be used primarily as a repository of the art and artifacts of the North American Indian tribes. According to the news release, "He [Waite Phillips] placed special emphasis on the importance of Indian collections to perpetuate the culture of a people to whom Oklahomans are especially indebted."

By the time the news release was made public, Waite and Genevieve were in New Mexico, continuing with preparations to donate portions of Philmont Ranch to the Boy Scouts of America.

Sept. 26 made trip to Philmont with G. E. P. to show Boy Scout officials the acreage to be offered as gift to Boy Scout organization.
~ WAITE PHILLIPS DIARY, 1938

The inspection team was there in response to the request Waite had made to Walter W. Head, president of the Boy Scouts of America, for the organization to take a look at the ranchland near Cimarron. Dr. James E. West, the chief Scout executive, sent an advance party made of Ray H. Bryan, assistant director of engineering service, L. L. McDonald, national director of camping, and James P. Fitch, regional Scout executive for Oklahoma, Texas, and New Mexico. A short time later, the group was joined by Dr. West, Walter Head, and Arthur A. Schuck, the BSA's director of division of operations. Waite led the men on a horseback tour of the ranch, spending most of the time in the Ponil country, the area that he considered the most suitable for a Boy Scout camping operation.

Waite, who long had been an admirer of Boy Scout programs, was more than pleased with the enthusiasm he saw in the eyes of the inspectors as they rode over his ranch. In early October, Head received a written communiqué from Waite that confirmed a prior promise to give a sizable hunk of property and a hefty cash donation to the Boy Scouts. The vast acreage Waite planned to donate to the Scouts was the most scenic portion of his ranch.

Waite wrote: "If this proposal were being made to any other organization, whose rating was inferior to that record of service made by the Boy Scouts of America, I would be inclined to be more particular in outlining a program, to be assured that the property would be put to full beneficial use as I visualize it, but I feel amply assured as a result of your record and in my contacts and conversations with you all, that the Executives and the advisory Board will not accept this property and cash gift unless they feel that it will be beneficial to the Scout program. . . ."

On October 20 received long distance call from Walter Head, President Boy Scouts of America, advising acceptance of land in New Mexico by their Organization, 35,857 acres and $50,000 cash for development. ~ WAITE PHILLIPS DIARY, 1938

On November 2, 1938, in a letter to Dr. James West, Waite wrote of the inspection tour conducted by Boy Scout officials and how they favorably impressed the entire Phillips family. "Our boy, Elliott, accompanied the inspection party by horseback on the last day at my special request," wrote Waite. "He is a fine lad, but like any other ordinary American boy who has had all the advantages of outdoor life from indulgent parents, he has hardly yet matured to the point of realizing what this project may mean to the lives of thousands of other boys who have not been similarly situated. In some ways he is not as fortunate as I have been in this respect for my early life was different as I was compelled to fight and work for such privileges."

After the BSA's national executive board accepted Waite's gift, they considered possible names for their new wilderness camping area. Only one made any sense. They named their New Mexico site the Philturn Rockymountain Scoutcamp. The word *Philturn* combined Waite's name with a key word from the Boy Scouts' popular slogan, "Do a good turn daily." It was a fitting phrase and a good name.

Waite once wrote, "Real philanthropy consists of helping others, outside our own family circle, from whom no thanks is expected or required." As 1938 grew to a close, those words of Waite's made sense, especially to all those that year who had witnessed Waite giving away sizable amounts of money, his fancy Tulsa residence, and a significant portion of his ranch.

Another epigram also seemed applicable. It was simple and to the point, and would end up the most remembered words Waite Phillips ever uttered: "The only things we keep permanently are those we give away."

CHAPTER THIRTY - ONE

PERMANENT CHANGE

On January 21, 1939 — a bright Sunday in
Oklahoma — Waite and Genevieve Phillips said good-bye to
their Villa Philbrook. They left behind the mansion that had
been their family's home for less than twelve years, and moved
into a lofty apartment in the eighteen-story Mayo Hotel in downtown Tulsa.

Opened in 1925 by brothers John D. and Cass Mayo, the luxury hotel with 601 rooms at Fifth Street and Cheyenne Avenue
survived the depression and remained a favorite of the oil crowd
and many others. Tulsa's social elite liked the ballroom chandeliers, marble stairs, brass fixtures, and fine furnishings. They
flocked to the hotel for dining and fancy parties.

Governors held court there, J. Paul Getty's favorite suite was
Room 816, and anyone who even smacked of celebrity stayed at
the Mayo when in town. The guest list included Will Rogers,
Charlie Chaplin, Katharine Hepburn, W. C. Fields, Wallace
Beery, Hedda Hopper, Eddie Cantor, Norma Shearer, Babe Ruth,
Mae West, Eleanor Roosevelt, Guy Lombardo, Gary Cooper,
Charles Lindbergh, Jack Dempsey, and Conrad Hilton. Even
Edna Ferber, the prize-winning novelist who had upset Waite so
much when she wrote about his wealth, liked the Mayo Hotel,
although she referred to the rest of Tulsa as "a cultural Sahara."
When Prohibition finally was repealed, the first bottle of legal

alcohol sold in Oklahoma was from the busy Mayo liquor store. None other than Sally Rand, the sensual entertainer and fan dancer, planned the hotel's 1937 Thanksgiving Day dinner menu.

Without question, the colorful Mayo, with its reputation as one of the finest hotels in the Southwest, was the natural place for the Phillipses to reside while they made arrangements for more permanent living quarters.

Actually, they spent little time at the hotel. That winter, Genevieve took Helen Jane to Miami Beach for an extended trip. Waite spent much of his time through the late spring taking care of matters at Philmont or in California. He had business activities in Los Angeles, San Francisco, and Oakland, and he visited with Elliott at Palo Alto, where he was completing his studies at Stanford. When Waite was in Oklahoma, there was constant activity.

> *On June 9 drove to Bartlesville with E. B. Reeser, Harry Campbell, and Fred Dunn to attend H. V. Foster's funeral.*
>
> *On June 14 tea at Philbrook for Board members of Tulsa Art Association, American Indian Foundation, University of Tulsa and Southwestern Art Association for inspection of completed Philbrook Museum.*
>
> *On June 17 to Ranch with G. E. P.* ~ Waite Phillips Diary, 1939

The Phillipses were flush with pleasure because of the ongoing transformation of Philbrook, due to open as a museum in October. Unfortunately, their joy was short-lived. They had barely settled in at Villa Philmonte that June when they received more bad news. It came with the unexpected arrival at the ranch of Helen Jane, her two sons, Phillips and Peyton, and their hired nurse.

Crying hysterically, Helen Jane related that on June 22, Bill Breckinridge had been driving an automobile which crashed into another vehicle on Route 66 near Chandler, Oklahoma. Bill was not seriously hurt but, according to newspaper reports, his "two women companions were injured." Helen Jane was furious with her husband, and once again wanted her father's help.

June 22, Bill Breckinridge in auto accident with a girl friend. Helen Jane and Mrs. Blyth brought children to the Ranch. Helen Jane insisted that we collaborate with her in getting another divorce from Bill which W. P. agreed to do on pledge from her it would be the last time. W. P. returned to Tulsa June 24 to work out divorce petition — G. E. P. and Helen Jane returning on June 28. ~ WAITE PHILLIPS DIARY, 1939

Helen Jane's divorce action against Breckinridge, handled by Waite's attorney, John Curran, quickly went to district court. On June 30, headlines in the *Tulsa World* blared: "Tulsa Attorney Sued for Divorce," and "Waite Phillips' Daughter Charges Breckinridge with Cruelty." The story related how Helen Jane alleged in her suit that Breckinridge "was an habitue of beer parlors and a confirmed user of intoxicating liquor and that he had broken a pledge to 'reform' after she divorced him January 31, 1938."

The petition also stated that Helen Jane suffered "embarrassing publicity at the time," and that she was forced to flee to her parents' ranch in New Mexico. On July 12, while the matter was under consideration with the court, Genevieve took her daughter back to Philmont. They returned on July 21 in a Phillips Petroleum airplane that had been dispatched to pick them up at Hutchinson, Kansas. On July 24, District Judge Leslie Webb signed the decree and Helen Jane's divorce was granted.

Curious Tulsans devoured the story that appeared the next day in the *Tulsa World*. "In an amended and modified petition Mrs. Breckinridge charged her husband with cruelty," said the newspaper. "Her only witness in the hearing held in the judge's chambers was Miss Constance Kates. The action was uncontested. There was no property settlement or alimony involved. . . . "

Judge Webb's decree stated, "the court finds both plaintiff and defendant are proper and fitting persons to share the custody of the minor children." Besides custody, the judge also ruled that financial support for five-year-old Phillips and two-year-old Peyton was to be divided equally between Helen Jane and Breckinridge.

On July 28, the Phillipses took Helen Jane back to Philmont. Waite wished to get the bad publicity about his daughter's failed marriage behind him. With no explanation, he noted in his diary, that "Otis McClintock and L. E. P. [L. E. Phillips] cooperated splendidly in this matter [the divorce]," which Waite described as "a distressing experience."

During the early summer of 1939, amid the hubbub surrounding Helen Jane's divorce, Waite and Genevieve moved out of their suite at the Mayo Hotel and into a newly finished apartment on the fourteenth floor of the Philcade Building. Called the penthouse, the Phillipses' luxurious apartment had 4,255 square feet of space, more than enough for three large bedrooms, five baths, formal dining room and kitchen, library, solarium, servants' quarters, and a conference room.

Many of the furnishings and fixtures for the penthouse came from Villa Philbrook. There were marble fireplaces and oak-paneled walls. One guest room was decorated with a nautical flair complete with portholes and bunk beds for visiting grandsons. The two roof terraces — ideal for cocktail parties or energetic little boys on tricycles — offered the Phillipses and their guests a commanding view of Tulsa whenever they were in town.

Sept. 1st to 14th on Ranch with G. E. P., Elliott and Helen Jane and children.

Sept. 28th left for New York with G. E. P., Helen Jane, Elliott,

Otis and Gladys McClintock. Stopped at Plaza Hotel, Henry
Lockhart and Tom Girdler called. Attended Century of Progress
Exposition, visited Metropolitan Museum and the American
Museum of Natural History.

Oct. 8 to Washington with G. E. P. and Elliott — Helen Jane
remained in New York with friends. Visited Congress, through
courtesy of Congressman W. E. Disney and returned to New York
Oct. 10. Visited Wall Street district with Elliott — Stock
Exchange — Auerbach, Pollak and Richardson's office and Chase
Manhattan Bank. Elliott left for Tulsa Oct. 11 and W. P. went to
Boston for some isolated rest and educational purposes. Stopped at
Copley-Plaza Hotel. G. E. P. and Helen Jane remained in New
York until Oct. 19, then G. E. P. went to Boston to join W. P.
and Helen Jane to Tulsa. ~ WAITE PHILLIPS DIARY, 1939

Waite and Genevieve were not in Tulsa for the formal opening
of Philbrook Art Center that autumn. Waite was still very much
involved with what he described in his diary as "educational purposes." In fact, what that meant was Waite's enrollment in formal
instruction at the school founded by best-selling author Dale
Carnegie. A Missouri native who had failed at most jobs he tried,
Carnegie published *How To Win Friends and Influence People* in
1936. The book went on to win the Pulitzer Prize and to win
millions of converts interested in self-improvement and a positive
lifestyle. Among those sold on Carnegie's concept was Waite
Phillips.

While Waite diligently pursued his course of study with
Carnegie in Boston, the rest of the nation learned more about the
Phillips family's tremendous gift to the city of Tulsa. On October
26, 1939, the doors to what first was called the Philbrook Art
Center were opened to the public. Oklahoma Governor Leon
Phillips and a distinguished company of guests were on hand for
the celebration.

Just days before the formal opening ceremony, a headline in

the *Kansas City Star* had heralded the big event — "Waite Phillips' Dream Home Becomes Tulsa's Ideal Art Center." The writer, E. B. Garnett, wrote in glowing terms of Waite and his gift of the Phillips mansion to the people of Tulsa.

"Today, from the young state of Oklahoma, comes the drama of a man who wrested a huge fortune from the earth," wrote Garnett. "But Waite Phillips is not one to let it go back to the earth, fading like a dream. He has given one of the most costly and sumptuous mansions in all the Southwest — his palatial Tulsa home, Philbrook, to this city, where he has lived since striking his great fortune in oil some twenty years ago.

"When the announcement of this munificent gift came last year, those who knew the story of Waite Phillips, the oil man who retired (temporarily) in 1926 with a fortune of 40 million dollars, may not have been greatly surprised. For Tulsa and the Southwest in the last decade had been recipients of other generosities totaling more than a million dollars, from the philanthropic Mr. Phillips."

Formal opening of Philbrook Museum on Oct. 26. We were in Boston, Mass. Nov. 2, G. E. P. left Boston for Tulsa — W. P. remaining to complete his studies. On Nov. 24 G. E. P., Elliott, Helen Jane and children went to Ranch for Thanksgiving and W. P. arrived there from Boston to surprise them on Thanksgiving Day. Came home from Ranch with G. E. P. on Dec. 7. Dinner dance at Southern Hills Country Club honoring Barbara Riley on Dec. 11. ~ WAITE PHILLIPS DIARY, 1939

Miss Barbara Riley, the lovely honorée at Southern Hills, was the young lady of Elliott Phillips' dreams. The daughter of Mr. and Mrs. Sheldon Riley of Los Angeles, Barbara was charming and gracious and met with the approval of Waite and Genevieve. Now that Chope, who would turn twenty-two years old in January 1940, was out of school and becoming serious about a relationship with Barbara, Waite decided it was time for his only son to become an oilman.

As the 1930s drew to a close, Waite established Hawkeye Oil Company for Elliott's benefit. Waite purchased oil properties near Winfield, Kansas, in which he carried one-third interest for Otis McClintock and one-sixth interest for Elliott. On January 2, 1940, Waite started the new decade by taking Elliott to Kansas to look over Hawkeye Oil Company's new properties.

Waite, due to turn fifty-seven years old on January 19, was feeling much better about the family's general state of affairs in 1940. Much of his satisfaction with life was because Waite believed Elliott, busy with Hawkeye Oil business in Kansas, was committed to becoming an oilman and had chosen a suitable young woman as his partner. If only Helen Jane could get her troubled life in order, Waite knew he would be satisfied.

Spending more time in Los Angeles, he purchased residential property in the fashionable Bel Air addition and began to shop around for an architect. That spring, he went back to the ranch in New Mexico, where the upcoming summer season meant more troops of Boy Scouts would appear at the developing Philturn facilities.

Upon arriving at Ranch, Bob Hefner was there by invitation of Helen Jane. Much to our surprise she announced, a few days later, that she had promised to marry him. . . . We both cautioned her not to be hasty about such important matters but finally gave approval. ~ WAITE PHILLIPS DIARY, 1940

Robert A. Hefner, Jr., Helen Jane's fiancé, was the son of Robert A. Hefner, a wealthy oilman and respected jurist with a long list of achievements to his credit. Besides his oil dealings, the elder Hefner had served as mayor of Ardmore, Oklahoma, for six years, followed by a nine-year stint as a justice of the Oklahoma Supreme Court. A friend of Waite's for many years, Judge Hefner voluntarily had retired from the bench in 1933 to resume the practice of law. In 1939, he was elected mayor of Oklahoma City, a post he would hold until 1947, when he returned to the oil business with his sons, Robert, Jr., and William.

Young Bob Hefner had known Helen Jane for many years. In their younger days, they had dated, although nothing serious developed. Helen Jane always had thought well of Bob, who had graduated with honors from Culver Military Academy and cum laude from Stanford, the same schools that Elliott Phillips later attended. Blessed with his father's sharp legal mind, Bob attended the Harvard University School of Law and was ranked at the top in his class when he earned his law degree at the University of Oklahoma in 1930.

A versatile young man who earned athletic letters in boxing, basketball, and golf at Stanford, Hefner also sang in the university chorus and was an award-winning violinist who played with the San Francisco Symphony from 1924 to 1928. Divorced since late 1939 from Louise Gunter, Hefner was the father of a five-year-old son, Robert A. Hefner III. The boy's godparents were Elliott and Minnewa Roosevelt, son and daughter-in-law of President Franklin Roosevelt.

In early May 1940, Genevieve, Helen Jane, and Bob Hefner departed Philmont Ranch, leaving Waite alone for a few days to ruminate about his future son-in-law and the Phillipses' plans to move to southern California.

Dr. West and A. A. Schuck arrived at Ranch May 14 for inspection of Philturn Headquarters Unit — were guests of W. P. until night of May 16. Roland E. Coate, architect from L. A., also visited on Ranch after having spent a couple of days in Tulsa conferring with G. E. P. about plans for house to be built in California.
~ WAITE PHILLIPS DIARY, 1940

That summer, after he dutifully attended the Republican

National Convention in Philadelphia and inspected the Hawkeye properties at Winfield with Elliott, Waite returned to Philmont for more conferences with the top brass of the Boy Scouts of America.

On July 16, at six o'clock in the evening, Waite and Genevieve watched as Helen Jane married Robert A. Hefner, Jr., on the patio at Villa Philmonte. It was thirty-eight years to the day since Waite's twin brother, Wiate, had died in Spokane. As always, Waite's mind turned to his long dead brother on that day, but he also was absorbed in the moment and the fact that his daughter appeared at last to be headed for happiness.

The villa and grounds were in splendid order for the big event. Guests in attendance included the groom's parents and brother, several members of the L. E. Phillips family, Otis and Gladys McClintock, John E. Curran and his wife, and Barbara Riley.

Immediately after the brief ceremony, Helen Jane and Bob left for California and a honeymoon trip to Hawaii. They sailed to the island of Oahu aboard the SS *Lurline,* staying in the ship's best cabin, which Waite had reserved for them secretly. After a brief stay in the islands, the newlyweds, accompanied by Helen Jane's two sons, returned to Evansville, Indiana, where Bob represented several large oil firms and had built a large home.

Many of the wedding guests stayed at Philmont for a few days. On July 18, Waite and Genevieve hosted a dinner party in honor of Judge and Mrs. Hefner's wedding anniversary and Barbara Riley's birthday. During the dinner that evening, Elliott and Barbara announced their engagement.

Throughout the rest of the summer and into the autumn of 1940, the Phillipses reviewed plans for their proposed residence in the fashionable hillside community of Bel Air, while they entertained family and dignitaries at their Tulsa penthouse and at Villa Philmonte. Waite and Genevieve also visited Elliott at the Hawkeye properties near Winfield, Kansas, and in late October, they arrived in Evansville to spend time with Helen Jane and Bob Hefner.

Shortly before this [visit to Evansville], W. P. learned through G. E. P., much to his surprise, that Helen Jane and Bob Hefner were not compatible with each other. To help correct, if possible, this situation was the object of this trip. W. P. pledged his son-in-law same consideration as if he were son. Left Evansville Nov. 1 for Tulsa, G. E. P. returned by train. Made trip to Oklahoma City for conference with Judge Hefner on Nov. 7.

On Nov. 13 had conference and lunch with Judge and Mrs. Hefner — they having just returned from Evansville. Helen Jane arrived for short visit Nov. 14, returning on Nov. 24. -
WAITE PHILLIPS DIARY, 1940

In December, Waite journeyed in a special railcar to Washington, D.C., as chairman of a delegation of Tulsa business leaders interested in securing a bomber airplane plant in the city. Back home for the Christmas holidays, Waite and Genevieve welcomed Helen Jane, Bob, and their two grandsons. Elliott came down from Kansas, but the day after Christmas he left for Los Angeles to get ready for his fast-approaching marriage to Barbara Riley. Bob Hefner went with him.

For the time being, at least, it looked to Waite as though Helen Jane and Bob had worked out their differences. This impression, coupled with Elliott's upcoming wedding, no doubt led Waite to believe his family was in harmony.

But unknown to Waite, trouble was brewing again, not only for the Phillips family, but for the entire nation. In the early 1940s, while the entire world once again erupted into open warfare, the children of Waite and Genevieve flexed their wings and attempted to come to terms with their own lives. The outcome was not always harmonious. Waite had raised a daughter and son who could be every bit as stubborn as their father.

And even Waite had to admit that first and foremost, no matter whom they married or what they did, his children — for better or for worse — would be his own forever.

CHAPTER THIRTY-TWO

LOVE AND WAR

On January 4, 1941, Waite and Genevieve left for Los Angeles to attend their son's wedding. Bob Hefner was already there, helping an excited Chope prepare for the big event. Helen Jane did not make an appearance. She stayed in Tulsa, where she was inexplicably bedridden or, as Waite put it, out of commission "because of her serious illness" — his euphemism for suffering from consumption of too much alcohol.

In Los Angeles, all the male guests flocked to a big bachelor-dinner bash that Waite threw for Elliott at the Town House, where the Phillipses also paid for the rooms for the entire wedding party. There were several out-of-town guests in attendance, including the L. E. Phillips family and the McClintocks.

The wedding ceremony took place at 8:30 p.m. on January 9 at Wilshire Methodist Church. Chope's first cousin L. E. Phillips, Jr., was his best man. "Mac" McClintock and several of Elliott's school pals served as ushers. After the vows were repeated, the Rileys hosted a reception at their residence. The following day, Elliott and Barbara sailed aboard the SS *Lurline* for Honolulu.

Within only a couple of months following Elliott's wedding, Waite realized that serious problems still plagued Helen Jane in her marriage with Bob Hefner. In late March, still not ready to give up on the couple, Waite consulted with his daughter and later with Bob about their troubled relationship.

April 6 left Los Angeles for Ranch with G. E. P., Barbara and
Elliott, Helen Jane, Mrs. Blyth and children. Bob Hefner came to
the Ranch from Evansville and plans were laid for Bob and
Elliott to participate in the handling of our estates — Bob to
handle Tulsa affairs and Elliott the ranch. All these to be put into
a Family Corporation — after which Bob and Helen Jane
returned to Evansville and Elliott and Barbara to Winfield.

On April 16 held annual meeting of Hawkeye Oil Company at
which time completed details in connection with sale of properties
to Leader Oil Co. and Zephyr Drilling Co., and R. Otis
McClintock, as Elliott decided to quit oil business in favor of
ranch life. This with Helen Jane's disagreement with Bob canceled
the Family Corporation plan. ~ WAITE PHILLIPS DIARY, 1941

By that May, Elliott and Barbara had moved from Winfield to
New Mexico. They took up residence in the Webster Cottage at
Philmont Ranch. About the same time, Helen Jane left Bob
Hefner in Indiana and took her two sons to live in Florida. Waite
was devastated again. Not only was he about to lose a son-in-law
whom he had trusted with some of his most important personal
affairs, but Waite's own son was turning his back on the oil patch
in favor of a cattleman's life. To Waite Phillips, all of that was
beyond comprehension.

In mid-June, Waite was busily contemplating the sale of the
rest of Philmont Ranch. A diary entry from Waite that month
noted, "Decided to sell [the ranch] on account of lack of cooperation of Helen Jane and Elliott."

Soon, more and more officials from the Boy Scouts of
America began to show up at Philmont, all invited by Waite, who
found that he had an ally in his effort to rid himself of Philmont
— his daughter-in-law, Barbara Riley Phillips. When Barbara's
parents came out from Los Angeles to visit Barbara and Elliott at
the Webster Cottage, Waite and Genevieve, with Helen Jane,
took them on an outing at Rayado Lodge.

*While there [Rayado Lodge] Helen Jane disclosed her plan of
returning to Florida to complete her plans for divorcing Bob
Hefner. We also learned through Helen Jane that Mrs. Riley and
Barbara were dissatisfied with ranch life. With these two problems, W. P. decided to put into effect a long time contemplated
plan of giving the central improved portion of Philmont Ranch to
the Boy Scouts of America with Philtower Building as an endowment.*

*Made arrangements for conference with Boy Scout officials in St.
Louis on Oct. 4. Conference with Walter Head, James E. West,
and Arthur Schuck, was held in Walter Head's office, at which
time proposal for gift to Boy Scouts of America of Philmont-
Philtower properties was presented.*

*Left St. Louis for Ranch on the 5th — had Ed Phillips out to
spend a few days. G. E. P. had accompanied W. P. to St. Louis
Oct. 4, then on to New York to meet Helen Jane who was coming
from Florida.* ~ WAITE PHILLIPS DIARY, 1941

Instead of meeting her mother in New York, however, Helen
Jane sent her a wire to advise that she once again had married Bill
Breckinridge. In a state of shock, Genevieve managed to tele-
phone Waite at Philmont. He also found the news of Helen Jane's
reconciliation with Breckinridge astonishing. He met Genevieve
in Kansas City, where they received comfort from old friend Ruth
Maher and Genevieve's sister, Helen, who returned with them to
Tulsa for a short stay.

Although he remained baffled by his daughter's seemingly self-
destructive relationship with Bill Breckinridge, Waite persevered
with his plans to turn over his major real estate properties to the
Boy Scouts and to get on with his own life. He was determined
that no family disturbances would darken his spirit.

Even the entry of the United States into the Second World
War did not stop Waite's negotiations with the Boy Scouts.

Meetings with Scout officials and a constant flurry of detailed correspondence outlining all the details of Waite's gift to the BSA continued until immediately after the Japanese sneak attack at Pearl Harbor on December 7, 1941. War or no war, for Waite Phillips, it was business as usual.

Dec. 6, Frank Phillips came down — took him out to Philbrook and had a few guests, the John Mayos and McClintocks, to dinner at apartment and attended a basketball game between Phillips 66 and Twentieth Century Fox afterwards. The night before Pearl Harbor. World War No. 2 declared on Dec. 11, 1941. The Phillips family group had 15 young men in this conflict and all returned — Frank 2, L. E. 2, Ed 1, W. P. 2, Nell 4, Fred 2, and Lura 2.

Dec. 13 went to St. Louis with Ed Gockel for conference with Walter Head re: Scout gift. Meeting with Boy Scout Executive Board held on Dec. 18 and they authorized Arthur Schuck to telephone that gift was accepted. Gave Jenkin Lloyd Jones and Lee Erhard news release pertaining to gift.

Dec. 20 dinner at apartment for Philbrook officials to announce plans for donating Beacon Building as endowment to Philbrook. Those attending — Rush Greenslade, Dr. Weatherby, Elmer Pollock, Otis McClintock, Dr. Pontius and John Curran.

Dec. 30 signed Quit Claim Deeds to Boy Scouts of America for 91,538 acres of Philmont Ranch and the Philtower Building. Made proposal to Mrs. Herbert Hoover to donate substantial sum if Girl Scouts and Campfire Girls would merge but could not get them to do so.

Upon completion of gifts to Boy Scouts of Philtower-Philmont with building equipment, ranch, livestock, machinery, etc. W. P. also released Moses and Cartwright to their service. He also recommended Mr. Schuck as liaison man, in New York office, to represent properties. W. P. agreed to actively manage them for a while . . . A continued program to sell balance of Philmont followed. Elliott was given full charge of acreage north of Cimarron and Leo Gates south of there. ~ WAITE PHILLIPS DIARY, 1941

The proposal for donating an even larger portion of his ranch, which Waite had initially made to the Boy Scouts in October 1941, included the 91,538 acres that Waite noted in his diary. In addition to the vast tracts of rugged mountain country and Villa Philmonte, Waite's Christmas present to the Scouts included all the other ranch buildings, facilities, livestock, and equipment. With Waite's previous gift of 35,857 acres for the Philturn camp, the donation of land alone totaled 127,395 acres.

Beyond all those gifts, the twenty-three-story Philtower Building, included as a permanent endowment, was netting more than $130,000 in annual office rentals. The total value of Waite's contribution to the Boy Scouts came to a staggering $5 million.

The headlines in the *Tulsa Tribune* of December 19 declared, "$5,000,000 Properties Stay Taxable" and "Tulsa Cherishes Generous Gifts From Philanthropist." The accompanying stories were glowing salutes to the Phillips family. "It has long been a habit of Waite Phillips to name his properties like the ships of a line — Philtower, Philcade, Philmont, Philbrook, Philturn," reported the *Tribune.* "By neat coincidence, Tulsans also know Mr. and Mrs. Phillips as the oil capital's greatest philanthropists."

The story went on to list some of the Phillipses' gifts to the community and nation, including Tulsa Children's Home, 1928; Waite Phillips Petroleum Engineering Building at the University of Tulsa, 1929, and other gifts totaling more than $700,00 during a period of years to the university; Wiate Phillips Memorial Clinic at St. John Hospital, 1936; Junior League Building, 1935; Community Fund Building, 1935; Philturn Camp, 1938; and Philbrook Art Center, 1938.

Waite, in confirming his gift for the newspaper, told the

reporter that in view of the current conditions, "I am impressed with the responsibility of this generation to adequately train its youth — physically, mentally and morally — to meet the problems they must face in the future.

"In my opinion, there is nothing more valuable to this generation than the enlargement of the scouting program, which develops self-reliance and dependability. It always has been my belief that the best contribution to that kind of development is by living close to nature and through learning to live in the great out-of-doors."

Just as he had when he donated the initial acreage used for Philturn, Waite placed no restrictions on the Boy Scouts except to ask that his gifts be used "for the advancement and development of the program of Scouting." Waite had only a couple of favors for the BSA officials concerning the land near Cimarron that they would christen Philmont Scout Ranch.

"I do not want to make any demand upon the Boy Scouts of America, but for twenty consecutive years, this Ranch has been part of my life," Waite had told the officials. "My son grew to manhood there. I would like to reserve for myself and members of my family the right to walk or ride over this property."

Other than that, Waite asked only that his favorite horse, Gus, more than twenty years old, be turned out on the ranch never to be ridden, to "live out his life in fields white with clover."

When the officials heard his simple requests, they quickly agreed. The deal was done. Once again, Waite Phillips had managed to follow his conscience and conclude what may have been the most important transaction of his life.

V
BRIGHT
LANDS WEST

Overleaf: The Phillips home in Bel Air, California, in the 1950s. Above, Genevieve, Chope's wife, Virginia, and Waite, on an Alaskan cruise in 1949. Right, the penthouse terrace, Philcade Building, 1944. From left to right are Waite, his grandson Phillips Breckinridge, Chope, on leave from the army, Helen Jane, Genevieve. Peyton Breckinridge stands in front of Helen Jane. Facing page, above, Waite and Genevieve celebrating Genevieve's birthday at a Los Angeles restaurant in 1950. Below, Waite with actress Yvonne DeCarlo and one of her costars at Waite's ranch north of Malibu, California, 1947.

CHAPTER THIRTY-THREE

LOOSE ENDS

In 1942, the war intensified in Europe and in the Pacific theater, where Japanese troops advanced on Manila. On American soil, Waite Phillips chugged along like the "Chattanooga Choo Choo," the Number One tune on the hit parade that first week of the year. Although he had one foot well out the door and was almost ready to make the leap westward to California, it would take Waite three more years to complete his move to the West Coast. Plenty of unfinished business awaited.

To that end, Waite began the new year with another major public announcement, at a January 3 luncheon meeting of the Philbrook trustees. After the dishes were cleared at the downtown Tulsa Club, Waite outlined his plan for giving the Beacon Building, located a few blocks away at Fourth Street and Boulder Avenue, as a permanent endowment for Philbrook Art Center. Besides bestowing the nine-story, half-million-dollar office building to Southwestern Art Association, Waite also announced that he would erase the 1941 operating deficit for Philbrook — approximately eighteen thousand dollars — and would pay all pending ad valorem taxes on the Beacon Building before transferring its ownership.

It was Waite's "abhorrence of waste," his belief that "property should be put to the most useful purpose," and his desire to aid Tulsa's cultural development that prompted his gift of the Beacon

Building. Waite was determined that Edna Ferber and other easterners no longer would refer to the city as a "cultural Sahara."

"I have developed a strong sense of responsibility for the ownership of property," Waite said in the January 4 edition of the *Tulsa World*, "and that same sense of responsibility goes with giving it away. My whole feeling is this: that the proper use of property is putting it to the most useful purpose, the most beneficial purpose possible. A vacant lot always worries me, whether I see it in Tulsa, Chicago, New York or Los Angeles. I always wonder who owns it, why they've neglected it and I'm always sorry to see its lack of use.

"I have a horror of waste. Now, what is the most useful purpose property can be put to? When I gave Philbrook to Tulsa as an art museum, I knew then it would require an endowment someday. But I believed then, just as I do now, that it would be much better for the public if the endowment came three years later than at that time. By now the art museum has challenged the public, it has taken a lot of work and effort to put it where it is today, it has gone through all the growing pains any progressive project or business must go through, and it has created a good deal of community interest. Now it's endowed."

One week later, a feature story in the *Tulsa World* revealed that the $100,000 endowment fund Waite had established for St. John Hospital in 1938 resulted in the development of a charity ward and one of the most modern X-ray clinics in the Southwest. Waite had made the gift as a memorial for his twin brother, Wiate.

To illustrate the 1942 newspaper story, the editors used a photograph of the X-ray unit at St. John and, for the first time ever, published the photo portraits of young Waite and Wiate taken in 1900 when they had worked as Western Union messenger boys in Salt Lake City. Waite, who continued to send money every year of his life to the good nuns at Sacred Heart Hospital in Spokane where his brother had died in 1902, also had high praise for the

Catholic sisters operating St. John Hospital.

"I've got a wholesome respect for these women and a high regard for them," said Waite in the January 11 *Tulsa World* story, "They work long and faithfully, devoting their lives to the sick and suffering, doing a tremendous service to the community. I'm sure their service is appreciated, but in this busy world of business today too many people are apt to forget them until they are sick. They deserve our appreciation at all times."

That winter, Waite huddled in Tulsa with Boy Scout officials, traveled to Kansas to look over oil properties, and visited Philmont in New Mexico. On February 1, he and Genevieve received good news from an excited Chope in Los Angeles, where Barbara had given birth to a healthy baby girl named Wendy Lee Phillips.

Barbara had been living at her parents' home in Los Angeles for the past two months, waiting to deliver her child. Chope spent most of January with his wife, and he was anxious to get mother and newborn daughter back to New Mexico. Barbara, who was never fond of ranch life, was in no hurry to leave.

After a lengthy conference and luncheon at the Tulsa Club with his friend Dale Carnegie, Waite prepared for the winter's vacation in California. On February 5, he and Genevieve departed for Los Angeles, anxious to see their first granddaughter. While there, the Phillipses also helped see Elliott through an appendectomy performed on February 16 at St. Vincent's Hospital. They dined at the Will Rogers ranch with Betty Blake Rogers and Irvin S. Cobb, the popular humorist who, late in life, had become known as an actor and writer for motion pictures.

Chope, tough as a cowboy boot, quickly recuperated and by February 28, he left Los Angeles with his parents for the ranch. Barbara and baby Wendy Lee remained behind.

March 3 had dinner at Villa Philmonte for various Boy Scout officials . . . March 5 Ed Vail and Mr. and Mrs. Jimmie Rogers [Will Rogers' son] arrived to inspect Ranch with idea of purchas-

ing a part of remaining acreage. Returned to Tulsa March 8 with G. E. P. On March 14 had cocktail party at apartment followed by buffet dinner at Tulsa Club for sixty guests, including the McClintocks before they left for Washington, D.C. where Otis was to take up his duties as Liaison Officer between War Production Board, Office of Petroleum Coordinator and Reconstruction Finance Corp. March 21 Elliott came to Tulsa with view of getting into some branch of the Army. Tried the Remount Service at El Reno and the Calvary at Ft. Riley as well as various other branches but was unsuccessful, so he decided to wait until he was drafted. ~ WAITE PHILLIPS DIARY, 1942*

On March 30, Waite and Genevieve observed their thirty-third wedding anniversary with a dinner party at their Philcade Penthouse. Some of their good friends, including Mrs. George Bole, William W. and Allene Michaels, and L. E. and Nora Phillips were there, along with Elliott. Michaels, Waite's stockbroker for many years, left his brokerage firm in 1942 to join First National Bank and Trust, where he stayed for twenty-six years. After the anniversary party, Waite took Michaels and the others to the Coliseum for a performance of the Ice Capades.

On April 5, while the Japanese resumed major attacks at Bataan and U. S. planes bombarded the enemy fleet off Burma, the Phillipses and their son drove out Route 66 toward the ranch in New Mexico. Ten days later, everyone was pleased when Barbara returned from Los Angeles with little Wendy. But within only a week or so, Barbara's mother also returned to the ranch. In his diary, Waite wrote, "She [Mrs. Riley] told us at Villa Philmonte of her disapproval of Elliott and next day Barbara left for Albuquerque, without notice to Elliott, to join her mother and return to Los Angeles."

Waite and Elliott were faced with the chore of moving out of the Big House and the Webster Cottage to make room for the Boy Scouts. They reestablished their ranch organization, moving the office to Rayado, where Leo Gates acted as superintendent. Waite purchased the the old Nairn place for himself and Genevieve, and the Bough house in nearby Cimarron for Elliott. Back in Tulsa, workers were preparing for the Boy Scouts to move their headquarters to the Philtower. By late April, Waite's office was moved from Suite 2104 in the Philtower across the street to Suite 210 in the Philcade.

> *Left on May 11 for ranch with G. E. P. Spent most of May and June repairing Nairn place and Bough house and moving Ranch office to Rayado. Moved from Villa Philmonte to Nairn place on June 15 and returned to Tulsa June 27 — G. E. P. and Elliott to Tulsa on June 11 to attend wedding of Allister Campbell and Connie Kates, returning to Ranch after the wedding on June 13.*

> *Had final settlement with Boy Scouts of America covering operation of Ranch properties and Philtower Building from Jan. 1 to May 1, 1942 — also gave them Bill of Sale covering gift of livestock, equipment, furniture, furnishings, etc. of Villa Philmonte and mountain lodges.*

> *Drove to Bartlesville with G. E. P. to celebrate July 4 with L. E. Phillips family. On July 15 received Silver Beaver award from local Boy Scout Council. . . . Left Tulsa on July 16 [the fortieth anniversary of Wiate's death] with G. E. P. for Ranch and then on to San Francisco at Mark Hopkins Hotel.* ~ WAITE PHILLIPS DIARY, 1942

Later that summer, Barbara once again went to New Mexico, where Chope worked cattle and waited to go off to war. In his journal from that period, Waite noted, "Barbara very reluctant to return to Elliott and their home in Cimarron but by persuasion and letters from W. P. she finally consented to come in August with Wendy Lee." Waite was still certain that once he disposed of more of the ranchlands, Elliott would forsake the cattle business and turn to some other endeavor. When that finally happened, Waite believed his son's marriage would be saved.

On September 11, Kate Smith, the popular singer identified by her theme song, "When the Moon Comes over the Mountain," paid a special tribute to Waite during her radio broadcast. Waite stashed a transcript of her broadcast in his files. "Givers of good gifts deserve our praise," Miss Smith told her listeners, "and so today our 'One Dozen Roses Department' singles out Mr. Waite Phillips, oil millionaire of Tulsa, Oklahoma, who has just turned over Philmont, his ranch estate of 127,000 acres, to the Boy Scouts of America! The mountain home lies in the loveliest country of New Mexico . . . and with this gift, Mr. Phillips has also included his Tulsa office building whose income pays the bills for the huge ranch estate. That's a wonderful gift. It means that any Boy Scout in the country can vacation at Philmont for $1.50 a week, or $2.25, if he doesn't want to supply his own food!

"For that nominal sum, he gets a bed under the stars and all the horseback riding, hiking, gold prospecting, and exploring he wants. He also gets lessons in first aid, wood lore, horsemanship, and general scout work. Yes, it's a boy's idea of heaven and it's not a fancy dude ranch, either. Philmont's stock of sheep and cattle is constantly being increased in the hope that some day the camp will pay for itself. . . . It gives me a glow to think of all the boys who will ride along the rocky trails at sunrise. If Mr. Phillips, generous donor of Philmont, has the privilege of witnessing their faces as they see the spot for the first time, I know he must feel well repaid for the magnificent gifts he's given the boys of America."

Indeed, Waite felt very well repaid for his major contribution to the Boy Scouts, but he also felt that he had no time to gloat or brood about the past. A world war was raging, there were still business deals to be concluded, property to be purchased and sold, and a family to oversee.

Throughout the autumn and winter of 1942, Waite worked intensely as head of a massive Community and War Fund Drive with other Tulsa leaders such as John Mabee, Bill Skelly, Horace Barnard, and Ed Moore, who was elected to the United States Senate that November. During those hectic months, Waite also went back and forth among Tulsa, Cimarron, and Los Angeles to negotiate the sale of the rest of his New Mexican ranch property.

Sept. 30 to Oct. 11 in Los Angeles at Town House — had various conferences with G. E. Kinsey and R. E. Fuller in regard to trade on ranch properties — inspected apartment houses that Kinsey wanted to put in on deal — decided not to accept properties and made Kinsey cash price — negotiations finally were terminated with no trade. . . . Oct. 11 left Los Angeles with G. E. P. and Emily [stenographer Emily Bramlette] on train for Ranch, arriving Raton Oct.12, and further work . . . on the Kinsey Ranch trade, returned to Tulsa Oct. 26.

About Oct. 15th to 20th while W. P. and G. E. P. were on ranch, at Nairn place, but while Elliott was in Ponil country with cattle work, Barbara again left without notice to join her mother in Denver and returned to Los Angeles. ~ WAITE PHILLIPS DIARY, 1942

Still not ready to concede that his son's marriage was kaput even though Barbara had left Elliott once again, Waite searched for a solution to the problem of having a daughter-in-law who wanted no part of life on a cattle ranch. Waite also completed the details of the management of the Philmont and Philtower properties with the Boy Scout officials and, in early December, signed the final contract selling his Philcade Building in Tulsa to the Stanolind Building Corporation.

By the end of the first week of 1943, Waite and Genevieve were at the Nairn place with a few friends to mark Elliott's twenty-fifth birthday on January 11. Only two days later, Waite received word that his older sister, Jennie Coan, wife of the man whom Waite once had clerked for when he was a youth, had died in Des Moines.

Just two days later, Waite was still saddened by his sister's death when he accompanied Elliott to Santa Fe, where he was given a final physical examination prior to his enlistment. Tired of waiting to be drafted, Chope had decided to cut to the chase and join in the fray. Waite was back in Tulsa, sick in bed with the flu, by the time his sixtieth birthday came on January 19. A few days later, Elliott reported to Fort Bliss, at El Paso, Texas, for duty as a private in the U.S. Army.

Just weeks after Chope marched off to basic training, Waite — in yet another attempt to contribute to the war effort from the home front — shipped his Malamute dog, Yukon, to Camp Rimini at Helena, Montana, to serve in the army's canine corps. Waite also devoted a great deal of his time to the American Red Cross fund-raising drive, while he continued conferences and inspections trips at Philmont and traded eighteen hundred shares of First National Bank stock for some Wilshire-Burnside property in Los Angeles.

The Phillipses quietly observed their thirty-fourth wedding anniversary that March with a few of their friends at the penthouse. As always, Waite's mind was going a mile a minute. He had to formulate a new sale program for the remaining ranch property, and see to it that his offices were moved from the recently sold Philcade back to the Philtower.

On April 13, Waite and Genevieve drove to Hot Springs, Arkansas, for a brief rest, interrupted a couple of days later when Otis McClintock phoned to tell them of the death of Henry Lockhart, a former business associate of Waite's in the 1920s. The next day, the Phillipses left to visit Elliott. When they arrived at his army camp in Texas, they learned that Chope's marriage to Barbara was just about to end.

On 16th ended vacation abruptly to go to Wichita Falls to see Elliott about his family affairs. Elliott urged Barbara to join him but she refused and wrote about her interest in another man. Therefore he decided to seek a divorce. W. P. and G. E. P. then went on to Ranch. On Ranch 20th to 22nd with Bob Fuller in connection with sale of property to McDaniel & Sons. Returned to Tulsa on 23rd.

Elliott came to Tulsa from Sheppard Field on March 29 for a three day furlough for conference re: divorce plans . . . it [divorce] was secured in Taos, New Mexico shortly after that time.

~ WAITE PHILLIPS DIARY, 1943

Waite was disappointed that his son's marriage had failed. Turning to his work, he pushed ahead with the sale of the ranch property in New Mexico, and continued to cut his ties to the business community in Oklahoma.

In early May, after visiting with Frank and L. E. in Bartlesville, Waite was driving back to Tulsa when he encountered rising floodwaters in the bottoms of Bird Creek, just east of Skiatook. He abandoned his automobile when water rushed inside over the seats. He waded through waist-deep murky water to a farmhouse, where he spent the night, and the next day finally returned home. The floodwaters remained high for some time. Later that month, Waite took a circuitous route to reach a train for New Mexico, where he closed the deal for the sale of his other ranchland to McDaniel & Sons. A short time later, Waite packed up all his personal belongings at the Nairn place and shipped everything to Tulsa.

That summer of 1943, which Waite spent mostly in Oklahoma, was taken up with the War Chest campaign and visits with L. E. Phillips. He had suffered a series of strokes that left his eyesight greatly impaired and paralyzed his throat and part of the right side of his body. About the same time, Waite sold 4,360 shares of his First National Bank stock to fellow Tulsa businessman John Mabee. By early fall, Otis McClintock had bought the rest of Waite's First National stock, amounting to about five thousand shares.

> *Canceled reservations to leave on 15th [July] for vacation in California on account of Elliott's divorce affairs. July 23, Los Angeles attorneys served divorce papers to Barbara. Left on 27th with G. E. P. for Los Angeles: Spent month of August in Los Angeles with G. E. P. Purchased Arroyo Sequit Ranch.*
> ~ WAITE PHILLIPS DIARY, 1943

Hurt by the breakup of his marriage, Elliott continued with his army training, and by late 1943 reported to Florida, where he entered Officer Candidate School at Miami Beach. A tenacious young man who could be just as immovable as his father, Chope wished to serve his country and then, just as soon as possible, get back to the work he enjoyed best — ranching.

"I loved that woman with all my heart," Chope Phillips said of Barbara Riley many years later when he was in his mid-seventies and still operating a ranch in New Mexico. "But when it came down to having to choose between her and ranching, I had no other way to go."

Besides the wounds he suffered from the divorce, Elliott also was deeply pained by his father's attempts to persuade him to leave the cattle business by selling off and giving away some of the family's best ranchland in New Mexico. As Elliott Phillips said many times in later years, "To say that Philmont means a lot to me is an understatement." Nonetheless, Chope never carried any grudge against his father, and eventually the two of them reconciled their differences over his career choices.

"You have to know that ever since I was a little kid, I never wanted to be anything else but a rancher and stay here on the land," Chope related when he was seventy-six years old. "In that way, I was very much like my mother. She was much more rooted than Dad and I was like that, too. I always knew that my place in this world was out on the land. But my Dad never could understand that about me. He had a real love for the land and for Philmont, but he had no patience when it came to ranching. He really wanted me to be a businessman.

"When Dad gave away that Philmont land to the Boy Scouts I was twenty-three years old, and I truly believe he thought he was doing me a big favor. I suppose he figured that by giving it all away, that would keep me from becoming a rancher. How I wish that I would have inherited this land — not so much the part that he gave to the Scouts — I think what he did for them was fine — but he also sold off a lot of the surrounding ranchland to others at that time and he sold it dirt cheap, he just about gave it away. That's what really got to me. I love this place. I grew up here. When I saw what he had done, it was as though someone reached right into me and tore my heart out."

CHAPTER THIRTY-FOUR

FAREWELL, OKLAHOMA

Waite Phillips welcomed 1944 sick in bed with the flu at his Philcade Penthouse. Within a few days, he rallied enough to meet with Ed Moore and John Mabee, first at Waite's Philtower office and then at Mabee's Okmulgee ranch. Always looking to make political hay, Waite's old friends tried to persuade him to consider a run for the U.S. Senate in the upcoming fall election against Elmer Thomas, the Democratic incumbent.

Waite chose not to pursue political office, however, and watched that November when the Republican nominee, William J. Otjen, went down in defeat like most other GOP challengers in Oklahoma.

A story circulated at the time that Waite was so disappointed at not having received the Republican nomination for the U.S. Senate that he decided to leave Oklahoma and move to California. But that was not the case. For several years prior to their move west, Waite and Genevieve had been spending more of their time in California, looking at homes, buying property, and establishing new contacts. They liked the climate, the lifestyle, and the pleasant surroundings in Beverly Hills, Brentwood, Bel Air, and the plushier neighborhoods of Los Angeles. Besides, Waite was simply ready to move on.

"My father really was a complex person," Chope Phillips said many years later. "He had little patience and he got bored very easily. Also, he was always looking for something new. It seemed to me that he spent every minute of his life putting all this effort into some aspect of his life and work, and then, when that was finished, he went on to something else. He had to keep moving; he hated to stand still."

Certainly Waite was never idle during those hectic times before he and Genevieve made their final move, to California. He continued with his fourth Red Cross War Fund drive, parleyed with bankers and realtors across the country, and kept up with his family. By the spring of 1944, Elliott, a freshly graduated lieutenant, was stationed at the army airfield in Amarillo, Texas. Helen Jane and her two sons lived in Virginia, while Bill Breckinridge served in the army at Fort Riley, Kansas, prior to being shipped overseas to Europe.

Besides his son and daughter, Waite also stayed in constant contact with his older brother L. E., who had suffered yet another stroke on April 10.

L. E. died at 10 a.m. April 16 — drove to Bartlesville but
G. E. P. unable to go as she was sick with flu. Back to Bartlesville
with Fred Phillips for funeral services on 18th. ~ WAITE PHILLIPS
DIARY, 1944

The death of Lee Eldas Phillips hit Waite hard. Always close to Waite, it was L. E. who had joined with Frank to help their younger brother get a start in the business world. Waite had lived with L. E. and Node for a while, and he chose L. E. to be best man at his wedding. In the months following his brother's passing, Waite called on Nora and her grown children, and he worked closely with them and their lawyers to settle L. E.'s estate.

In June, Waite left for Chicago with Bill Skelly to attend the Republican National Convention. Waite conferred with several of his political party's heavyweights at the convention, including Charles Dawes and Alf Landon. He also met with Governor John Bricker of Ohio, who had wanted to run for the presidency but withdrew. On the first ballot he was selected as running mate for the GOP's presidential nominee, Governor Thomas E. Dewey of New York. Bricker made the snide statement, "Truman? I never can remember that name," when asked about the Missourian who became the Democratic vice presidential candidate with perennial favorite President Franklin D. Roosevelt, ultimate winners of the 1944 general election.

July 16, accompanied by G. E. P., went to to Phillips Memorial Building at St. John Hospital as it was 42nd anniversary of twin brother's death — then to Rose Hill Cemetery in memory of Harry Campbell — to Memorial Cemetery east of Bartlesville where L. E. is buried — then a visit with Frank and Jane in their home. ~ WAITE PHILLIPS DIARY, 1944

But there was more on Waite's mind than politics and family duties. He was determined to be California bound as soon as possible. That July, August, and September, he and Genevieve spent most of their time at the Mark Hopkins Hotel in San Francisco, the Del Monte Lodge at Pebble Beach, and one of their favorites, the Town House in Los Angeles.

Waite and Genevieve shopped the real estate market until they found exactly what they wanted. In November, the story hit the newspapers — the Phillipses finally had found a suitable California abode. Waite, who already owned other properties in the Los Angeles area, including ranch acreage and choice real estate in the Beverly Hills business district, settled on a large residential estate in tony Bel Air.

The Phillipses forked over $125,000 to Phyllis and Abe Miller for the residence at 10659 Bellagio Road, with part of the purchase price covered by the transfer of two tracts of real estate on

Saint Cloud and Saint Pierre roads in Bel Air. Willard J. Lewis, a prominent Beverly Hills realtor, represented both parties in the transaction.

An announcement from Coldwell, Banker & Company in Los Angeles, released to the press in early November, revealed more details about Waite's two Beverly Hills properties. According to the report, those large tracts Waite had purchased just prior to buying the Bel Air estate, with the addition of improvements to be made, involved an investment of more than $3 million.

"The property at the north side of Wilshire Boulevard, between Beverly Drive and Rodeo Drive, with frontage of 400 feet on the boulevard and 450 and 250 feet on Beverly and Rodeo Drives, respectively, was bought by Phillips from the Lloyd Corp. Ltd.," reported the *Tulsa Tribune* on November 2, 1944. "At the same time, Phillips bought from George Taylor the southwest corner of Beverly Drive and Dayton Way, adjoining his other purchase at the north, with 150-foot frontage on Dayton Way and 50 feet on Beverly Drive, thus giving him ownership of the entire block with exception of the southeast corner of Rodeo Drive and Dayton Way.

"The area acquired by Phillips is one of the best known and most important in the Wilshire Boulevard section of Beverly Hills. It is in the neighborhood of the Beverly-Wilshire Hotel and large business concerns, and not far from Hollywood and large developments in westerly Los Angeles."

During the last few months of 1944, the Phillipses returned to Tulsa to clean up their business affairs and personal matters. They came back to bid farewell to their many friends and to a community that owed them a debt of gratitude for everything the couple had contributed during several decades.

November 8 gave dinner party at Tulsa Club for Executive Committee of Southwestern Art Association, composed of Fred

Haddock, C. I. Pontius, R. Otis McClintock, Dr. B. B.
Weatherby, Victor C. Hurt, Mrs. Allman Blow, Mrs. Warren D.
Abbott, in order to present proposed gift of Elliott Building, cash
and additional art objects. . . . November 24 attended dinner on
Roof Garden of Tulsa Club in connection with Golden
Anniversary expansion program of University of Tulsa. . . .
Harvey Heller brought movie star, Leo Carrillo, up to office for
visit — Carrillo in Tulsa in connection with Sixth War Loan
Drive.

December 20 talked to Walter Head at St. Louis making
arrangements for conference . . . to discuss Philtower-Philmont
affairs — planned luncheon at Tulsa Club for Boy Scout officials
and some Tulsa citizens. . . . Attended dinner party with G. E. P.
given by the Skellys in our honor. This was large party at
Southern Hills Country Club. W. P. made farewell talk after
dinner. ~ WAITE PHILLIPS DIARY, 1944

Even as he spent his final days in Tulsa, Waite continued to work not just on his personal business but also on projects that affected the community at large. On Christmas Day, Waite made an inspection trip through the North Greenwood Avenue area, a black district that had been the scene of the white mob's wrath and terrible violence during the infamous Tulsa racial conflict of 1921. The day after his tour, Waite summoned several powerful white Tulsans to a luncheon meeting at the Tulsa Club to discuss the welfare of the city's black citizens. At yet another conference he called before the year's end, Waite established what he called the Carver Memorial Fund for the creation of a black community center. He appointed as trustees Johnson Hill, Ralph Talbot, H. B. Dowell, H. A. Heller, Bill Skelly, Harry Clarke, and W. K. Warren. To make sure the project got off to a good start, Waite donated a $100,000 cash gift.

As he prepared to move to his new home in Los Angeles and close out the year, Waite made a final entry in his journal for

1944: "In all my years of business life I never had a mortgage on any property owned by me and I owned approximately 700,000 acres of land in Colorado and New Mexico at one time in the 1920s. Also, millions invested in city properties including Philtower and Philcade and seven homes in Bartlesville, Okmulgee, Tulsa and Los Angeles."

Waite devoted most of New Year's Day 1945 to dictating memos and letters. The Phillipses had only about seven weeks left before the move to Los Angeles. Practically every one of those days was filled with farewell activities, tribute luncheons, and appreciation banquets. Nora Phillips came to the penthouse, and there were fancy spreads at Southern Hills, where Waite was given a life membership. The Johnson Hills, the Fred Phillipses, the R. E. Fullers and F. B. Parriotts and many others gave dinner parties for Waite and Genevieve.

Frank Phillips showed up to say good-bye. But that particular dinner did not conclude on a harmonious note. As sometimes happened throughout their lives, fireworks erupted. The two Phillips brothers, so much alike in so many ways, came to verbal blows.

"I'll mention one more incident of having a serious argument with Frank that could and should have been avoided by me," Waite wrote in his 1958 memorandum which explained the key incidents in his life. "Shortly before we left Tulsa, he [Frank] came to our Philcade apartment for dinner and unfortunately was not in a very good mood and I regret to report as follows.

"His particular complaint that evening was directed toward associates of mine in Tulsa and in some respects about the unworthiness of Tulsa people in general. Therefore, when he made a special example of Otis McClintock I unfortunately asked him how he would like to have one of his associates, such as W. C. Smoot, President of the First National Bank in Bartlesville, referred to in like manner. By that time we both lost our tempers and in consideration of the many generous favors provided by him to me in past years I should not have allowed that acrimonious discussion to continue. The results were that he misunderstood my analysis and thought I was making detrimental remarks about Smoot comparable to those he had made about McClintock."

Loyal to the end to his best friends such as Otis McClintock, Waite also remained steadfast to Frank. Eventually the two bull-headed brothers patched up their differences, just as they had done ever since the days of old in Iowa and later in the oil patch of Oklahoma where they had made their fortunes.

At last, as February came around, final tributes and toasts were held for Genevieve and Waite. There was a dinner party for them on February 17, the day General Douglas MacArthur's troops landed on Corregidor. It was given in the Phillipses' honor at the Mayo Hotel by the John Mayos. On February 19, Otis and Gladys McClintock hosted the last farewell dinner at their home. Those who were there recalled later that tears flowed with the champagne.

That evening was the very last one Waite and Genevieve spent in Oklahoma as official citizens of the state. When morning dawned, they left their penthouse and were driven to the depot. It was a Tuesday, and the sky was clear and cloudless.

Feb. 20 left for Los Angeles to establish permanent residence.
~ WAITE PHILLIPS DIARY, 1945

CHAPTER THIRTY-FIVE

WEST OF THE WEST

Waite and Genevieve Phillips arrived in Los Angeles aboard the Santa Fe Chief on February 22, 1945. That afternoon, they promptly drove up the coastal highway along the Pacific toward the Santa Monica Mountains north of Malibu and out to their Arroyo Sequit Ranch. By evening, they had settled into a spacious apartment at the Town House, their temporary home for the next sixteen months while their newly purchased Bel Air residence on Bellagio Road underwent extensive remodeling.

The southern California and greater Los Angeles area that greeted the Phillipses in 1945 was a far cry from the sprawling, smog-covered and crime-ridden megalopolis that evolved in the next half-century. As some observers from that past era put it, if California was the land of dreams, then Los Angeles was the dream factory. Since its founding as a Spanish pueblo in 1781, the city continually recast itself as everything from a health paradise to the motion-picture capital of the world and a major financial center. Many residents considered their "city of angels" to be the promised land and the city of the future.

In a book entitled *Southern California Country*, published in 1946, just after the Phillipses arrived, Carey McWilliams wrote, "No region in America . . . is dominated by one city to the extent that Los Angeles, with its 450 square miles of territory, dominates Southern California."

Early visitors were drawn to the geography of the place and the fact that southern California was insulated climatically, shut off from the rest of the continent. Writer Helen Hunt Jackson had noted, "It is a sort of island on the land." Many years later, another author, John Gunter, called Los Angeles "Iowa with palms." Frank Lloyd Wright said, "If you tilt the whole country sideways, Los Angeles is the place where everything loose will fall."

Always a magnet to all sorts of migrants from across the nation, from south of the border, and from the Orient, the Los Angeles area grew tremendously in the years following World War II. The war itself helped set up the pattern. During the fiscal years of 1940 to 1946, the federal government spent $360 billion in the United States. Of that sum, about $35 billion went to California. Shipyards and aircraft plants flourished. At the war's end, thousands of additional residents came to the "Golden State," where — thanks to government spending — the personal income level was more than three times greater than prewar figures.

Waite and Genevieve enjoyed being Angelenos. Although Waite wished he had moved to California in the 1930s, their timing was still almost perfect. They moved to Los Angeles before the air degenerated and rust began to creep up the edges of the city, and the tangled jungles of boulevards and freeways sprouted. The Phillipses came before, as one journalist wrote, people began to "make daily deals with the devil."

Waite and Genevieve preferred the climate, the fauna and flora, and the hidden retreats in the surrounding mountains. Like so many others before them, they loved watching the sun vanish into the Pacific each evening, as yet another chronicler of the city wrote, "like a lost and bloody cause."

But perhaps the description of this sovereign empire by the

western shore that best suited the Phillipses' attitude about their adopted home was a quote from Theodore Roosevelt, one of Waite's favorite Americans. "When I am in California," Roosevelt said during a speech delivered there in 1905, "I am not in the West. I am West of the West."

Those could have been Waite's exact words. This land beyond the hills and mountains and deserts was as far west as Waite Phillips could go without leaving the continent that had been home to his family since their ancestors arrived centuries before. It was as far as Waite needed to go. They would continue to travel and journey to new places, but California was the Phillipses' home for the rest of their lives.

Unlike the midwestern cities the Phillipses had known so well, where residents were proud of roots that ran deep in the soil, in Los Angeles almost everything and everyone was imported or improvised.

"This was a lovely makeshift city," pointed out Frank Fenton in *A Place in the Sun.* "Even the trees and plants did not belong here. They came, like the people, from far places, some familiar, some exotic, all wanderers of one sort or another seeking peace or fortune or the last frontier, or a thousand dreams of escape." As far as Waite was concerned, that was a description of heaven on earth. He wasted no time in quietly making his presence known.

March 7 new office headquarters established at 3275 Wilshire Boulevard. Hugh Shinn of Coldwell, Banker & Co. first caller. . . . Lunch with Arch Anderson and Frank King at California Bank on [March] 20th to acquaint G. E. P. with bankers. No. 1 check drawn on W. P. and G. E. P. Los Angeles bank account issued to American Red Cross. ~ WAITE PHILLIPS DIARY, 1945

Throughout that first spring season in Los Angeles, despite a severe case of neuritis in his shoulder that kept him working out of his Town House apartment for several weeks, Waite showed no signs of slowing his pace. He knew he was living in a moneyed oasis. As real estate values soared, Waite snapped up more and more investment property or sold it off for an enviable profit.

In late May, he sold the million-dollar block of property in Beverly Hills which he had purchased from the Lloyd Corp., Ltd., as an investment the previous year for what was reported to be "in excess of $1,000,000." The buyer was E. L. Cord, former automobile magnate and financier, who announced his intentions to develop the property into a major retailing center.

Waite dropped his plans for a major business development on the Wilshire Boulevard land because of what were described as "construction difficulties." The flood of new residents created housing shortages and put a great strain on the construction industry and builders throughout southern California. Waite stressed, however, to inquiring reporters that he still intended to improve his residential property and maintain his other real estate projects in southern California.

While Waite kept up with his business and financial matters on a daily basis, he constantly churned out lengthy letters and memos to Boy Scout officials in Tulsa and at Philmont, to old friends in Tulsa, and to his family. Most of the correspondence was filled with Waite's personal observations and plenty of advice for the person on the receiving end. For instance, earlier that year, he had sent a three-page letter to Lieutenant Elliott Phillips at the Amarillo Army Air Field, in which Waite explained that "the sound rules to follow for business success lie in the ability to VISUALIZE, ORGANIZE, DEPUTIZE, and SUPERVISE."

In a letter to Otis McClintock dated June 25, 1945, Waite admitted, "Of all the pesky habits I have acquired over the years — about which you are mostly acquainted — probably the worst is that of annoying friends and associates by issuing epigrams and philosophical letters to them." With that said, Waite on to send McClintock a complete list of his favorite inspirational epigrams, including one Waite had found only recently — "To build a business that will never know completion." It was chiseled in stone over the main entrance of the Bullocks-Wilshire Store in Los Angeles. "Not only is this a good motto for a commercial enterprise," Waite wrote to McClintock, "but it is likewise a valuable and wholesome rule for human beings to follow."

During their years in California, the Phillipses received a steady flow of guests from across the country, including business associates, dignitaries and celebrities, and family members. The McClintocks, John Mabee, Bill Skelly, and many others came calling. There were constant lunches and dinners at the Biltmore, the Los Angeles Country Club, the Florentine Gardens, and the original Brown Derby, just across Wilshire from the Ambassador Hotel.

Some of the more frequent family visitors were Genevieve's sister, Helen Pine, Frank and Jane Phillips, L. E.'s widow, Nora, Helen Jane and her two sons and, of course, Elliott. He spent much of his furlough time with his parents, at their apartment and horseback riding with Waite at the Malibu ranch.

On August 6, 1945, the United States dropped an atomic bomb on Hiroshima and, three days later, dropped a second bomb on Nagasaki. That same day, August 9, Sidney Dickinson, an artist commissioned by Philbrook to paint portraits of Waite and Genevieve, arrived in Los Angeles from New York. As Dickinson prepared to begin his work with the Phillipses, the Japanese called for an end to the war.

Aug. 14 Japan surrendered unconditionally — end of World War II. W. P. had first sitting for portrait that day. In evening went to church with G. E. P., Helen Jane, and Emily [Bramlette] before going downtown and Pershing Square to witness Victory Celebration. Closed office 15th and 16th — National Holidays — in observance of end of war. Week of August 15 started remodeling work on Bel Air residence. On Aug. 21 G. E. P. had her first sitting for portrait by Mr. Dickinson which he completed

25th. G. E. P. down with flu and unable to attend cocktail supper party next evening, Sunday, at apartment to display finished portraits — those present, Sidney Dickinson, the artist, L. W. Craigs, L. L. Gradys, Howard Shermans, George Cordinglys, Joe Blanchard, and Helen Jane.

W. P. put Helen Jane, Mrs. Blyth and boys on "Chief" next day for Lexington, Va. — after having made two month visit in L.A.

~ WAITE PHILLIPS DIARY, 1945

That fall, Waite contributed twenty-five thousand dollars to the Los Angeles War Chest before leaving with Genevieve on a series of trips to Santa Barbara, San Francisco, Big Bear and Arrowhead lakes, and the Mojave. In November, Waite moved his office from 3275 Wilshire to a new office building at 6366 Wilshire Boulevard, and kept up with his various real estate dealings.

Elliott, still serving in the army, had left Amarillo and was stationed at Peterson Field near Colorado Springs. He continued to visit as often as possible, to be with his parents and see his daughter. Chope maintained a close relationship with Wendy Lee, and Waite and Genevieve frequently visited with their granddaughter, as well as with Barbara, their former daughter-in-law.

The Phillipses were pleased to learn that while he was stationed at the airfield in Amarillo, their son had met a young woman who apparently caught his eye. Elliott seemed quite serious about her, and everyone kept fingers crossed that the couple's romance would continue. Her name was Virginia Ward. When Genevieve and Waite found out that she was a pure-born Texan, not at all disinclined to the notion of spending her life on a cattle ranch, they were ecstatic.

Anxious to get out of uniform and back into jeans and cowboy boots, Chope also wished for a wife who was willing to share all his hopes and dreams. Part of that desire came true for Chope in early 1946 when he received his discharge from the army. The rest would come true in the near future.

After he made a thorough inspection of potential ranches in Arizona and New Mexico, Chope went to Los Angeles to discuss the possibilities with Waite, who called on some of his business contacts for their advice. It was not his cherished Philmont, but it looked as though Chope was finally was going to get his New Mexico ranch.

April 1 Elliott left for Albuquerque for conference with R. J. McCanna re purchase of a ranch. . . . Talked to Elliott about ranch deal . . . on April 13.

April 16 talked to Fred Dunn at First National Bank in Tulsa re transferring money from Elliott's Trust for purchase of a ranch, also talked to Fred Phillips who was in Dunn's office. . . .

May 10 conference with Elliott — recommended cancel deal with Tommy Crenshaw and secure combination local man for office and handy-man, also make suitable arrangements for housing records. Took the Gradys, Blanchard, Elliott, and Emily to Mocambo for dinner. Lunch at the apartment with Wendy and Elliott — talked to Roger Randolph in Tulsa and Chas. Donnelly re Wendy Lee Trust. Elliott left for Albuquerque May 15. ~WAITE PHILLIPS DIARY, 1946

That same month, at their annual meeting in Saint Louis, the Boy Scouts bestowed Silver Buffalo awards on General Dwight Eisenhower, Admiral Chester Nimitz, and Walt Disney. Waite thanked the Scouts for also offering him their highest honor, but for the second time, he turned it down.

As he busied himself with a combination of family and office matters and shipped Elliott's personal files to New Mexico, Waite prepared for Genevieve's approaching fifty-ninth birthday. On the big date — June 17 — Genevieve got the best gift she could have asked for when a team of workers began to move some of the furniture into the Phillipses' new home. There were still many details to take care of, but the residence on Bellagio Road was almost ready. Waite thought they would be completely in by August.

The Phillipses spent most of July trying to keep their minds on other matters as they anxiously awaited the time when they could settle into their Bel Air house. First they went to the Del Monte Lodge at Pebble Beach, and from there to the Mark Hopkins in San Francisco. After adjusting their itinerary because of Genevieve's brief illness, they ended up at the Santa Barbara Biltmore. Finally, that August, just as Waite had promised, their Bel Air estate was ready. With little or no fanfare, the Phillipses moved in.

He may have known in his heart at the time that it was to be the last residence where Waite Phillips — the man who never stayed in one place too long — would ever live. This secluded home on Bellagio Road was where he would spend the last seventeen-and-a-half years of his life. It would be the longest time he ever had lived anywhere.

CHAPTER THIRTY-SIX

BEL AIR

The Phillipses' newly refurbished residence was in the hills bordering Bellagio Road, a narrow blacktop lane that twisted through Bel Air, the sleek residential community filled with winding roads that curved past palatial homes.

Developed during the 1920s by Alphonzo Bell, an oilman and entrepreneur with a sense of elegance, Bel Air was subdivided into plots of several acres, which limited buyers to only the very wealthy. During Bel Air's infancy, movie people, many of whom were Jewish, were excluded from living in the elite community.

That all changed with the Great Depression, as other businesses suffered and Hollywood prospered. As one cynical writer wrote, "Bel Air's greed proved stronger than its bigotry." Before very long, many of the residents were high-powered motion-picture producers, directors, screenwriters, and movie stars. Huge estates appeared along roads with names such as Saint Pierre, Tortuoso Way, Sunset, Saint Cloud, Copa de Oro, Strada Corta, Stone Canyon, and Bellagio.

The dashing Errol Flynn once lived in the mansion at 345 Saint Pierre Road, built in 1927 by silent screen star Colleen Moore. During the 1950s when the Cold War was at its most frigid stage, actress Kim Novak paid ninety-five thousand dollars for her home at 780 Tortuoso Way and then proceeded to have a fallout shelter dug in the backyard. For a time, Judy Garland resided on Stone Canyon Road. Not too far from the Phillips home, Loretta Young, the exquisite actress who won the Academy Award in 1947 for her performance in *The Farmer's Daughter,* lived with her family in a colonial-style Bel Air residence.

Not everyone living in Bel Air made his mark on the big screen, however. Some, like Waite, had earned huge fortunes in business and industry. At 750 Bel Air, Lyn Atkinson, the engineer who built the Hoover Dam, erected a palace for $2 million dollars. His wife thought it was so pretentious she would not even move in, forcing her husband to sell it for a fraction of its cost to hotel mogul Arnold Kirkeby. Years later, the same mansion was used for eight seasons as the Clampett family home in the television series, "The Beverly Hillbillies."

After 1950, another well-known hotelier, Conrad N. Hilton, also was one of the Phillipses' nearby neighbors. Connie Hilton, the king of innkeepers who became the largest hotel operator in the world in 1954, called his Bel Air place Casa Encantada, enchanted house. Situated on nine acres complete with swimming pool and manicured gardens, the sixty-room house was home for Hilton and his thirteen servants.

Hilton's grand home adjoined Bel Air Country Club, another of Waite and Genevieve's preferred places to dine or entertain. But perhaps one of the Phillipses' favorite spots for quiet dinners was the Hotel Bel Air, at 701 Stone Canyon Road, just a few blocks from the entrance to their home. Set off the beaten track on a dozen acres of heavily wooded canyons, the mission-style main building with its graceful arcade and scores of garden bungalows painted pink offered the ideal setting for well-heeled patrons. Waite and Genevieve found the hotel charming, and they frequently brought family and friends there to dine.

They also enjoyed entertaining at their new home. It not only was spacious and well-appointed, but there were also terraces and patios, a split-level garden and, of course, a large swimming pool for their visiting grandchildren. Like the rest of Bel Air, the

Phillipses' property was cloaked with bougainvillea, beds of ivy, thick ferns, and towering palms and eucalyptus trees. Waite liked to stand outside and look at the distant snow-capped Sierras, or turn and peer out over the terraced hillsides toward Westwood Village, a mecca for students. It was nestled at the foot of the 411-acre campus of the University of California at Los Angeles.

Best of all, the Phillipses discovered that their residence on Bellagio Road was not only a perfect place for relaxing but also for making plans with friends, associates, and family. And through the later years, Waite never ceased to confer with his daughter and son about their prospects for the future.

Spent New Year's Day at Bel Air with Elliott — discussed relationship with Bill Breckinridge and proposed trip of Helen Jane and family out here — also reviewed Elliott's proposed marriage. Elliott left on California Limited for Las Vegas, N. M.
~ WAITE PHILLIPS DIARY, 1947

Elliott, a mature and vigorous twenty-nine-year-old, worked hard at his New Mexico ranch while he prepared to wed Virginia Ward, the young woman he had met during the war while stationed in Amarillo, in the Texas Panhandle. As he watched his daughter Wendy grow into a healthy and happy little girl, Chope was delighted that he had found Virginia, who appreciated his love for the wide-open spaces and the rigors of life on a working cattle ranch. Waite and Genevieve were glad for their son and his bride-to-be.

April 19 Elliott was married to Virginia Ward at Amarillo, Texas. On 21st Elliott and his new wife arrived in L. A. On 23rd took Elliott and Virginia to inspect McClatchie Ranch — in evening gave party at Earl Carrolls for Elliott and Virginia. Present were the Posts and Gradys. On 24th Elliott and Virginia came to office and met with W. P. and Mr. Maynard Toll re their wills — later Elliott and Virginia left in W. P.'s Chrysler for trip

*to northern California. April 29 had an important conference
with Elliott . . . In evening had dinner at Bel Air Hotel with
Elliott and Virginia and then to Ice Capades. On 30th went with
G. E. P. to see Elliott and Virginia off for Las Vegas [New
Mexico].* ~ WAITE PHILLIPS DIARY, 1947

Distressed that they had not been invited to Elliott's wedding, the Phillipses got over their hurt as soon as they met their new daughter-in-law.

"I had not met Dad and Genevieve before we were married," Virginia remembered more than forty-six years later. "They were kind of upset that they had not been invited to the wedding, but Chope and I discussed it and decided with both of us having been married before, we just didn't want a big ceremony. We just had a few friends, none of my family and none of his.

"I don't recall being overly nervous about going to meet them. I think they were just grateful when they saw that I was fairly normal and didn't have two heads. They really did put themselves out to welcome me into the family, and that never stopped, not ever. Both of them were always very kind to me."

A vivacious and beautiful woman with plenty of Texas charm, Virginia was everything the Phillipses had hoped for in a wife for their only son. She quickly was accepted by the entire family and became like another daughter to Waite and Genevieve.

Other than not having been at the ceremony, Waite's only regret was that on February 14, 1946, more than a year before Chope and Virginia's marriage, burglars had entered Waite's Wilshire Boulevard office building through a rear window. The thieves broke open his safes and made off with some of the family's heirloom jewelry. One of the items stolen would have been the ideal wedding gift for Virginia.

"The Phillipses told me the story of Helen Jane's birth in Bartlesville, and how they were at first going to name her Virginia but then at the last minute they instead decided to name her for two of her aunts," recalled Virginia Phillips. "It seems that L. E. Phillips, Waite's brother, was only aware of the first name they were going to use, so he brought the baby a gold necklace with a locket, and the name Virginia was inscribed on it. The Phillipses had kept that locket and chain all those years until it was stolen in that office burglary on Wilshire Boulevard.

"I still can remember Mr. Phillips telling me that story. He said he was so sorry that the locket was lost because he would have liked to give it to me. But he said that they were pleased that at last they had a Virginia in the family. It made them happy."

Throughout that time, Waite also kept up with Helen Jane and her family. She and her two sons, who were fast growing into young men, were frequent visitors at the Bel Air home. Mostly they came without Bill Breckinridge. The Phillipses took them to movie premieres and fancy dinners at the Bel Air Hotel. Sometimes Waite was able to slip away with his daughter to discuss family matters during a long walk along the quiet streets of the neighborhood. When Elliott and Virginia were in town at the same time as Helen Jane and her boys, Waite arranged for tours of motion-picture studio lots and chartered a deep-sea cruiser for fishing trips in the coastal waters off Malibu.

Many other visitors came to California to share a meal or sometimes a few days with the Phillipses, either at their home or at one of the many swanky clubs, hotels, and restaurants in the area. It was an impressive list. Waite dined at the California Club with former President Herbert Hoover, attended a Beverly Hills stag party in honor of the prince of Yemen, and entertained Dale Carnegie and many other notable persons.

One of Waite's friends in his later years was actor Leo Carrillo. A reporter and cartoonist before becoming a dialect comedian in vaudeville and later on the legitimate stage and in motion pictures, Carrillo first had met Waite during a war bond drive in Tulsa. The two men built a friendship after the Phillipses moved to California. In the early 1950s after retiring from the screen,

Carrillo played the affable character named Pancho, Duncan Renaldo's sidekick in "The Cisco Kid" television series.

In the autumn of 1947, Waite and Genevieve took a long vacation. First they went to New York on the Santa Fe Chief and spent a month at the Plaza Hotel. They got together with many old friends and associates at the Stork Club, the Twenty-One Club, and the Pierre. After seeing the musical *Brigadoon,* they wrapped up their visit and headed to Iowa. They went to their old hometowns. While in Gravity, Waite drove to the cemetery to pay his respects to his parents and other kinfolk resting there, especially his twin, Wiate. Sometimes Waite considered moving his twin's coffin to California, but he never did do it. He allowed Wiate to remain in his native state. From Iowa, the Phillipses journeyed to Kansas City and then to Oklahoma for visits at Bartlesville and Tulsa.

In Tulsa, Otis McClintock gave a luncheon in Waite's honor at the First National Bank dining room. Among the many guests were some of Waite's old friends — Fred Dunn, Senator Ed Moore, John Mabee, John Mayo, Dr. C. I. Pontius, W. K. Warren, J. L. Shakely, Victor Hurt, Ralph Talbot, W. M. Bovaird, and Bill Skelly. On October 22, 1947, the *Tulsa Tribune* made note of Waite's being in town for his first visit since moving to California more than two years before, to invest heavily in Los Angeles and Hollywood real estate. The newspaper quoted him as saying that he came back "just to look around a bit and check up on some of my friends. . . . No business, none at all. Just going to spend a few days here."

After stops in New Mexico to see what was going on at Philmont and to take a peek at Chope and Virginia's ranch, Waite resumed his fast pace in California that autumn and winter.

On December 6, Waite and Genevieve attended a special invitation luncheon hosted by the hierarchy of the University of Southern California, and then watched the USC versus Notre Dame football game. Just two days later, Waite received one of the first warnings that his lifestyle was due for a drastic change.

*Dec. 8 after arriving at office was stricken by a heart attack —
Coronary Thrombosis. Went home immediately and was ordered
to bed for one month by Drs. Lanphere and Langly, with day and
night nurses in attendance.*

*Elliott and Virginia arrived on 21st to spend the holidays.
During the time Elliott was here — until Jan. 3 — we discussed
some matters affecting our respective plans for the future and I
outlined program whereby he could, in my opinion, be more
serviceable to himself and family and also to us by broadening his
business interest to include a part-time residence in California. It
was agreed that he would consider the proposal and come to visit
us with his answer the latter part of January or early February
1948. Elliott and Virginia celebrated New Years Eve at Beverly
Hills Club.*

*Jan. 1 W. P. and G. E. P. had luncheon conference, upstairs in
W. P.'s room, about Elliott and Helen Jane and other family
matters. . . . From Jan. 1st to 6th W. P. still confined to bed.
Balance of month convalescing in room and upstairs yard.*
~ WAITE PHILLIPS DIARY, 1947- 1948

The heart attack Waite suffered in late 1947 served as a wake-
up call. Realizing that he needed to slow down, Waite tried one
last time to convince Elliott that he should devote at least part of
his time and energy to business matters other than the raising of
beef cattle. But Waite's compromise plan, calling for Chope and
Virginia to split their time between their ranch in New Mexico
and a home in California, did not work.

Elliott boarded a train at Las Vegas, New Mexico, and arrived
in Los Angeles on February 5 with his response to his father's
proposed program. That answer was a polite but firm no. It came
following a conference about family wills and estates. "He

[Elliott] declined the plan suggested by W. P. in December, 1947 in preference to devoting entire time to his own ranching business," was how Waite recorded the incident in his journal. Chope returned to New Mexico a couple of days later. On February 11, Waite returned to the office, his first time back at work there in more than two months.

Conscious of his health, Waite still tried to keep up with business matters and social obligations. He and Genevieve enjoyed getting together with Mary Pickford and her husband, Charles "Buddy" Rogers, at their home, Pickfair, and at the Phillipses' residence. Waite also remodeled his office, and continued to hire and fire personnel at both his office and home. For the remaining years of his life, Waite's personal diary was littered with curt entries concerned with the termination and rehiring of employees.

"There's no question that Dad was a very difficult man to work for," remembered Chope. "I know this; he fired some pretty good folks over the years. But that was the reality of working for Dad. Remember, he demanded perfection, both in himself and in those who worked for him, and that included people at his office or the household staff. If he believed someone wasn't doing their job, they were gone."

But for all his toughness when it came to employees, the aging oil tycoon continued to demonstrate his gentler side. This was especially true when it came to his beloved wife, his sweet Genevieve. During their many years together as man and wife, Genevieve tucked away many of the cards and notes she found attached to gifts or bouquets which her husband sent to her. The messages in themselves offer yet another facet of Waite.

"To my Valentine of 1903 ..." "Dear Genevieve, Your favorite flowers for my favorite wife ..." "The loveliest flowers for the loveliest girl I know ..." "To Genevieve, A wonderful and gracious helpmate throughout all these years since 1909, especially during these troublesome times ..." "To my best girl ..." "To the girl who is forever young ..." "To Genevieve, Merry Christmas if such is possible with an old man husband ..." "To Genevieve, the girl I've known since 1903 and I still think she's the best for me ..." "To my Genevieve, Just as lovely as 39 years ago ..." and "To Genevieve, She is just as attractive to me at 62 as she was at 16!"

To Waite, his abiding relationship with Genevieve and the futures of his children and grandchildren were more important than all his real estate deals rolled into one. With each passing year, he became more aware of his own mortality. In August 1948, the death in Bartlesville of Waite's sister-in-law Jane Phillips, after she had suffered a heart attack, certainly got his attention. So did his brother Frank's medical problems and Waite's continued ailments.

Nov. 2 Election day! Dewey defeated — Truman elected. W. P. and G. E. P. at Scripps Clinic, La Jolla — 14th thru 18th — for medical checkup, then to Coronado Hotel, San Diego for couple of days.

... Dec. 20 Elliott and Virginia arrived from Las Vegas [New Mexico] to spend Christmas holidays. Elliott and Virginia, Parriotts and Gradys at residence for Christmas dinner. Dec. 28 W. P. and G. E. P. attended cocktail party at Frank King's home in evening. On evening of Dec. 29 Elliott, Virginia, G. E. P. and W. P., with Gradys, had dinner at Biltmore Hotel and then to theatre to see "Show Boat." W. P. became quite ill before dinner and Elliott brought him home. Dec. 30 Fred Phillips telephoned that Frank Phillips had another stroke. Canceled reservations on steamship Lurline to sail Feb. 21 for Honolulu — also reservations at the Royal Hawaiian Hotel — this on account of business matters and on account of Frank Phillips illness.

~ WAITE PHILLIPS DIARY, 1948

In late January 1949, after his sixty-sixth birthday, Waite spent time with his big brother Frank in Boca Raton, Florida, when both of them were feeling much more fit. Just to be sure, on his way to see Frank, Waite threw away his Chesterfields and gave up smoking for the duration of the stay in Florida.

Returning to Los Angeles, Waite went home to Genevieve and several hectic months of social and business activities, including the purchase of more ranch acreage in Mandeville Canyon. They also made sure there was time for some good old-fashioned fun.

In August that year, Elliott and Virginia joined Waite and Genevieve for a trip to Canada and Alaska. The two couples took the train northward to Vancouver and from there sailed to Skagway, Alaska. Next they went via rail to Whitehorse, returned on a steamship to Vancouver, and finally made their way back to Los Angeles.

"Our Alaska trip was one of the best ever," recalled Virginia Phillips. "Dad, especially, really had a good time on that trip. The best part of it was that we all got along so well whenever we were together. All the way up to Alaska and all the way back, we played games of pitch every night. We played on the train or wherever we were. It would be me and Dad against Genevieve and Chope, and they'd win every single time. I can still see Dad throwing his cards down and saying, 'I am not going to play anymore,' and that very next night he'd be back there ready to play again.

"When we got back from that trip we still played pitch, but I don't believe that Dad and I ever let them win another game. My, we had fun! We'd play games, and have our drinks together, and travel. Every Sunday we'd go to movies. It was more like the four of us were contemporaries rather than parents and in-laws."

In Los Angeles, life went smoothly for Waite. He was pleased to meet Jennifer Jones, who had won an Oscar in 1943 for her performance in *The Song of Bernadette.* Married to film producer David O. Selznick in 1949, the actress had been born Phyllis Isley in Tulsa in 1919, about the time the Phillips family had moved there. Miss Jones and Waite compared life in Oklahoma and California over drinks in the comfort of the Bel Air Hotel.

That December, there was good news from Tulsa. Ground had been broken for the Carver Memorial Center, made possible by Waite's setting aside $100,000 in 1944 for the erection of a community center for black Tulsans. It was yet another monument to Waite's generosity, and it made him feel good as the holidays approached.

But sadly, for Waite and all the Phillipses, the close of the year and of the 1940s ended on another sour note that reverberated into the next decade and beyond.

Dec. 17 Elliott and Virginia arrived from Las Vegas to spend holidays at Bel Air residence. Wendy Lee and her mother over for luncheon on the 20th. Dec. 25 Christmas dinner at residence. . . . Wendy Phillips spent afternoon Dec. 29 and stayed overnight at residence with family, including Elliott and Virginia. Dec. 31 as guests of the Gradys, W. P. and G. E. P. and Elliott and Virginia went to Bel Air Club for New Year's celebration.

Helen Jane called from Tulsa. She appeared ill and mentally disturbed. W. P. and G. E. P. talked to Mrs. Blyth and asked that she [Helen Jane] be taken to hospital and we would call Dr. Sheppard the next day. ~ Waite Phillips Diary, 1949

January 1st — spent day at home with Elliott and Virginia. Called Dr. Sheppard at Tulsa about Helen Jane's condition — asked that she be kept in hospital until Elliott and Virginia arrived. They left for Las Vegas on the 2nd, and on the 7th made trip to Tulsa in interest of Helen Jane's welfare. ~ Waite Phillips Diary, 1949-1950

Concerned about Helen Jane but also aware of their own health needs, the Phillipses kept up frequent visits to their physicians and periodic stays at Scripps Clinic. Besides a flurry of medical checkups, Waite was busy with plans for the development of the Mandeville Canyon property, while he continually tried to trim down any more personal commitments. Later that year, Waite declined an invitation from banker Frank King to become a trustee at the University of Southern California. Instead, the Phillipses took their postponed Hawaiian cruise, sailing on the SS *Lurline* to Honolulu for reunions with old friends at the Royal Hawaiian Hotel.

While the Phillipses vacationed in Hawaii, Elliott took Virginia east to Johns Hopkins Clinic. Virginia was not ill, but wanted to have a child. As Waite noted in his journal, "This was result of my suggestion last winter after reading that a doctor there made a specialty of conditioning women to bear babies."

Back on the mainland, Waite spent considerable time at his California ranch and turned down opportunities to become more involved in additional business or political endeavors.

On May 11, 1950, Waite wrote to his friend Frank King, at California Bank. Waite spelled out some of his thoughts about world conditions, government, and the world economy. Like the staunch Republican he was, Waite mostly reviled those he called the "New Dealers" and others who supported the policies of Roosevelt, as well as the "Fair Deal" administration of Harry Truman.

"For the last forty years I have been responding quite liberally to emergency political solicitations for 'saving the country' to now find it burdened with debt and harassed by enemies from without and within," Waite wrote to King. "Considerable pressure has already developed for political contributions for the primaries this summer and undoubtedly will follow for the elections this fall. In moving our residence to California about five years ago for semi-retirement purposes — without business profit motives — it was my idea to avoid assuming new responsibilities of burdensome nature. Therefore, I'd like to pass these political responsibilities over to the young Republicans — native sons — out here. Certainly until such time as I am convinced that the Republican Party and its individual candidates will openly and energetically oppose Fair Deal policies it is my intention to withhold any and all donations to them."

Instead of politics and big business deals, Waite took care of real estate transactions and tended to his family. Another significant trip Waite made that year was in July when he went off once again to visit with his oldest brother, Frank Phillips. For some time, Frank had distanced himself from running the powerful oil firm he had founded, and he was spending the summer at Atlantic City, New Jersey.

Left for Atlantic City via Union Pacific to visit Frank Phillips. Quit smoking for the duration of the trip, same as on trip to Florida last year to visit brother Frank. At Traymore Hotel in Atlantic City. ~ WAITE PHILLIPS DIARY, 1950

Waite spent several days on the Jersey shore with Frank at the grand Traymore on the Boardwalk. It was a good visit. The two brothers discussed their lives and talked of their past. They remembered L. E. and their parents and Wiate, who had died so young.

Waite thought Frank did not look very well. As Waite left, he told some of Frank's entourage that he was worried and asked them to keep him advised about his brother's condition. Then Waite said good-bye. It was, as Waite secretly feared, the last time he saw his brother and mentor alive.

On August 23, Waite recorded in his diary, "Received word that afternoon of the death of Frank Phillips in Atlantic City." With Genevieve by his side, Waite left on the Super Chief for Oklahoma. They went to Bartlesville to bury his big brother.

It was a huge funeral. All the Phillips Petroleum offices across the nation and every business in town closed for twenty-four hours. Flags were at half staff, and soft chimes sounded over Bartlesville. Many friends and employees paid their respects. Condolences and floral offerings came from Harry Truman, Rudy Vallee, Alf Landon, Cardinal Francis Joseph Spellman, Pierre du Pont, and many others. Waite knew Frank would have been pleased by the outpouring of sympathy.

Outside Frank's town house on Cherokee Avenue after the service, a crowd of more than three thousand people stood in silence. Waite watched as the coffin was carried to the hearse that would take Frank to his final resting place at Woolaroc, his ranch in the Osage. With tears streaming down his face, Waite turned away.

Those nearby heard him say, "Frank may have had his faults but his averages were high. There goes my best friend — I loved him so much."

CHAPTER THIRTY-SEVEN

FLEETING YEARS

The 1950s — the decade that yielded Joe McCarthy, Disneyland, and Elvis — became a time of conservative politics, social conformity, and economic prosperity. Nowhere was this more true than in California, where the population, especially in Los Angeles, continued to swell.

During the 1950s, Los Angeles County was inundated by more than a million newcomers. All of them sought food, jobs, education, and shelter — not necessarily in that order. In the greater L. A. area, so many large tracts of land were being subdivided and covered with look-alike houses that *sprawl* was still an acceptable word. Within a few years into the decade, that would change, as a shortage of private housing evolved into a major economic and political problem.

High above the urban sprawl in his well-groomed Bel Air retreat, Waite Phillips plugged along. Still feeling the effects of the death of Frank Phillips, Waite was further stunned in January 1951. Just two days before Waite's sixty-eighth birthday, he found out that Frank's only son, John Phillips, had died at sea of a heart attack aboard the *Queen Mary* while returning from Europe.

The following year, on April 30, 1952, Waite's brother Ed Phillips died. Accompanied by Chope, a grieving Waite went to Okmulgee for the funeral. Tears brimmed in his eyes as Waite buried yet another of his big brothers. Standing in the spring sunshine while the casket was lowered into the ground, he realized he was the oldest surviving Phillips sibling.

As he always had done whenever he was troubled, Waite occupied his mind with a variety of projects. He spent time on the sale of his Wilshire property, construction work on mountain roads and buildings at his Mandeville ranch, conferences with Boy Scout officials, and frequent out-of-town trips. They included visits to New Mexico, where Elliott and Virginia maintained the Conchas Ranch. Periodic stops at Philmont also remained important to Waite.

July 10th — Left with [Arthur A.] Schuck [chief Scout executive]
and G. E. P. for New Mexico for inspection of Philmont Scout
Ranch and for two weeks visit with Elliott and Virginia at their
Conchas Ranch near Las Vegas. ~ WAITE PHILLIPS DIARY, 1952

Late that year, Waite's disposition brightened noticeably when, at long last, his Republican Party took back the White House, and the succession of five Democratic presidential victories came to an end. On November 4, 1952, Dwight D. Eisenhower was elected president of the United States, swamping his Democratic opponent, Adlai E. Stevenson, in a landslide that also put Senator Richard M. Nixon of California into the office of vice president.

After the excitement of the election subsided, life for Waite remained untroubled for the rest of the year. In early December, he sold the Arroyo Sequit Ranch to the state of California for use as a public park, and he joined with his family and a few friends in welcoming the new year. As far as Waite was concerned, 1953 got off to a great start. Some of his favorites in sports and politics were coming up winners. First of all, Southern Cal posted a 7-0 victory over Wisconsin in the Rose Bowl, followed the next day by Robert Taft's election as the United States Senate Republican leader. On January 19, a birthday dinner was staged at the Phillipses' home for Waite, who turned seventy years old that day, and to celebrate Elliott's thirty-fifth birthday on January 11. The following afternoon, Waite and his GOP cronies applauded the inauguration of Dwight Eisenhower as the nation's thirty-fourth president, carried across the country via television.

Although hostilities continued in Korea, that summer the Phillipses went ahead with their two-month cruise to the Orient. They made ports of call in Honolulu, Yokohama, Manila, Hong Kong, and Kobe. They returned to California less than a week after an armistice took effect, ending the three years of Korean warfare. In late September, Waite sold three of his Wilshire properties. Only a few weeks later, on October 28, more medical problems surfaced when he suffered another heart attack.

Confined to the Bel Air residence, Waite was told by attending physicians that the heart attack was very similar to the first one he had had almost six years before, in December 1947. The doctors again diagnosed his condition as coronary thrombosis, the formation of a clot in a coronary artery, resulting in an obstruction. After a few weeks' rest, Waite went back to work, but angina pains forced him to return home. The very next morning, however, he was back at his desk.

Dec. 18 — Dr. C. E. Fronk of Honolulu stopped in office. 22nd — W.P. attended Lee Combs luncheon at Beverly Hills Club in honor of Judge Hefner [father of Waite's former son-in-law]. 23rd — Virginia and Elliott arrived for Christmas holidays. 25th — Christmas — W. P., G. E. P. and Elliott and Virginia spent day at home. Entertained the Gradys for dinner. 30th — Wendy Lee Phillips arrived at Bel Air residence for visit. 31st — Had New Year's Eve dinner at Bel Air Hotel with Elliott and Virginia.
~ WAITE PHILLIPS DIARY, 1953

Jan. 2nd — Elliott and Virginia left for Las Vegas. 18th — Helen Jane arrived from Tulsa for visit — left for home Jan. 31st. 19th — W. P.'s 71st birthday — dinner at residence. 24th — W. P. &

Helen Jane called on Dick Powell and June Allyson at Mandeville Canyon home. 25th — Signed sale agreement for Lot 27 (old office) with doctor group. 26th — Mrs. Nettie Hale (cousin) & family called at office. 30th — Helen & Clarence Pine arrived Long Beach from Iowa for winter vacation. ⁓ WAITE PHILLIPS DIARY, 1954

With each new day, it looked as though Waite's schedule was becoming filled again with all sorts of engagements and social obligations. He also sold off much of his Wilshire-Warner property during the year. However, he listened to his doctors' advice and went in for periodical physical checkups. Waite also made sure that he and Genevieve escaped now and then to New Mexico or another destination, as they did in May 1954, when they went to New York by train via New Orleans and Washington, D.C.

That summer, Waite became worried when he again experienced chest and abdominal pains. By August, when the pain persisted, he went to the Beverly Hills Clinic for an examination and consultation. After three days of tests and electrocardiograms, Waite's physicians strongly recommended the removal of his gallbladder, an operation he had put off in the past. Elliott and Helen Jane rushed to California to be with their parents. On August 27 at 7:30 a.m., Waite's gallbladder was removed successfully at St. John's Hospital in Santa Monica.

"Waite Phillips, former Tulsa oil man and philanthropist now living in Los Angeles, is reported recovering satisfactorily today from a gall bladder operation," reported the *Tulsa World* on August 30. "R. Otis McClintock, president of the First National Bank & Trust Co., returned today from the West Coast, where he had visited Phillips. He reported that the former Tulsan was in good condition following surgery."

Escorted by a watchful nurse, Waite left the hospital in Santa Monica on September 3 and went home to Bellagio Road. By September 28, the attending nurse was long gone and Waite was moving into another new office, at 6242 Wilshire Boulevard.

In early October, barium tests revealed a deep postoperative ulcer in the wall of Waite's stomach. His physicians prescribed medication and a gentle diet. Everything seemed to be fine until the day after Thanksgiving, when Waite felt stabs of pain in his chest and left arm. The pain increased the next evening, but attending doctors said it was a virus infection. It soon cleared up. Although Waite would be bothered by further ulcer and stomach ailments in later years, further testing on December 2 showed that his initial ulcer problem was almost entirely healed.

But the next day, December 3, Waite was stricken with another heart attack. Although they considered it a mild attack, his physicians ordered Waite to bed for the next four weeks. He did his best to comply, although he found it most difficult to lie there doing nothing. Bedridden or not, he still managed to see several visitors, terminate an employee and, for the first time since his heart attack, come downstairs on Christmas Day to join the rest of his family for a holiday dinner.

Jan. 1st — W. P. recuperating from heart attack at home.
~ WAITE PHILLIPS DIARY, 1955

Waite would continue to experience a gradual decline in health for the rest of his life, but that did not totally restrict his busy daily regimen or put a damper on the lifestyle he had become so accustomed to. A small army of personnel came in and out of what seemed like a perpetually revolving door, as Waite never diminished the high standards and work ethic he insisted on for all in his employ, and for himself.

Waite took frequent visits to Philmont to see how well the Boy Scouts were treating his old ranch. He enjoyed riding horseback over the meadows and inspecting abandoned mountain trails. Oftentimes he would talk with some of the thousands of Boy Scouts who came there every summer. He seldom told the boys who he was, but seemed to get more pleasure out of a quiet chat or watching them at work or play.

By the close of 1955, Waite had disposed of much of his southern California property. That included the Whitney Canyon Ranch and, in Los Angeles, all the remaining Wilshire tracts including the Warner houses, with the exception of what were known as the Carthay and Crescent properties. Those were sold at a later date, as was the Mandeville ranch, in late 1956. Waite purchased new ranches to ensure that he had a place for his horses and a retreat when he and Genevieve wished to escape Bel Air for an afternoon.

Throughout the 1950s and well into the 1960s, Waite's daily diary was filled with notations concerning property transactions. There were scores of entries such as: "Sold San Diego property to M. L. Holzman thru Coldwell, Banker & Co."; "Lunch with Joseph Shelton at California Club re Westwood property"; "Whitney Canyon Ranch sold to Jacob Albert of L. A."; "Dan Duggan submitted written offer for Carthay property from Franklin Life Insurance Co."; "Signed suit papers re clearing title for parking lots on Warner lots–Crescent property"; "Signed sales agreement to sell Crescent property"; "Signed contract to purchase Ventura Ranch"; and "Escrow closed on sale of Crescent property to Atlas Terminals, Inc., of New York."

On January 2, 1956, the *Tulsa World* published a column that discussed the Phillipses' life in California and gave a summary of their many contributions to Tulsa, including the Philbrook Art Center, various downtown building endowments, the engineering building at the University of Tulsa, and much more. "Mr. and Mrs. Waite Phillips reside at Bel Air, a suburb of Los Angeles, Calif. Mr. Phillips still dabbles a little in real estate but he has been reducing greatly his extensive holdings which he acquired shortly after going to Los Angeles from Tulsa. The daughter, Helen Jane Breckinridge, resides in Tulsa, and the son, Elliott Phillips and his wife, reside on a ranch near Las Vegas, New Mexico."

*Jan. 19th — Helen Jane arrived for W. P.'s birthday. Had dinner
alone with parents. On account of unusual circumstances, she
returned home evening of Jan. 21st by Santa Fe Super Chief
train.* ~ WAITE PHILLIPS DIARY, 1956

Waite and Genevieve continued to be fearful for their daughter's well-being. Her abuse of alcohol grew worse in later years, and her marriage to Bill Breckinridge would always be stormy at best. Still, the Phillipses sought ways to bring some semblance of order and comfort to Helen Jane's life. She never stopped going to California for visits with her parents. As her two sons grew into young men, they also continued to spend time with their maternal grandparents in Bel Air.

*Aug. 31st — Phillips & Peyton [Breckinridge] arrived by airplane to spend Labor Day weekend. Returned home by plane on
Sept. 3rd.*

*Sept. 5th — We left by train for Canadian vacation via
Vancouver, Banff, Winnipeg to Minneapolis by Canadian
Pacific. W. P. returned via Missoula, Montana to visit Fish Creek
and via San Francisco to visit Aunt Cora — 90 years old this
fall. G. E. P. returned via Knoxville and Las Vegas to visit sister
and E. W. P. [Elliott] and Virginia.* ~ WAITE PHILLIPS DIARY,
1956

Those years saw the deaths of more and more of Waite's former associates and old friends from those bygone years in the oil patch and the boardrooms. In early 1957, Otis McClintock called Waite to tell him of the passing of F. B. Parriott. On April 11, Waite received word of the death of W. G. Skelly, one of the remaining pioneers of the oil industry and someone whom Waite greatly admired.

One by one, the remnants of the old guard slowly were leaving the scene they had helped to create through their bold and sometimes extravagant moves. Out in California, battling a bad heart and a troublesome stomach, Waite Phillips was one of the last ones left — and he knew it.

CHAPTER THIRTY-EIGHT

INDOMITABLE SPIRIT

Life in California appeared to be unclouded for Waite. With each passing day, he became more aware of his own mortality, yet he tried very hard not to allow every new ache and pain to hinder his movements or slow his pace. He did not wish to miss a minute of the grand adventure that he had been living since he and his twin, Wiate, had been born so many years in the past.

Each of Waite's remaining years on earth was just like all the others — full of both ups and downs. Whatever came his way, Waite took his licks, administered a few of his own, and rolled with the punches.

In 1958, for instance, Waite had high and low points. So did the United States, as the country experienced a national recession that deepened and then slackened. It was the year that John Kenneth Galbraith's book *The Affluent Society* described the materialism and conformity that by that time characterized the United States. During the year, Richard Nixon was stoned in Caracas, Pat Boone and J. Edgar Hoover had best-selling books, and the Giants and Dodgers fled New York for the West Coast.

It was the year when Senator William F. Knowland, who had represented California in the United States Senate since 1945, seemed the highly probable winner in the gubernatorial race that autumn. Waite spent time talking about issues and strategy with

Knowland, whose political mentor was Robert A. Taft. But beyond the conversations, Waite also contributed large sums of money to Knowland's campaign fund.

It turned out to be money down the drain. Instead of an easy victory, Knowland was thrashed in the election of November 1958, when the Democratic candidate, Edmund G. Brown, won nearly 60 percent of the votes and carried fifty-four of California's fifty-eight counties.

Waite did not blink an eye. For every defeat, he knew the sweet taste of success. That was the year that Waite turned seventy-five years old. Throughout all those years, he had had mostly victories to his credit.

In July, Waite paid $500,000 cash for a ranch home and acreage on Lake Sherwood, in the Hidden Valley area of Ventura County in southern California. Waite, who bought the property from Mr. and Mrs. James R. Canterbury, announced that the ranch was for his cattle and horses. The two-story ranch house, often referred to as the "Castle of Sherwood Forest," was surrounded by stables, garages, and a swimming pool.

Waite also knew the ranch would be ideal for his growing family. In 1957, the Phillipses' younger grandson, Peyton Breckinridge, had wed Sylvia Joan Aker in Tulsa. Later that year, the couple's first son, William R. Breckinridge II, was born in Houston, where Peyton attended school before earning a degree at the University of Tulsa. Then on June 14, 1958, Waite and Genevieve's older grandson, Phillips Breckinridge, wed Patricia Flint of Tulsa. Also a graduate of the University of Tulsa, Phillips went on to earn his law degree there in 1959.

Waite had high hopes for both of his grandsons. He also still believed in Helen Jane. In March 1958, before their older son's summer wedding, Helen Jane and Bill were guests at her parents' Bel Air residence on a one-day stopover en route to a vacation in Australia. It was the last time Waite and Genevieve would see their son-in-law alive.

In the early hours of August 23, 1958, William R. Breckinridge, after two weeks of hospitalization, died of what the Tulsa newspapers described as a heart ailment. Hard living and alcohol had taken their toll. Born into a pioneer legal family, he had pitched major-league baseball, attended Dartmouth and other universities, run for political office, and served in World War II, but he never really achieved the success so many people had expected of him. Despite being the son of a respected judge and the son-in-law of a multimillionaire and possessing a brilliant mind, Bill Breckinridge — at least as far as Waite was concerned — had failed to live up to his potential. Bill was less than two months away from his fifty-second birthday when he died.

The Phillipses were greatly saddened by the death of their son-in-law. But Waite especially felt badly for Helen Jane. Her sons and their families lived in Tulsa, but essentially she was alone at her home, an attractive ranch-style residence located just off South Lewis Avenue at 3810 Terwilleger Boulevard, only a few miles from Philbrook. When Bill's last will and testament finally was probated in 1959, records showed that he had left an estate of $130,510, including many oil and gas mineral interests. Of course, Waite would continue to provide additional funds for his daughter's needs. He also contributed to his son's ranching endeavors.

Dec. 1st — Elliott and Andrew Marshall here for several days re purchase of Ft. Union Ranch land [in New Mexico]. Signed agreement to purchase south half of 40,000 acres and option for later purchase of north half. Purchase completed Dec. 16th, by W. P. and G. E. P., for later conveyance to Elliott. ⁓ Waite Phillips Diary, 1958

That Christmas, Elliott and Virginia came to Bel Air with a surprise of their own — their newly adopted baby daughter. After years of waiting, the couple at last had a child. They named the newborn infant Julie. She was the center of attention in the Phillipses' household during the holidays, as Helen Jane arrived and Elliott's older daughter, Wendy Lee, came to meet her new half-sister. Elliott, Virginia, baby Julie, and her Aunt Helen Jane stayed until January 5 of the new year, when they all departed for their respective homes and Waite and Genevieve prepared for the next wave of houseguests, including the Talbots and McClintocks.

By early March 1959, Waite had established trusts totaling $400,000 in First National Bank of Tulsa for Helen Jane and her sons. At the same time, Waite gave Elliott the $600,000 needed for purchase of the Fort Union Ranch in New Mexico. Before year's end, Chope sold his Conchas Ranch and exercised his option to purchase the north half of the Fort Union.

With their new wills drafted and signed and the financial gifts for their children and grandchildren taken care of, the Phillipses boarded a ship in New York on March 27 for a South American cruise. On March 30, as the SS *Argentina* cut through the sea bound for Rio de Janerio and other ports in Brazil and Argentina, Waite and Genevieve observed an important date in their lives — their fiftieth wedding anniversary. It was a glorious trip. When they went back to New York on April 28, Helen Jane was there to greet them. Genevieve stayed with her daughter in New York for several days while Waite rushed back to Los Angeles to move his office yet again — this time to 10904 Wilshire Boulevard in Westwood, not far from his Bel Air residence.

June 17th — G. E. P.'s birthday spent at home — she was recuperating from flu. 18th — started working on History of Philbrook and Southwestern Art Association. Completed Nov. 27th.

June 27th — Helen Jane, Phillips & Pat arrived as house guests at Bel Air residence. Left July 5th. 30th — Dinner at Beverly

Hills Club with Helen Jane, Phillips & Pat, the Gradys and the
Fullers to celebrate G. E. P.'s, Helen Jane's, Pat's, and Mr. Grady's
birthdays. July 1st — Lunch at Beverly Hills Brown Derby with
G. E. P., Helen Jane, Phillips & Pat in honor of Helen Jane's
birthday. . . . 31st — Helen Jane, Peyton & Joan and Robbie
house guests until August 9th. ~ WAITE PHILLIPS DIARY, 1959

The 1950s ended on a high note. Waite found out that a brand-new elementary school dedicated in Tulsa had been named after him, and Helen Jane and Elliott and his family came to spend the holidays and help their parents bring in the 1960s.

On January 7, after she signed her new will, Helen Jane had a thorough physical examination at the Beverly Hills Clinic. Later that month, at St. John Hospital in Tulsa, doctors removed from her breast a tumor that turned out to be benign. Nevertheless, Waite was worried and continued to confer with physicians in Beverly Hills about his daughter. She became a grandmother again on March 29 when her son Phillips and his wife, Pat, had their first child, a son they named Flint.

After several months of work involving the various family trusts, handling more real-estate transactions, and keeping up with unceasing social engagements, Waite was proud when the Boy Scouts bestowed an unusual honor on him. A grade school had been named after him and part of his surname had been emblazoned on countless buildings and monuments, but now Waite's name was to be given to a mountain. The ceremonies at Philmont changing the name Clear Creek Mountain to Waite Phillips Mountain were conducted by Dr. Arthur A. Schuck, chief Boy Scout executive emeritus, and other Scout officials on July 31, 1960. Waite was not able to attend, but he sent a telegram to be read aloud by Schuck to all gathered there.

"To you and all others participating in the dedication ceremonies of renaming Clear Creek Mountain, I send greetings. It has been a long time since I had the pleasure of riding my faithful old gray horse over the trails, foothills, divides, valleys and then up the slopes of this high mountain to enjoy the majestic view from its summit. While I cannot attend in person, be assured I will be there in thought and with grateful appreciation to those who have protected and preserved this magnificent ranch for the benefit of Explorer Scouts and their volunteer adult leaders.

"Furthermore my blessings go to those Boy Scouts with the hope that they will receive as much physical betterment and mental inspiration as I did in exploring the rugged, natural beauty of Philmont. For these reasons I reaffirm my statement of 20 years ago that this property referred to as the 'Great University of the Out-of-doors' should not be selfishly held for the benefit of the few but made available for the benefit of the many, as nothing in the meantime has caused me to change that opinion."

After Waite's wire was read, a group of Boy Scouts standing at the peak of the mountain unveiled a bronze plaque embedded in the ledge rock. Inscribed on the plaque were the words: "Waite Phillips Mountain is dedicated this 31st day of July, 1960, in appreciation of Waite Phillips whose generosity has opened new horizons to the Scouts who travel the Philmont Trails."

A few weeks later, more good tidings came to Waite and Genevieve from New Mexico. Elliott and Virginia had expanded their family further. Overjoyed with their daughter, Julie, the couple had decided she needed a little brother. On August 17, after completing adoption proceedings in Las Cruces, they received their newborn son. They named him John Elliott Phillips. The next day, his proud grandparents left Bel Air, eager to see the newest addition to the Phillips clan.

Back in Los Angeles, before the close of 1960, Waite conferred with officials concerning the Community Chest campaign for the coming year, and made final payment to architects for the remodeling of the Ventura Ranch buildings. That ranch and some Westwood property were put up for sale. But at the same time, Waite made several trips through the San Gabriel Mountains and up the Malibu coast, looking for additional land suitable for a small ranch.

That autumn, the deaths of Ralph Pringle and Gillette Hill, two of his dearest friends and closest colleagues from his Oklahoma days, left Waite despondent. His mood changed, however, as it always did, around the holidays. Both of his children and Chope's two little ones came for Christmas. The family hosted a dinner at Bel Air Country Club in honor of Wendy Lee Phillips and her fiancé, William Wallace Drewry III, who announced their intention to wed. They were married on September 2, 1961.

Jan. 19 — W. P.'s birthday spent quietly at home. 20 — John Rebold (90 yrs. old) made special trip from Okmulgee, Okla. to ask donation to Okmulgee Hospital. Gave substantial amount in June. 25 — Received word of death of John Mabee. 31 — R. E. Fuller resigned account of ill health. ~ WAITE PHILLIPS DIARY, 1961

Waite's own health remained troublesome. During a long trip on the Santa Fe Super Chief, he had a mild congestive heart attack after the train pulled out of Fort Dodge, Kansas, the morning of March 15. A few days later, while aboard the Southern Pacific en route to Los Angeles, he had another mild attack, requiring him to convalesce at home until the end of the month, when most of the immediate family turned up for Waite and Genevieve's anniversary.

In early April, Otis and Gladys McClintock arrived after a round-the-world cruise. The McClintocks, their granddaughter Patricia, known as Trish, and her husband, Conrad N. (Nicky) Hilton, Jr., were dinner guests of the Phillipses. Young Hilton, son of hotel magnate Conrad Hilton, the Phillipses' neighbor, had been the first husband of movie star Elizabeth Taylor, from whom he was divorced in 1951. Nicky and Trish had been mar-

ried in 1958. That event caused the senior Hilton, out of defer-
ence to the McClintocks — his son's grandparents-in-law and the
Phillipses' best friends — to remove a large tree on his property
that partially blocked Waite's view of Los Angeles from his library
window. The tree had been a source of contention between the
two neighbors for several years. A few days after Trish and Nicky
dined with Waite and Genevieve in 1961, they returned for
another visit, along with Conrad Hilton. In his diary for April 12,
1961, Waite noted the occasion, but made no mention of
whether Hilton took advantage of the clear view of the city from
the Phillipses' library.

The tide of guests, mostly family but also many people connected to various business dealings, never ceased to appear at the
Phillipses' Bel Air home. But while Waite held many conferences
with real estate brokers, bankers, and Scout officials, he also mon-
itored his and Genevieve's health. She underwent an emergency
appendectomy in October 1961, but quickly recovered and generally had far fewer medical problems than her husband. Waite
especially continued to have difficulties with his heart. He suffered another mild attack in late 1961. Although he bounced
right back after only a week away from the office, he knew that
eventually the situation could easily become critical. It did so in
the coming year.

A look at just a few of Waite's diary entries for 1962 explains a
lot about his everyday life as he approached his eightieth birthday.

*May 2 — W. P. & G. E. P. signed sales agreement to sell
Ventura Ranch to Barney R. Morris et al for $1,250,000.
Broker — L. O. Kittle — sold at profit.*

*June 22 — Lord & Lady Baden-Powell visited in office & were
luncheon guests at Bel Air residence. [He was the son of the
founder of the Boy Scouts. He died in Deccember 1962 in
England.]*

July 4 — Otis & Gladys McClintock at Bel Air residence for din-
ner, enroute to La Jolla. Traveling with nurse due to Otis having
heart attack in January.

Aug. 18 — Lud L. Grady, partner in Harris, Upham & Co.,
stock brokers, died of heart attack at his home. ~WAITE PHILLIPS
DIARY, 1962

Late that October, Waite and Helen Jane spent some good
time together. They took a long drive along the Malibu coast, visited Marineland, and spent a day at Knott's Berry Farm. Just a
few days later, Waite had a congestive heart attack late one
evening while reading in bed. His physicians ordered twenty-
four-hour nursing supervision and complete bed rest. Within a
week, Joseph A. Brunton, Jr., chief Scout executive, was at the
residence for a conference. Only about two weeks after the attack,
Waite was back at work in his office. Throughout the year, he had
made numerous trips to Malibu and outlying areas in search of a
small piece of property for a ranch site. Always a realist, Waite
also made what he called "an inspection trip" with Genevieve that
December to various area cemeteries, including Forest Lawn.

Jan. 1 — New Years Day spent quietly at home — with G. E. P.
& Helen Jane. Jan. 6 — W. P. had 3 hour conference at residence
with Dr. George C. Griffith, heart specialist, and another one on
Jan. 12th. Jan. 18 — Phil Phillips [L. E.'s son] arrived in L. A.
for W. P. birthday. Elliott & Virginia also arrived at Bel Air resi-
dence. Jan. 19 — W. P.'s 80th birthday — celebrated at home
with G. E. P., Elliott, Virginia, Helen Jane and Phillips.
~ WAITE PHILLIPS DIARY, 1963

Throughout the winter and spring, Waite continued to look
at new ranch property and to search for a final resting place, as
more friends and associates died. One of them was Arthur
Schuck, the retired chief executive of the Boy Scouts of America,

who died of cancer at Santa Barbara. Several weeks later, Waite and Genevieve looked at Westwood Memorial Park. They then met with an architect about plans for a private mausoleum, but those plans were postponed.

On May 11, Waite and some real estate brokers looked at ranch property. That evening, Dr. Bernard Pearson came to the Bel Air residence to continue a discussion about Waite's health that had started over lunch the day before. Pearson did not mince words. He told Waite that fluid was on his lungs and gave him an injection to remove it. Two days later, another of Waite's attending physicians, Dr. John C. Egan, came to the residence and ordered complete bed rest for Waite.

Although he reluctantly went along with the doctors' orders, Waite knew his daughter was due very soon for one of her visits. When his Helen Jane got to Bel Air, Waite would get her to go with him and they would drive along the Pacific. They would look in the foothills and search the canyons for new ranchland. Helen Jane was due to arrive in California on the following Sunday, May 19. She was going to stay for an entire month. Waite counted the days until her arrival.

But when May 19 came, there was no Helen Jane. Instead, Waite and Genevieve received a telephone call from Elliott. Their son sounded distraught, and for good reason. He was bringing his father and mother the most devastating news any parents can ever receive.

Helen Jane — their firstborn child and only daughter — was dead.

Early that morning in Tulsa, her body had been discovered by her loyal housekeeper. Helen Jane was lying on her bed at the Sophian Plaza, an eight-story apartment building on Frisco Avenue, overlooking Riverside Drive and the Arkansas River. There were some questions about the contributing factors of her death, but county investigator Ray Bachus said expiration "resulted from natural causes, probably a heart attack." Helen Jane would have turned fifty-two in July. She was the exact age her husband, Bill Breckinridge, had been when he died in 1958.

After her husband's death, Helen Jane had left their home on Terwilleger Boulevard for the security and comfort of an apartment in the Sophian, a stately building erected in the late 1920s, a twin of another Sophian Plaza built in Kansas City in 1923. She had belonged to Southern Hills Country Club and Trinity Episcopal Church, and served on the board of the Children's Home and Welfare Association, founded long before by a gift from her father. In the years since Bill's passing, Helen Jane also had participated in the Foster Parents' Plan, Inc. In 1959, she had adopted financially a four-year-old Italian girl, a seven-year-old Chinese girl, and a seven-year-old French boy.

After breaking the grim news about Helen Jane to his parents, Chope rushed to catch an airplane and was in Los Angeles by early evening. Dr. Egan came to the house twice that day to tend to both of the Phillipses. He ordered the nurse left on night duty to pay special attention to Waite.

"Helen Jane surely wasn't born an alcoholic, but she became one later in her life and she was married to an alcoholic," recalled Chope Phillips. "That's what killed both of them.

"It all caused my parents much grief. And finally, I all but gave up on Helen Jane and I think my mother finally gave up too, even though we still loved her. But my father never stopped trying to help Helen Jane. Right down to the very end, he tried to get her to turn her life around. He never gave up on her."

CHAPTER THIRTY-NINE

JOURNEY'S END

Chope Phillips left the Bel Air residence for Tulsa on May 21, 1963, to attend his sister's funeral and represent his grief-stricken parents, neither of whom could make the long trip. The following day, Chope returned to Los Angeles to find that his father was out of bed. Just four days after his daughter's death, Waite was up and dressed and headed to his office.

He managed to spend only a few hours there. It was the first time he had been out of the house since he had been taken ill on May 11, and the doctors ordered him to bed. They insisted that his poor health, combined with the shock of Helen Jane's death, was sufficient reason for Waite to stay put. He did not totally agree, arguing that work was the best medicine, even for pain as deep as that caused by the death of his child.

The following day, Waite underwent further tests, including X rays, and Dr. John C. Egan found fluid on his lungs and an enlarged heart. The doctor immediately ordered bed rest and a daily intake of oxygen. That was, of course, much easier to prescribe than to enforce — especially the part about resting in bed.

May 25 — With Mr. Westmoreland, attorney, & Bernis at residence. Wrote codicils to W. P. and G. E. P. wills for signature same day. Elliott returned home in evening.

*June 1 — W. P. ill during night with attack of spasm of the
colon. These attacks continued and worsened. On June 6th
doctor insisted W. P. go to hospital for X-rays. He went to St.
John's in Santa Monica in afternoon & remained there until the
8th. X-rays indicated obstruction of the colon. Elliott arrived on
the 7th and Virginia on the 15th. A night nurse was kept on
duty at the residence.* ~ WAITE PHILLIPS DIARY, 1963

On June 17, Genevieve's birthday, Waite went to his
Westwood office for an hour or so, the first time he had been
there since May 24. That afternoon, he went home for a birthday
lunch with Genevieve. He then devoted the entire afternoon to a
conference with Russell Hunt, of First National Bank of Tulsa,
regarding Helen Jane's last will and testament. The value of Helen
Jane's estate was listed at "more than $20,000 real estate and more
than $20,000 personal property."

She bequeathed fifteen hundred dollars to Edna Anderson, a
Tulsa friend, and ten thousand dollars to Mary E. Blyth, who had
cared for Helen Jane and her family for so many years. Peyton
and Phillips Breckinridge, who by then was an assistant U.S. district attorney, were given their mother's automobile, belongings,
furniture and furnishings, and all other personal effects. Each also
received one-fourth of her remaining estate split in equal shares,
with the remaining three-fourths set aside for them in trust with
the First National Bank and Trust Company.

Despite his poor health, Waite maintained a regular schedule
of business meetings and conferences. On June 29, Leroy Garrett,
Waite's former attorney and a close friend, came to the Bel Air
home to discuss a list of Waite's personal matters. Garrett came to
the Westwood office on July 1 to resume their discussions, but a
recurrence of Waite's intestinal pain was so severe that Garrett
accompanied him home to be sure he arrived safely. At six o'clock
that same evening, after he left the Phillipses' house, Garrett suffered a heart attack and died.

Waite was jolted, but managed to attend the funeral on July 3. Then two days later, Waite received word that another longtime friend, John C. Long, the builder from Kansas City, also had died. Waite coped. Thankfully, the McClintocks arrived in Los Angeles on their way to La Jolla and spent some time with the Phillipses. Waite also arranged for several meetings with business contacts and officials from the University of Southern California.

On July 31, the first entry appeared in Waite's journal of his difficulty in sleeping at night because of severe pain in his legs and feet caused by poor circulation. A variety of remedies was prescribed, but none brought relief. As Waite noted in his diary for that date, "A neurologist, the doctors and chiropodist all prescribed but nothing helped, and the condition caused much aggravation and depression." The month of August was much the same. Waite tried to conduct business, but his physical condition would not allow it.

August 24 — W. P. could not get to sleep due to pain in feet. Doctor called and administered 'shot.' Night nurse called on duty. Restlessness & inability to get to sleep continued until August 27 when W. P. had congestive heart attack about 6:00 A. M. Elliott arrived August 28th, & Phillips and Peyton came from Tulsa on the 30th, to spend Labor Day weekend at residence. They all returned home on September 2nd. The day nurse was discharged Sept. 4th and the night nurse Sept. 8th. ~ WAITE PHILLIPS DIARY, 1963

By early September, Waite had regained enough strength to get to his office. But after only a couple of days, he experienced more breathing difficulties and returned home. More nurses were hired and placed on duty at his side, as he greeted his granddaughter Wendy and her new husband and, along with Genevieve, signed an agreement to sell the Westwood properties to Joseph and William Horton. Waite managed to go to the office by the end of the month, but the unseasonably hot weather — with temperatures as high as 108 degrees — forced him back to the comfort of his home office.

During October, Waite lunched with friends and associates and held several conferences, ranging from sessions with Boy Scout executives to a meeting with a Salvation Army official. The Phillipses signed yet another set of freshly drafted wills. Late in the month, they felt cheered when Virginia and little Julie came from New Mexico to spend several days.

On the evening of November 5, Waite had a congestive heart attack. His doctors immediately tended to him and ordered additional day and night nurses. A few days later, Waite's younger sister, Lura, arrived at the Bel Air residence for a visit. Soon after that, Waite was able to spend a few hours at his office. He conferred with Ellsworth Augustus, president of the national council of Boy Scouts of America. Waite was pleased to hear that his granddaughter Wendy Lee Drewry had given birth to a son. But Waite's pain continued.

A night nurse remained on duty, frequently administering injections to induce sleep and to quiet nerves agitated by what Waite described as his "restless feet." Ironically, his own words for that chronic ailment — "restless feet" — were also the best description of the unyielding urge that had kept Waite Phillips on the move all his life.

In early December, representatives from the Boy Scouts came to Bel Air to show the Phillipses a new motion picture about Philmont Scout Ranch. The film seemed to brighten Waite's spirits. Then on December 12, Waite, tired of having to work at home, went to his office. It would be for the last time.

Dec. 14 — W. P. suffered congestive attack in the night. Dr. Smith came to residence and spent several hours. He ordered day nursing in addition to night nurse who had been on duty since Dec. 7th.

Dec. 20 — Elliott, Virginia & children arrived to spend a
month. An apartment was rented in Santa Monica for them,
although Elliott stayed at the residence most of the time at night.

Dec. 25 — W. P. had another mild attack in the morning after
being downstairs to have Christmas breakfast with the family. Dr.
Smith was called and administered shot and W. P. remained in
his room under sedation the rest of the day. ~ WAITE PHILLIPS
DIARY, 1963

For much of his remaining time, Waite stayed under heavy
sedation. In spite of that, he could not sleep through the night,
leaving him groggy and unable to concentrate on business matters
during the day. As a result of all the medication for dehydration,
Waite felt weak and lost a great deal of weight. Still, he insisted
that all his mail be brought to his bedside, and he issued instructions about answering every single piece of correspondence.

Another year was upon him — 1964. Waite would turn
eighty-one years old on January 19. On New Year's Day, his condition remained generally the same, but by week's end there
appeared to be a little improvement. He was still somewhat
depressed, but he took more interest in the activities around him.
Occasionally he watched television in the evening. During the
day, he enjoyed brief walks around the yard and gardens, sometimes by himself but often with Tony Frenchmore, his trusted
employee who took care of the property.

Since he could not travel, Waite dispatched Elliott to Philmont Scout Ranch on January 8 to make a special inspection for
him. Chope was happy to go. He returned to California four days
later to help the rest of the family prepare for Waite's birthday.

Jan. 19 — W. P.'s 81st birthday. He had a very difficult time
during the previous night, due to pain in feet and inability to
sleep, but managed to go downstairs for a birthday dinner with
G. E. P., Elliott and Virginia. ~ WAITE PHILLIPS DIARY, 1964

On January 22, Elliott, Virginia, and the two children left for home. Waite rallied some, and by January 24, he was able to dictate a few letters. The following afternoon, he went outside and walked around the grounds alone. Then he and Tony Frenchmore discussed some yard work that Waite thought needed to be done. The next day was Sunday, and Waite made plans to return to his office on Monday morning.

At about 1:30 a.m. on that date, January 27, Waite had another heart attack. All the doctors and nurses, the medicines and treatments could do no more for him. At 10:15 a.m., Waite Phillips died at his home. His time on earth was over; his long journey was done. Those restless feet were still at last.

Chope and Virginia rushed to Bel Air to comfort their mother. Shortly afterward, Phillips and Peyton Breckinridge arrived. Genevieve had met Waite when she was a girl of sweet sixteen and had never loved anyone on earth as she loved him. They had been man and wife for almost fifty-five years. They had gone through some hard times together in the oil patch but they had enjoyed so many more years of happiness. They had buried a daughter, but lived to see the successes of their son and grandchildren. They had built an empire on oil and real estate and lived to see it all transformed into the public good.

The family withheld news of Waite's passing until late in the afternoon. By Tuesday, headlines across the country told the story of the final chapter in Waite's colorful and full life. "Philanthropist Waite Phillips Dies On Coast," was the bold headline in the *Tulsa World* on January 28. "Waite Phillips, oilman, industrialist and probably the most generous philanthropist ever to live in Tulsa, died Monday in Los Angeles, his home for the last 18 years," ran the lead of the accompanying story. "A man of great wealth who believed wealth carried responsibilities with it, he contributed millions in cash and property to the community he called home for more than 27 years."

In a separate editorial, on January 29, the *Tulsa World* declared

Waite a great humanitarian. "Tulsa has never had the equal of this man — an altruist who believed in doing things for his community. The one-time Iowa farm boy scaled financial heights seldom equaled by others. . . . His interest and concern were deeply rooted in the heart of humanity. That, perhaps, explains the munificence of his benefactions.

"Waite Phillips was not the sort who wanted an exuberant rush of words. He sought no compliments. A person of calm strength and constancy, he was self-effacing and modest to the point of shyness. As a restraining and conservative force his mark has been stamped indelibly in the life of Tulsa. It was a happy and compensating experience to share for a quarter of a century the philanthropist's fruitful life. Benevolence was the distinguishing characteristic of Waite Phillips. As embodied in his life, it was the path of duty."

Tributes poured in from all across the nation. Some came from former associates. Waite would have approved of their assessments because they were truthful and came straight from their hearts. B. B. Blair, a longtime Tulsa oilman and former employee, labeled Waite as a true "individualist" who was never afraid of taking a risk. "He took big oil strikes in stride and they didn't seem to bother him very much. Waite had been through some lean years so big gushers didn't necessarily go to his head."

Of all the accolades and remembrances, probably the best was the editorial that appeared in the *Tulsa Tribune* on January 28. It was penned by Jenkin Lloyd Jones, a premier journalist who knew his subject well.

> Like most rich men Waite Phillips was glad to be wealthy. But he was not a light-hearted rich man. His wealth concerned him. He spent a lot of time brooding about what he ought to do with it. And he thought well and to good purpose.
>
> When Waite Phillips died at his Los Angeles home

Monday at the age of 81, Tulsa was only one of the many places that had been changed by his generosity. But Waite Phillips thought beyond mere giving. Gifts cost money to maintain. He endowed his Philmont Scout Ranch in New Mexico with the income from one Tulsa office building, and Philbrook Art Center in Tulsa with the income from another. He was a prudent man.

Waite Phillips never had much sense of humor. He was as introverted as his brother, Frank, was outgoing. Waite Phillips bruised easily and was always worried about what people might think of him. Frank, confident and proud of his millions, laughed easily, steered a bold course and didn't mind the winds. Both did a lot for Oklahoma.

In his later years Waite Phillips would lead guests up to the long study behind his mansion and lecture at length on the pictures of long-forgotten tool pushers, wildcatters and Indians with whom he had lived and worked after he left his job hawking coal in Iowa and followed his brothers to the last frontier. He thought a lot about the good, poor, early years.

Not that Waite Phillips wasn't proud of all the money he made, or of the fact that at an age when most men retire he went out to California and made a lot more. But Waite Phillips found his fun in the hunting of a dollar, not in the possession of it. Every dollar he owned bothered him a little, and he kept looking around to see where it might do some good. The world could use a lot more Waite Phillipses.

Waite's funeral was held the afternoon of January 30 at Westwood Memorial Park in West Los Angeles. The services were conducted by his friend, the Reverend Ray W. Ragsdale, former minister of Westwood Community Methodist Church, who came from Tucson at Genevieve's request. Some old friends, including

B. B. Blair and Gene Hayward, also were there. When the prayers were over, they laid Waite to rest in a temporary crypt until the completion of a private mausoleum.

Later that year, after his final will was probated in Los Angeles, it became clear that Waite still had much more to give. The bequests totaled a staggering $7.5 million, with most of the money going to charities, hospitals, colleges, and, of course, the Boy Scouts.

Waite bequeathed to his widow all of his interest in their Bel Air residence and all the remaining real estate he owned. He provided $1,350,000 to relatives and staff members, including $500,000 each to Genevieve and Elliott; twenty-five thousand dollars to Virginia; fifty thousand dollars to his surviving siblings, Nell Phillips Walker, Lura Phillips Hill, and Fred Phillips; fifty thousand dollars to his brother Ed's widow, Anna, who died only a week after Waite; twenty-five thousand dollars to each of his five grandchildren; and twenty-five thousand dollars to his last secretary, Bernis Crandall. Beyond those gifts, he also left one thousand dollars each to five residential employees — Tony and Lilly Frenchmore, Gertrude Bassey, Albert and Lola Babineau. He also provided a year's salary to each of his business employees who had been with the Phillipses for more than two years immediately previous to his death.

But the vast majority of Waite's great fortune went to many others. The largest single specific bequest was for $1 million to the Boy Scouts of America "to provide financial assistance to underprivileged Boy Scouts in order that they may receive the benefits of camping experience on Philmont Scout Ranch."

After payment of all the specific bequests, estate and inheritance taxes, and administration expenses, the residue amounted to approximately $3 million for the University of Southern California, for the purpose of constructing the "Waite Phillips Hall of Education for the education of teachers for all levels of education."

Other bequests in the southern California area included $250,000 to the Southern California School of Theology, Claremont; $250,000 to the Children's Hospital and Clinic, Los Angeles; $200,000 to the Braille Institute of America, Los Angeles; $200,000 to the Los Angeles Community Chest; $200,000 to the Salvation Army, Southern California Division; $200,000 to the Los Angeles Heart Association; and $200,000 to St. John's Hospital Association, Inc., Santa Monica.

Back in Oklahoma, where the Phillips family already had made so many monetary and property contributions, Waite willed $2 million more to a variety of institutions. Those gifts included $650,000 to Southwestern Art Association to further endow Philbrook Art Center; $500,000 to the University of Tulsa; $250,000 to St. John Hospital; $200,000 to Tulsa's YMCA; $200,000 to Okmulgee City Hospital; and $200,000 to the Jane Phillips Memorial Episcopal Hospital in Bartlesville.

Unquestionably, one of Waite's most cherished epigraphs best summed up the legacy he left behind — "The only things we keep permanently are those we give away."

Genevieve Phillips, the quiet wife and gracious hostess who had a mind of her own, continued the tradition of giving to charities, educational institutions, the arts and cultural community, and a variety of needy causes as she gracefully lived out her life in southern California. She died at her home on June 19, 1979, just two days after her ninety-second birthday, and was laid to rest next to Waite in Westwood Memorial Park. The statue of two playful cupids in a fountain that once graced the family's breakfast room at Philbrook was placed inside the mausoleum.

Chope and Virginia stayed on at their New Mexican ranch, where their daughter and son grew into adults and the Phillipses continued to do what they loved best — raise and sell beef cattle.

Many years after Waite's death, Chope decided there was something he could do for his father, even though he was gone. It was a simple but very profound act. Chope chose not to discuss what he did for a long time, and when he finally did talk about it, there was not much to say.

"Just after my Dad died in Bel Air, Virginia came across some old stuff that you could put in one hand," Chope recalled. "Those few things were all together stuck away in Dad's dresser drawer. There was an old tobacco tin with some rolling papers, a few trinkets, tintype pictures of girls and one of my father and his twin brother. Dad had held onto those things all through the years and kept them close by.

"We figured out that those were the things he took out of Wiate's pockets when that boy died in Spokane. Those were his brother's last possessions. They were the things that Dad would get out every single year when their birthday came around and he'd go into a bit of a decline. Then he'd get those things of Wiate's and go off by himself and he'd think of those old times. I brought that stuff with me back to my ranch and one day I gathered it all up and went up to Philmont."

Chope saddled a horse and rode off toward the Sangre de Cristos. He moved through the high grass and made for the trails that led toward the Tooth of Time, and to the mountain named for his father, and the high meadows and cow camps and fishing lodge that Waite had loved so much. When he reached a place he knew his father had liked, Chope reined up his horse and dismounted. All around him were endless blue sky and woods that smelled like freedom. Chope dug out some earth from beneath a big Ponderosa pine and he put those special things — those last possessions of that dead twin boy — in the ground and he covered them all up. He buried them deep, and afterward he scattered some pine needles and grass over the dirt.

He did not say a word — his deed alone was like a prayer. There was no need for more. Then Chope got back on his horse and rode away without looking back.

Badger, Anthony J. *The New Deal: The Depression Years, 1933-40.* New York: Farrar, Straus & Giroux, Inc., 1989.

Bean, Walton. *California: An Interpretive History.* New York: McGraw-Hill, Inc., 1978.

Bernstein, Michael A. *The Great Depression.* Cambridge: Cambridge University Press, 1987.

Bird, Caroline. *The Invisible Scar.* New York: David McKay Co., 1966.

Bogan, Samuel. *Let the Coyotes Howl: A Story of Philmont Scout Ranch.* New York: G. P. Putnam's Sons, 1946.

Bowman, John S. *The World Almanac of the American West.* New York: World Almanac, an imprint of Pharos Books, 1986.

Brooks, Elston. *I've Heard Those Songs Before.* Vol. 2. Fort Worth: The Summit Group, 1991.

Chandler, Lester. *America's Greatest Depression, 1929-1939.* New York: Harper and Row, 1970.

Debo, Angie, and Oskison, John M., eds. *The WPA Guide to 1930s Oklahoma.* Originally published by the University of Oklahoma Press in 1941 under the title *Oklahoma: A Guide to the Sooner State.* University of Kansas, 1986.

Faulk, Odie B., and Laura E. Faulk. *An Oklahoma Legacy: The Life of Robert A. Hefner, Jr.* Oklahoma City: Oklahoma Heritage Association, 1988.

Franks, Kenny A. *The Osage Oil Boom.* Oklahoma City: Oklahoma Heritage Association, 1989.

_____. *The Oklahoma Petroleum Industry.* Norman: University of Oklahoma Press, 1980.

_____, Paul F. Lambert and Carl N. Tyson. *Early Oklahoma Oil: A Photographic History, 1859-1936.* College Station: Texas A&M University Press, 1981.

Gentry, Curt. *The Last Days of the Late, Great State of California.* New York: G. P. Putnam's Sons, 1968.

Gibson, Arrell Morgan. *Oklahoma: A History of Five Centuries.* Norman: University of Oklahoma Press, 1981.

Gordon, Lois, and Alan Gordon. *American Chronicle: Seven Decades in American Life, 1920-1989.* New York: Crown Publishers, Inc., 1987.

Gregory, Robert. *Oil in Oklahoma.* Muskogee, Oklahoma: Leake Industries, Inc., 1976.

Haralson, Carol, and Raakel Vesanen. *Villa Philbrook.* Tulsa: Philbrook Art Center, 1976.

Inhofe, Marilyn, Kathleen Reeves and Sandy Jones. *Footsteps Through Tulsa,* 1984.

Jones, Billy M. *L. E. Phillips: Banker, Oil Man, Civic Leader.* Oklahoma City: Oklahoma Heritage Association, 1981.

Keleher, William A. *The Maxwell Land Grant: A New Mexico Item.* Santa Fe: The Rydal Press, 1942.

Knowles, Ruth Sheldon. *The Greatest Gamblers.* New York: McGraw-Hill Book Company, Inc., 1959.

Lasky, Jane E., and David Reed. *Crown Insider's Guide to California.* New York: Crown Publishers, Inc., 1988.

Logsdon, Guy William. *The University of Tulsa.* Norman: University of Oklahoma Press, 1977.

Lohbeck, Don. *Patrick J. Hurley.* Chicago: Henry Regnery Company, 1956.

Mathews, John Joseph. *Life and Death of an Oilman: The Career of E. W. Marland.* Norman: University of Oklahoma Press, 1951.

Murphy, Lawrence R. *Philmont: A History of New Mexico's Cimarron Country.* Albuquerque: University of New Mexico Press, 1972.

Okmulgee Historical Society and the Heritage Society of America. *History of Okmulgee County, Oklahoma.* Tulsa: Historical Enterprises, Inc., 1985.

Perrett, Geoffrey. *American in the Twenties.* New York: Simon & Schuster, 1982.

Phillips, Cabell. *From the Crash to the Blitz, 1929-1939.* New York: The New York Times Company, 1969.

Phillips, Waite. *Epigrams.* ed. Elliott W. Phillips. Privately printed, 1964.

Rieger, Ray. *Hidden Southern California.* Berkeley: Ulysses Press, 1988.

Schlesinger, Arthur M., Jr., ed. *The Almanac of American History.* New York: G. P. Putnam's Sons, 1983.

Stuever, Mary, and Daniel Shaw. *Philmont Fieldguide.* Irving, Texas: Boy Scouts of America, 1985.

Trafzer, Clifford Earl. *The Judge: The Life of Robert A. Hefner.* Norman: University of Oklahoma Press, 1975.

Wallis, Michael. *Oil Man: The Story of Frank Phillips and the Birth of Phillips Petroleum.* New York: Doubleday, 1988.

Williams, Joe. *Philmont: Where Spirits Soar.* Irving, Texas: Boy Scouts of America, 1989.

Wilson, Terry P. *The Underground Reservation: Osage Oil.* Lincoln: University of Nebraska Press, 1985.

Yoch, James J. *The Philbrook Museum of Art: A Guide to Villa Philbrook & Its Gardens.* Tulsa: The Philbrook Museum of Art, 1991.

Zimmer, Stephen, and Larry Walker. *Philmont: An Illustrated History.* Irving, Texas: Boy Scouts of America, 1988.

MICHAEL WALLIS is a historian and biographer of the American West. He is the author of *Oil Man: The Story of Frank Phillips and the Birth of Phillips Petroleum, Route 66: The Mother Road, Pretty Boy: The Life and Times of Charles Arthur Floyd, Way Down Yonder in the Indian Nation: Writings from America's Heartland, Mankiller: A Chief and Her People, En Divina Luz: The Penitente Moradas of New Mexico,* and *Songdog Diary: 66 Souvenirs of the American West.*

He has been nominated three times for the Pulitzer Prize and was also a nominee for the National Book Award. In 1994, Wallis was honored by Rogers State College, in Claremore, Oklahoma, as the recipient of the prestigious Lynn Riggs Award, given for his deep and lasting commitment to the perpetuation and improvement of the arts in Oklahoma. He was also the first inductee into the Oklahoma Route 66 Hall of Fame.

A Missouri native, Wallis has lived and worked throughout the Southwest and Mexico. He and his wife, Suzanne Fitzgerald Wallis, have made their home in Oklahoma since 1982.